Mastering Active Directory

Mastering
Active
Directory

Robert R. King

San Francisco • Paris • Düsseldorf • Soest • London

SYBEX®

Associate Publisher: Guy Hart-Davis
Contracts and Licensing Manager: Kristine O'Callaghan
Acquisitions and Developmental Editor: Maureen Adams
Editor: Suzanne Goraj
Project Editor: Elizabeth Hurley
Technical Editor: Don Meyers
Book Designer: Bill Gibson
Graphic Illustrators: Tony Jonick, Todd Rinker, and Jerry Williams
Electronic Publishing Specialist: Rhonda Ries
Production Editor: Jennifer Durning
Indexer: Matthew Spence
Cover Designer: Design Site
Cover Illustrator/Photographer: Sergie Loobkoff, Design Site

Library of Congress Card Number: 99-69763
ISBN: 0-7821-2659-6

Manufactured in the United States of America

10 9 8 7

To my wife and best friend, Susan

Acknowledgments

I'm fairly new to the whole publishing game. I've been involved in a few other projects (namely the Sybex Exam Notes series), but I'm still surprised by the number of people and the amount of work that go into producing any kind of high-quality material. There are numerous people who helped get this book into your hands—and each of them was critical to the process.

My family deserves the most thanks. Every time I start a new Sybex project, I promise them that I'll "work a normal schedule," and every time I end up working into the wee hours more often than not. This book could not have been finished without their love and support.

I also would like to thank the fine folks at Sybex. I have never worked with a more supportive and understanding group of people. Both Maureen Adams, the book's developmental editor, and Elizabeth Hurley, the book's project editor, were understanding when I ran over deadlines. Editor Suzanne Goraj was insightful and really helped to ensure that I held to some sort of consistent style! Production Editor Jennifer Durning and electronic publishing specialist Rhonda Ries from Publication Services made the final product look sharp. Finally, my technical editor, Don Meyers, ensured that I didn't embarrass myself—something I really appreciate! To these, and to all of those who helped put this book together, I'd like to say one big "Thank you."

Contents at a Glance

Table of Contents

Introduction

Over the last few years, Microsoft Windows NT 4 has become the hottest "new" technology to hit the networking market. This has always surprised me, since the networking portion of Windows NT 4 is based on a domain model that is over 10 years old. In other words, Microsoft's newest technology isn't really all that new. That has changed, however, with the release of the newest version of NT—Windows 2000 Server.

Windows 2000 Server moves Microsoft networking away from the dated (and limiting) domain-based architecture of earlier releases and toward the true directory service–based architecture necessary in today's complex networks. Microsoft provides this service through the addition of Active Directory Services (ADS), an open, standards-based, X.500-compliant, LDAP-accessible network directory. (Don't worry—we'll talk about X.500, LDAP, and what seems like an endless list of industry acronyms throughout this book.)

ADS provides the power and flexibility you need in today's changing computer world, but it provides these at a price. A large portion of that price will be the steep learning curve that administrators will need to climb in order to fully understand and utilize the potential of Microsoft Windows 2000 and Active Directory Services.

The first commercially viable directory service–based operating system to hit the networking industry was Novell's NetWare 4 with NetWare Directory Services (NDS). At the time of its release, I was working as a senior technical instructor for a company in Minneapolis, Minnesota. In order to be one step ahead of the competition, my company sent me to the prep classes taught on the beta version of the software. After two weeks of intensive training on NDS, I returned home and started to reevaluate my career choices. It seemed as if everything I knew about networking was about to become out of date, and I would be forced to master this new paradigm known as a "directory service." I have to admit that when I first saw Novell's directory service I didn't get it, didn't think I would ever get it, and wasn't sure I wanted to get it. I felt safe with earlier versions of NetWare, and I couldn't understand why *anyone* would want to add the complexity of a directory service to their network.

I'm hoping that this book can help you avoid being caught by surprise by Microsoft's newest technology—Windows 2000 Server and Active

Directory. While a network directory is a new paradigm in networking, try to remember that at its most basic, networking technology—whether Windows 2000, ADS, or anything else—is still just moving bits from one place to another. All of the knowledge you have gathered about networking is still valid; you'll just have a few more options available to you.

What's in This Book?

When I was planning the table of contents for this book, I struggled with how best to present a new paradigm for Microsoft networking—the concept of a network directory. It was suggested that I just write about Active Directory Services and leave it at that, but I wanted to give you a conceptual overview of the technology as well as a look at ADS. I decided that a three-part book would suit my goals. Read on to learn what's in each part.

Part I: The Background and History of Network Directories

No matter what Microsoft would have you believe, network directories have been around for quite some time. Understanding earlier implementations (both their strengths and weaknesses) can help us understand why ADS works the way it does—and perhaps help us realize some of its weaknesses. Part I is fairly short, but it is filled with conceptual information that can really help you tie ADS to your environment. Part I contains four chapters.

Chapter 1: An Introduction to Directories   This chapter gives a basic overview of what a directory is and compares directories to older technologies.

Chapter 2: Anatomy of a Directory   In this chapter, you will learn what a directory is by looking at examples of existing technologies, starting with basic paper-based directories and working up to the directories used in today's networks.

Chapter 3: The X.500 Recommendations   Read this chapter for an overview of the X.500 recommendations, which are used to create the structure of the Active Directory database.

Chapter 4: Accessing the Directory   Chapter 4 explains DAP and LDAP, the two protocols used to access the information stored within the ADS database.

Part II: Microsoft Active Directory Services

Once we have a firm grounding in directory technology, we can look at ADS with a critical eye, trying to find its strengths and weaknesses. With this information, we can better apply the technology within our own environments. There are nine chapters in Part II.

Chapter 5: Microsoft NT without ADS To fully appreciate Windows 2000 Server, and especially Active Directory Services, it is important to understand earlier versions of NT. If you are an NT expert, this chapter will be a review. If you are a newcomer to the NT world, this chapter should prepare you for some of the topics you will encounter later in the book.

Chapter 6: Microsoft NT with ADS Just as NT was originally designed to overcome the weaknesses of server-centric environments, Windows 2000 Server with ADS was designed to overcome the weaknesses of domain-based environments. In this chapter, we will discuss how ADS fits into the overall Windows 2000 philosophy.

Chapter 7: Alphabet Soup: ADS, TCP/IP, DNS, WINS While Microsoft 2000 Server can utilize many different protocols for communication, ADS depends on TCP/IP. Before you can begin to install and configure an ADS environment, you must have a strong foundation in TCP/IP tools and techniques.

Chapter 8: Building the Active Directory Tree In this chapter, you will read about the theories of designing a stable ADS structure that does not place undue stress on any single component of your network.

Chapter 9: Implementing Your Design Read Chapter 9 to find out about the mechanics of ADS installation and building your ADS structure.

Chapter 10: Securing the Active Directory Database If the ADS database is going to be of any real use in a network, the information it contains must be secure. In this chapter, we will look at the various security options available with Windows 2000 Server.

Chapter 11: Implementing Group Policies Group policies are used to define user or computer settings for an entire group of users or computers at one time. As such, they will be a very important concept for administrators of networks based on Windows 2000 Server. In Chapter 11, we will discuss the concept of group policies and look at the procedures used to implement them.

Chapter 12: Modifying the Active Directory Schema The ADS database contains object classes, which define *types* of network resources, and attributes, which define *parameters* of those classes. The default list of classes and attributes might not be sufficient in some environments. Chapter 12 discusses the process of extending the design of the ADS database to include custom object classes and attributes.

Chapter 13: Understanding and Controlling ADS Sites and Replication For any network operating system, no matter how logical we make the structure or how graphical we make the interface, when all is said and done, everything comes back to the plumbing—the "pipes" we use to move data. This chapter looks at design issues with an eye on available bandwidth and communication costs.

Part III: The Future of Active Directory Services

For the last section of the book, I look into my crystal ball and predict the impact of ADS on various aspects of the networking industry. This final section contains three chapters.

Chapter 14: ADS and BackOffice It appears that ADS will become the backbone of the Microsoft network arena. As such, it will have a great impact on the design of other Microsoft network products. In Chapter 14, we will examine the possible effect of ADS on Microsoft Exchange Server, Microsoft Proxy Server, Microsoft Site Server, Microsoft Systems Management Server, Microsoft SNA Server, and Microsoft SQL Server—those products that make up what is commonly referred to as the BackOffice Suite.

Chapter 15: ADS and Third-Party Products Numerous companies offer products that add to or enhance the functionality of the NT networking environment. As Microsoft moves to a directory-based operating system, these companies will be forced to move along with it. Chapter 15 looks at the various changes that third-party vendors will have to make in order to stay current with Microsoft's vision of networking.

Chapter 16: Directory-Enabled Networks (DENs) A directory service database is designed to hold information about network resources. The network infrastructure—routers, switches, gateways, and the like—is just another set of resources to be managed. This chapter considers the impact of a network directory on the management of these kinds of resources.

Who Should Read This Book?

This book was written for the experienced network administrator who wants to take a look at Microsoft's Active Directory Services. I'm going to assume a basic level of knowledge of networking in general, but no (or little) knowledge of directory-based technologies. It seems as though whatever Microsoft is doing is what the industry moves toward—and Microsoft is doing network directories in a big way! If you run a Microsoft house, you'll need to come up to speed on ADS quickly. If you run a non-Microsoft house (or older versions of Microsoft NT) you can bet that sooner or later you'll need to understand how Microsoft views network directories.

I guess the bottom line is this: If you are in networking today and you plan to be in networking tomorrow, you will have to master the concepts of a network directory at some point in your career. This book is designed to give you the information you need to understand and implement Microsoft's interpretation of that technology.

In Short

Microsoft Windows 2000 Server is going to be the next big wave in networking technology. We will have to rethink how we characterize network resources and services. The days of putting in the network and *then* considering the environment are long gone! With today's technologies, each network will have to be designed around a "total business solution"—providing the resources and services necessary without unduly taxing the budget, staff, or infrastructure of the host company.

One last word of advice: Enjoy what you do. New technology can be exciting, challenging, and downright fun. If you spend more time complaining about the technology than being amazed by it, perhaps a vacation is in order!

As with all my books, if you have questions or comments about the content, do not hesitate to drop me a note at `bking@royal-tech.com`. I always look forward to hearing from you.

PART

I

The Background
and History of
Network Directories

CHAPTER

1

An Introduction
to Directories

The computer industry, especially in the networking arena, generates more acronyms, terms, phrases, and buzzwords than any other business in the world. The latest craze is the phrase *network directories*. Directories are nothing new—they have been around in one form or another since the late '60s. Now, however, they are about to enter the mainstream with the release of Microsoft's long-awaited Active Directory Services in Windows 2000 Server. To get the most from this technology, you must have a firm understanding of what directories are, what they are not, and how they can be used to ease the management of your network. That is the goal of this book—to give you enough information to implement, manage, and utilize the services provided by Microsoft's Active Directory Services (ADS).

PC-based networks have become an integral part of the business world. They started out as simple solutions for the sharing of a few physical resources—hard disk space, printers, and so on. Over time, though, networks have become quite complex—often spanning multiple sites, connecting thousands of users to a multitude of resources. Today, networks control everything from payroll information to e-mail communication, from printers to fax services. As networks offer more services, they also demand more management. Easing the use and management of networks is the real goal of a directory service.

Understanding Network Directories

To understand and appreciate the power and convenience of a directory-based solution, you must have an understanding of the technologies that it will replace. Before the advent of directories, most network operating systems

(NOS) were "server-based." In other words, most account management was done on a server-by-server basis. With older NOS software, each server maintained a list of users who could access its resources (the *accounts database*) and the users' permissions (the *Access Control List*, or ACL). If a system had two servers, then each server had a separate accounts database, as shown in Figure 1.1.

F I G U R E   1.1

Server-based NOS

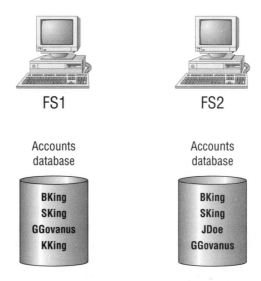

FS1   FS2

Accounts   Accounts
database   database

BKing   BKing
SKing   SKing
GGovanus   JDoe
KKing   GGovanus

As you can see, each server in Figure 1.1 maintains its own list of authorized users and manages its own resources. While this system is simple and easy to understand, it becomes unwieldy once a system grows past a certain point. Imagine trying to manage 1,000 users on 250 servers—the user and resource lists would soon overwhelm you! To get around this limitation, some NOS software, such as Microsoft NT 4, was configured so that small groups of servers could share one list of users (called a *central accounts database*) for security and authentication purposes, as shown in Figure 1.2. This central accounts database gave administrators a single point of management for a section of their network, known as a *domain*. Once again, however, this system becomes cumbersome after it reaches a certain size.

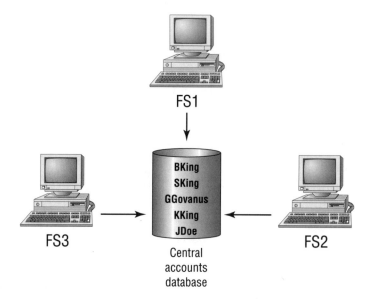

FIGURE 1.2

NT 4 security
accounts database

The shift from server-based to domain-based networks was the first step in creating an environment where all users and resources are managed through a single database. In a domain, all user information is stored in a single place and managed with a single set of tools, and users can access the network via a single account (no more having to remember multiple account names and passwords). Network directories take this approach to the next phase: a single database to hold *all* user and resource information across your entire network.

I'm using the phrase "user and resource" to refer to the records within a directory database because that is how traditional administrators see their world: users accessing resources. In a directory-based environment, however, users become nothing more than another resource. This subtle shift in philosophy is critical in understanding the strengths of a directory-based network. This distinction should become clear as you become more familiar with directory concepts.

Network directories are just databases that hold network information. They can contain many different types of information:

- User account information (logon name, password, restrictions)

- User personal information (phone number, address, employee ID number)

- Peripheral configuration information (printers, modem, fax)

- Application configuration (Desktop preferences, default directories)

- Security information

- Network infrastructure configuration (routers, proxies, Internet access settings)

If you can imagine it, a network directory can store it!

Once this information is stored in a centrally controlled, standards-based database, it can be used in many different ways. Most commonly, administrators will use such information to control access to the network and the network's resources. The directory will become the central control point for many different network processes. Here are examples of some of these processes:

- When a user attempts to log on to the network, the client software will request authentication from the directory. The directory service will ascertain whether the account name is valid, check for a password, validate the password submitted, and check any restrictions on the account to determine if the logon request should be granted.

- Once a user has logged on to the system, the directory will be queried each time that user tries to access a network resource. The directory will authenticate the request to determine if the user has the appropriate permissions to use the resource. The directory will also return the resource's physical address to the client.

- Individual users can use directories to store personal preferences. Each time a user logs on to the network, his Desktop settings, default printer, home directory location—even his application icons—can be downloaded to whatever computer he happens to be at. Users will no longer have to re-create their environment each time they use a new computer. All of their settings will be centrally located to ensure a "universal environment" and, if you desire, centrally controlled to lock them down.

▪ As directories mature, you will also be able to use them to monitor and control traffic across network devices. When a user attempts to access a remote network, for instance, the directory could be used to determine whether the request is valid for that user. Imagine controlling Internet access with the same tool you use to control other security settings. Or perhaps the directory could query various devices to determine the least congested network path to the destination. You might even be able to grant higher network priority to certain users, groups, applications, or services, allowing you to provide a guaranteed level of service.

Traditional Networks vs. Network Directories

Many network tasks can benefit from the capabilities of a network directory. Many of the hardest configuration issues of earlier networks will become a piece of cake when you use a network directory as the central controlling point for the network.

Traditional Network Solutions for Common Administrative Tasks

As food for thought, let's consider a few common networking tasks and the non-directory solutions to them. Each of these scenarios is a "real world" implementation that I have been asked to complete on production networks. As you will see, the non-directory-based solutions often border on the ridiculous. In some cases, the service provided could not justify the time spent to provide the requested solution. In other words, the constraints placed upon networks by traditional management techniques often limit the services that a network can realistically provide.

Scenario 1: To Trust or Not to Trust

Your company's marketing department has a Color Wax Thermal Transfer Graphics printer, which is used to create camera-ready art for the company that prints your sales brochures. Because of the cost of consumables, which is somewhere in the neighborhood of $3.00 per page, you have been very careful about who is allowed to print to this device. Luckily, the marketing department is its own domain, so security has been fairly easy to maintain. Over in the engineering department, Susan has decided that she needs to print drawings of prototypes on this printer. Your job is to arrange the appropriate permissions.

In a multidomain environment, there are two basic ways to handle this situation:

- You *could* create a trust between the marketing domain and the engineering domain, create a global group in the engineering domain, place Susan's account in the group, and then place that global group in the appropriate local group in the marketing domain. While this solution is great for Susan, it does mean that you now have to keep track of another trust relationship, not to mention the associated local and global groups.

- You *could* create a local account for Susan in the marketing domain and teach Susan to "Connect As" to use the printer. Now, of course, you've lost one of the biggest benefits of a multidomain design—one user, one login.

Scenario 2: Where's Joe?

An executive calls to inform you that a user named Joe in the sales department has been overheard discussing confidential information, including future product designs and marketing strategies. This executive would like a detailed explanation about where Joe has permissions and how they are acquired. She would also like you to ensure that Joe only has rights to resources appropriate for salespeople.

In a multidomain environment, this problem can be overwhelming. Your first inclination is probably to delete Joe's account and start from scratch—but you want to ensure that no other salespeople have been granted inappropriate permissions. You'll have to track down every group that Joe is a member of, and then check the permissions of each group. For each global group, you'll have to check to see which local groups it has been made a member of (including those local groups in other domains). You'll also have to search for any local accounts that might have been created for Joe in the marketing and R & D domains. Finally, you'll probably want to institute an auditing policy to track who is accessing the confidential data.

Of course, this scenario assumes that you have administrative rights in the other domains of your environment. If not, you will have to coordinate your actions with those of the other administrators.

When you have completed your search, you will have to implement a corporate-wide policy that defines how permissions should be granted, who should be able to grant rights to various types of resources, and the appropriate naming standards for things like global and local groups (this will make the next search a little easier). In a multidomain environment, enforcing these policies can be an administrative nightmare.

Scenario 3: The Search for Information

An expensive and mission-critical printer refuses to print. You know that the printer was purchased in the last few months, but you need specific information for dealing with the vendor. In a traditional office, you must contact purchasing. The purchasing agent will have to dig up the paper-based purchase order using the serial number or approximate date of purchase. If all goes well, the purchase order will contain the check number and date of purchase, as well as the name of the salesperson who sold you the device. Once that information is at hand, you can call the vendor and negotiate repairs or replacement.

Scenario 4: Setting Limits

Your company has just adopted a policy to control Internet access: Certain users have unlimited access, other users are allowed to surf the Web during non-business hours, and some users are allowed to access only an approved list of Web sites. It's your job to make sure this policy is implemented. Luckily, all of this functionality is built into the new routers you have purchased. Unfortunately, those routers are not "NT aware," so you must enter all of the specifics (including usernames) in the vendor's proprietary format.

Scenario 5: Company Information

You've been asked to design a database that can serve as a company phone book. The CEO would like to have the following information available for each employee:

- Company phone extension
- Home phone
- Company mail stop
- Home address
- Birthday
- Hire date

While all of this information is already in a series of databases controlled by the human resources department, the CEO would like this to be a company-wide application. She also realizes that some of this data is confidential, so you must control access to certain fields based upon job function.

One solution might be to create a series of databases: one for non-secure information and another for secure information. Each user would access the database that is appropriate for his or her needs. Not an elegant solution, but it is probably the quickest. The biggest problem will be keeping the information up to date.

Network Directory–Based Solutions

Most administrative tasks can be broken down into two basic functions:

- Providing resources
- Securing those resources

With that in mind, let's look at the five scenarios just described. You've been asked to:

1. Secure access to an expensive resource (a printer).
2. Provide security for confidential information.
3. Organize information (the purchase order for the printer).
4. Secure and control access to the Internet.
5. Provide (and secure) access to employee information.

Balancing the availability of resources with the need to secure those resources represents a large percentage of what LAN administrators do for a living. The implementation of a network directory service can help to make these tasks as straightforward as possible.

Scenario 1: To Trust or Not to Trust

Because a network directory provides a single database to manage all network resources, the directory-based solution to this problem is fairly straightforward. The users and the printer are no longer "separated" by any type of administrative grouping; in other words, both the user account and the printer now exist in the same database. When you use a directory, the solution can be as simple as giving Susan account permissions to use the printer.

Scenario 2: Where's Joe?

Once again, the single point of management provided by a network directory offers a fairly simple solution to this problem. Since all groups exist in the same database, you can query that database for a list of all groups of which Joe is a member. Rather than checking each group by hand, you can use the database as a tool to limit your workload.

Once you've discovered the source of Joe's extra permissions (and fixed the immediate problem), you should be able to implement a directory-wide policy to correct the errors that caused the problem in the first place. You might, for example, limit the administrator of the sales department so that he can only administer resources listed as belonging to the sales department. With this type of policy in place, the sales administrator could never grant permissions to non-sales resources.

Scenario 3: The Search for Information

Many people get so hung up on the fact that a directory "manages the network" that they forget that a directory is just a database. Why not store resource-related information as a part of that resource's record? A directory can easily store things like the serial number of a printer or any purchase information that you might need later.

If this information is in your directory, the directory-based solution would be to query the database for the printer's record. You can base your query on any known attribute—since the printer is not working, you probably have access to its serial number. Search the directory for a matching entry.

Scenario 4: Setting Limits

Once the networking industry settles on a standard format for network directories, it should not be difficult to manage a multivendor environment from a single point. You should be able to import the configuration information for things like a proxy server or router right into your network directory. Once such integration is possible, you might be able to drag and drop user accounts onto the router and configure limits for each user. Another option might be to create a series of groups in Active Directory Services, and then assign permission to various router functions to those groups. The router can then query the ADS database to determine what groups a particular user belongs to.

Scenario 5: Company Information

The company phone book is probably one of the easiest tasks an administrator can accomplish in a directory environment. Most directories (ADS included) will store most of the information that the CEO requests in this scenario. Directories also have built-in security so that users can be limited to viewing only certain data from the directory.

ADS is accessible by most of the industry-standard directory tools. Once you have imported the information into the directory, you can use any of these tools to query for things like phone numbers and addresses. The internal security will determine whether or not the request is honored.

In Short

As you can see from the scenarios presented in this chapter, moving to a directory-based environment should make administration of large networks a lot easier. The directory can act as:

- The central point of management for the network

- The central point of access for users

- A repository for administrative information that would otherwise be hard to manage

As we discuss the capabilities of ADS, you will probably come up with some solutions for your own administrative nightmares.

In Chapter 2, we will dig a little deeper into the internal workings of network directories. There are many directories currently being used throughout the networking world, and we'll take a look at a few of them. As we examine these other directories, we'll build a "wish list" for ADS. Later, we'll see how closely the reality of ADS matches the potential of directory-based networks.

CHAPTER
2

Anatomy of a Directory

The simplest definition of a *directory* would be a device used to store and organize data. According to this definition, we all use directories on a daily basis. Perhaps the most common directory would be the plain old phone book. You might not see the telephone directory as a marvel of technology, but consider the services it provides.

Paper-Based Directories

The telephone directory acts as a repository of information, storing the names, addresses, and telephone numbers of the residents of your town (or state or nation, depending on the book you are using). This information is presented in an easy-to-use format—in most cases, as a paper-based book that can be used by anyone with a basic level of literacy. The book's information is organized in an easily understood manner: an alphabetical listing. All in all, as a directory, the telephone directory fulfills its purpose admirably, as evidenced by how long it's been around and how little its design has changed.

The telephone directory has become a standard piece of our culture: consider how many companies now offer such directories to the public. Many of these offerings are specialized—business-to-business listings, neighborhood directories, even restaurant listings organized by type of food. Having such specific directories means that you don't have to search through page after page of information in order to find that great Mexican restaurant or a pizza parlor near your home.

An example of a common directory that is specific in scope would be the list of physicians in a particular health-care system. This is an example of a directory that is a little more "directed": a list of physicians, their specialties, their locations, and sometimes even their office hours. This information targets a specific audience. If you do not participate in the appropriate health-care plan, this information would be of no use to you. If, however, you belong to the plan, the information is critical to the health of your family. Once again, this information is presented in a manner that is appropriate for its use: usually a paper-based solution where the physicians are listed alphabetically by specialty.

The biggest problem with both of these examples—the telephone directory and the physician directory—is that a paper-based solution is usually out of date before you receive it. Think about the number of times you have dialed the listing for a local pizza parlor, only to find that it has gone out of business. While the list of physicians might be correct and current, wouldn't it be nice to have a list of physicians who are currently accepting new patients? Better yet, wouldn't you prefer to have a list that is so up to the minute that you could check to see how far behind schedule the doctor is running today?

Computer-Based Directories

Paper-based directories illustrate the kinds of services that a network directory can provide, but they fall short of explaining the true benefits of a real-time, software-based solution.

A better example of a directory would be a personal information manager (PIM), such as Microsoft Outlook. PIMs store, organize, and display information that is specific to an individual. You can use a tool like Outlook to hold your addresses, keep track of appointments, and even warn you about important dates such as birthdays or anniversaries. PIMs are starting to take the place of paper-based address books because they store more information, they can display that information in more convenient ways, and they can be customized (and all without forcing you to write really small in the margin).

It is not unusual for someone to use a PIM to organize a day's activities, add a list of friends' birthdays to her to-do list, send a copy of a good joke to all her friends, and automatically fax a sales announcement to her clients. A good PIM not only stores information but also makes information usable in real-world applications. With Outlook, for instance, you can use your contacts list (which contains names, addresses, telephone numbers, and other information about people) as the data list for a mail merge into a document created in a word processor.

While PIMs are convenient, they do have their drawbacks. To retrieve the information in your PIM, you must have access to both the software and a computer. Also, stand-alone PIMs, such as Palm Pilots, are not convenient for sharing information because their information is not stored on a central server. If your schedule is stored on your laptop or sitting in your pocket, your colleagues can't access it to find out whether you can attend an important staff meeting.

These limitations are being overcome by moving PIMs from the status of stand-alone applications to groupware products. *Groupware* can be defined as an application that is specifically designed to allow users to share and/or collaborate on projects or data. Most of today's groupware packages started out as e-mail applications and have grown from there. This makes sense; e-mail is a basic way to share information, and most collaboration is just that—shared information.

Microsoft has entered the groupware market in a big way with Microsoft Exchange Server. As an e-mail package, Exchange is about par for the course, although some might argue that Microsoft's traditional graphical interface makes it easier to configure and manage than many others on the market, such as Lotus Notes and Novell's GroupWise. Exchange really shines, though, in its collaborative tools. In an Exchange system, the administrator (or any user with the appropriate permissions) can create *public folders* that hold data. That data can be in just about any form you desire— from traditional e-mail messages to form-based, threaded conversations to executables. All of this data can be made available to users of the system based upon an internal security system.

The Exchange system is managed through a series of containers and subcontainers—just like most network directories. Its access features include the following:

- It has an internal security system so that only specific individuals can access certain data.

- It can be accessed from various types of clients (from mail clients like Outlook, using Internet browser software, and even from LDAP-enabled applications).

Exchange was Microsoft's first attempt at a directory-based system.

We'll talk about directory organization later in this chapter.

While all of these examples—the telephone directory, a listing of physicians, a personal information manager, and even Microsoft Exchange Server—indicate the kinds of services that a network directory can provide, none exemplifies the true depth of the service that such a system can provide. A network directory encompasses all of these examples—and offers even more.

Network Directories

A *network directory* is a database that contains information used to access, manage, or configure a network. As thus defined, network directories have been in use for quite some time. Some examples of mature network directories would include:

- Domain Name System (DNS)
- Windows Internet Name Service (WINS)
- Novell Directory Services (NDS)

Each of these directories holds information that is used to access or manage a network and each works in a slightly different manner. Let's look at each of them to determine what each does, how it is configured, and how it accomplishes its tasks. Each of these examples will include good traits and bad traits: things to be embraced or avoided by any new directories that enter the market, such as Active Directory Services. From each example, we will build a list of desired capabilities in a directory service.

Domain Name System (DNS)

The basic function of DNS is to resolve user-friendly domain names into IP addresses. When a client enters a fully qualified domain name (FQDN), the DNS server is queried for the IP address of the corresponding server. DNS is the tool most commonly used to find resources on large IP networks such as the Internet. While DNS has been working as the main name-resolution service on the Internet for quite some time, it does have a few weaknesses. For our discussion, we'll look first at how DNS is structured, then at a few of its weak points.

Why DNS?

Before the Internet was created, there existed a network known as the ARPAnet. This network tied together a few university and Department of Defense sites so that they could share research material.

> This is a bit simplistic, but it will suffice for our discussion. For an overview of Internet history from the perspective of network security, see *Mastering Network Security* by Chris Brenton (ISBN 0-7821-2343-0, Sybex, 1998).

Since the network was small, each computer on the net had a small text file, known as a *hosts file*, that listed a user-friendly name for each host (computer) and its IP address. When another host was added to a site, the hosts file on each computer that might need to communicate with the new computer was updated with its address.

As an example, suppose that two networks were tied to this network—KingTech and PS Consulting. Each of these networks has five hosts that must be accessed across the network. The hosts file for each client device must include a "friendly name" and the IP address of all 10 hosts. A sample hosts file is shown in Table 2.1.

T A B L E 2.1 Sample Hosts File	IP Address	Host
	131.107.2.100	Localhost1
	131.107.2.101	Localhost2
	131.107.2.102	Localhost3
	131.107.2.103	Localhost4
	131.107.3.100	Remotehost1
	131.107.3.101	Remotehost2
	131.107.3.102	Remotehost3
	131.107.3.103	Remotehost4
	131.107.3.104	Remotehost5

Each computer needing to access hosts on these two networks needs a hosts file with the IP address of all of the hosts it might access. In other words, keeping these "simple" text files up to date could require quite a bit of management.

What Are DNS Domains?

DNS was created to alleviate some of this management overhead. Basically, DNS is this text file, broken into logical units known as *domains* and distributed across multiple computers known as DNS *servers*. The logical domains are organized in a hierarchical structure, much like the DOS file system. There is a very specific format for the names used in a DNS system, known as the *namespace* of the DNS system. The concept of a namespace will be very important in understanding how ADS is accessed by clients, so let's define the term for future reference:

> A *namespace* is a set of rules governing how objects (DNS records in this case) are formatted within a directory.

On the Internet, domain names are registered with a central consortium to ensure that they are unique and that their format follows the namespace rules set forth for the Internet. This consortium, known as InterNIC (short for Internet Network Information Center), controls the last section, or "upper level," of domain names and has created a specific set for use on the Internet. Domain names on the Internet will end with one of the following, based on the purpose of the domain:

.edu	Educational institutions
.com	Commercial organizations
.org	Nonprofit organizations
.net	Networks
.gov	Non-military government organizations
.mil	Military government organizations
.num	Telephone numbers
.arpa	Reverse DNS
.XX	Two-letter country codes (such as .ca for Canada)

Any directory service must include a set of clearly defined, standard rules for naming the objects that it contains.

Actually, this list is not really complete. Most of us are used to typing in domain names like www.royal-tech.com, and we are taught that this is the resource's complete name. In this case, www represents the host (my Web server) and royal-tech.com is the domain. In reality, the full name of any domain ends in a period. The period represents the root of the domain namespace, much like DOS paths should really start with C:\ but are rarely typed that way.

When a domain name is registered, InterNIC will determine if the requesting agency has chosen the appropriate upper-level domain. If so, and if the name is not already in use, InterNIC will reserve the name for the requesting party and add a record to DNS for the new domain. The following steps show how a DNS request is translated into an IP address during a typical query:

1. The client requests a resource; for our example, let's assume it's the Web page www.royal-tech.com. One of the configuration parameters for IP clients is the IP address of a DNS server. The client software will query this server for the IP address of the corresponding resource.

2. The DNS server will process the query, first checking to see if information for the royal-tech.com domain is included. If not, it will check a local cache. The local cache contains the IP addresses of resources that have recently been resolved to IP addresses. If the IP address for www.royal-tech.com is in the cache, the server will return this information to the client.

The DNS cache is a physical file that holds the IP addresses that the DNS server has resolved; if someone accesses a site once, he might want to do so again. Caching the IP addresses speeds up response time, since the DNS server will not have to query any other servers for the information the second time. Because the Internet is a dynamic environment, these cached entries are given a Time To Live (TTL) so that they will be re-resolved every so often. In the Microsoft implementation of DNS, the default TTL for cached entries is 60 minutes.

3. If the information is not available locally, the DNS server will forward the query to a root server. Each DNS server on the Internet contains a *public cache* file that holds the IP addresses of the root servers for each top-level domain tree (.com, .edu, .org, and so on).

4. The root DNS server will search its database for the record of a DNS server registered for the .com domain. If such a record exists, it will return the IP address to the local DNS server.

5. The local DNS server will then query the .com DNS server for the IP address of a resource named royal-tech. If such a record exists, the remote DNS server will return the IP address to the local DNS server.

6. The local DNS server will query the royal-tech.com DNS server for the IP address of a host named www. If such a record exists, the remote DNS server will return the IP address of the www server to the local DNS server.

7. The local DNS server will then return the IP address to the client. The client will then begin the process of connecting to the royal-tech.com Web server. This process is depicted in Figure 2.1.

The DNS Structure

The example in Figure 2.1 demonstrates both the distributed nature and the hierarchical design of DNS. Each DNS server contains only records for resources in the domains for which it is responsible. If the DNS server receives a request for information that it does not contain, it will pass that request up or down the structure until the appropriate DNS server is found.

FIGURE 2.1

A typical Internet
DNS query

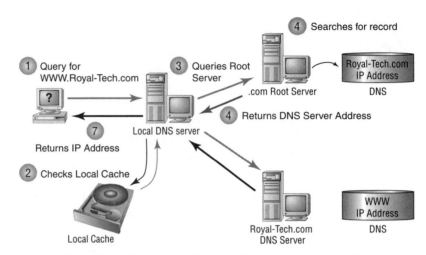

Steps 5, 6, and 7 result in local DNS servers walking the DNS structure until the proper IP address is returned.

You could see DNS as a DOS-like structure—a series of directories (or domains) organized in a tree-like format, as shown in Figure 2.2.

FIGURE 2.2

The DNS hierarchical
structure

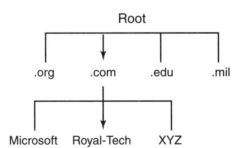

DNS "Tree" Structure

The hierarchy of domains within the DNS structure allows the database to be broken into smaller sections, which can, in turn, be distributed across multiple servers. This reduces the hardware required at any given server, as well as the network bandwidth required to support queries.

Imagine a system that was *not* broken into smaller pieces. First, the database would be huge (a record for *every* resource on the Internet). Few companies would be able to afford the kind of equipment that would be required: large hard drives, tons of memory, and multiprocessor servers would be mandatory. With fewer DNS servers available, each would have to handle more queries from clients. This would result in more network traffic, which would, in turn, require more bandwidth on the link to the Internet. Without the ability to distribute the workload across multiple servers, DNS would probably not work for name resolution on large IP networks.

This ability to break the database into logical pieces and distribute those pieces across servers is critical to any network directory that hopes to serve in medium or larger environments.

A network directory should include the ability to split the database (this is called partitioning) in order to distribute the maintenance and access overhead across multiple computers.

DNS Records

Due to the various services that can be listed in the DNS database, the format of each record can get quite complex, but the bottom line is that DNS is a series of text files containing IP addresses for hosts in an IP-based network. This text file must be created and maintained manually—a task that can consume a lot of time in a large environment. If a company is forced to change its IP addressing scheme, the DNS records for each resource must be updated in DNS. If a resource is added (another mail or Web server, for instance), a record must be added to the DNS database.

The manual nature of DNS management is both a blessing and a curse. On one hand, the simplicity of a text file offers advantages in a mixed environment. On the other hand, a database that does not offer any automation will require a lot of person-hours in a large environment.

A network directory should have the ability to dynamically confirm the validity of some of the information it contains.

DNS Fault Tolerance

In order to provide fault tolerance, DNS defines two types of DNS servers:

- Primary servers
- Secondary servers

Primary servers copy the domain information that they contain to secondary servers on a regular basis. Clients can be configured with the IP addresses of multiple DNS servers. If the client attempts to contact a DNS server and receives no response, it will proceed to the next DNS server in its list. This ensures that clients will continue to function normally even if the network loses a DNS server to some catastrophe, as shown in Figure 2.3.

F I G U R E 2.3

Primary and secondary DNS servers

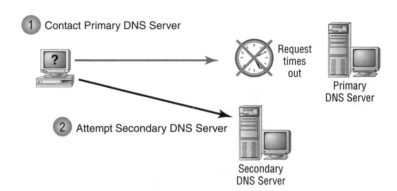

① Contact Primary DNS Server

Request times out

Primary DNS Server

② Attempt Secondary DNS Server

Secondary DNS Server

While the primary/secondary arrangement of servers provides a level of redundancy, it is configured in a limited manner known as a *single-master environment*. All changes to the DNS database *must* occur at the primary (or *master*) DNS server and be propagated to the secondary. If the master DNS server should fail, no changes can be made to the database until one of the secondary servers has been promoted to the status of master.

A network directory in a large environment must be completely fault tolerant. The loss of a single server should in no way affect network functionality.

DNS in Short

The Domain Name Service is a database used to resolve host names into IP addresses. The namespace it defines follows a set of rules, which is the industry standard. The database can be broken into smaller pieces (domains) and distributed across multiple servers. The service provides a mechanism for combining these separate files into a logical whole. Using a series of primary and secondary servers, the service adds a limited amount of fault tolerance to the database by replicating domain information to multiple servers.

All in all, DNS is a success. It has fulfilled its purpose in a large environment (the Internet) for quite some time. While there are a few things that might need improvement, for our purposes it acts as a very good example of a working directory.

You might be wondering, "If DNS is so great, why don't we use it as our network directory instead of implementing Active Directory Services?" The answer to this question revolves around functionality. DNS was designed for a specific purpose: resolving a host name into an IP address. DNS handles its intended function very well—so well, in fact, that ADS incorporates DNS into its own design—but DNS could not handle the extra functions that would be placed upon it in an expanded role. DNS is based on a series of text files that are seen as a flat-file database. Adding additional functionality (holding the configuration information for a router, for instance) would stretch the limits of such technology.

Windows Internet Name Service (WINS)

WINS is another network directory currently used in Windows NT environments. Like DNS, WINS is used to resolve names into IP addresses. Unlike DNS, though, WINS is used to resolve NetBIOS names rather than host names. *NetBIOS names* are the unique identifiers, or computer names, given to resources on an NT network. Since these names identify computers on the network, each computer must have a unique NetBIOS name assigned to it.

Registering a Name

NetBIOS is a *broadcast-based protocol*. As each client is initialized, NetBIOS sends out a broadcast announcing the name it intends to use. If another station is already using the intended name, that station will return a negative acknowledgment to the newcomer. Basically, this boils down to the first station yelling, "I intend to join the network as WS1—anyone mind?" If no response is returned, the station will assume that the name is unique on the network and will continue its initialization.

While this sounds like a simple but effective technique, it is of limited use in a routed network. Most of today's routers are configured so that they do not pass broadcast packets. In effect, this means that the NetBIOS station is limited to confirming the uniqueness of its name to the local network. Conceivably, there could be another station with the same name on a different network.

The first function of a WINS server is *name registration*. In a WINS environment, clients are configured with the IP address of a WINS server. Instead of using the broadcast method to announce itself (and determine if its name is unique), each client sends a registration request directly to the WINS server. The WINS server builds a database of the names of those workstations that have registered themselves. When the server receives a new request, it compares the requested name to those that have been registered. If the name is unique, it sends back a positive response; if not, it sends back a negative response. Since all of the traffic is made up of directed packets, routers will pass the request to a WINS server on another network.

Unlike DNS, the WINS server builds the database dynamically, adding records as workstations register with the service. The net effect is that the database is updated without intervention from a network administrator, greatly reducing the administrative overhead for networking staff.

Figure 2.4 depicts the four steps in the name registration process:

1. The client sends a message to the WINS server requesting registration.

2. The WINS server checks its database to ensure that the name is unique.

3. The WINS server sends a positive response to the client and adds the client's name and IP address to the database.

4. The WINS server adds the NetBIOS name and IP address to its database.

In a large environment, a directory service should have some mechanism for dynamically adding information to the database.

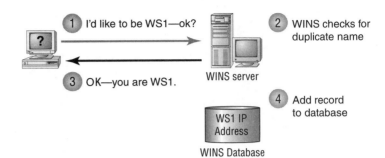

FIGURE 2.4

WINS name
registration

① I'd like to be WS1—ok?

② WINS checks for
duplicate name

③ OK—you are WS1.

WINS server

④ Add record
to database

WS1 IP
Address

WINS Database

Name Resolution

Once a station has determined that its name is unique, it can begin to communicate on the network. In a traditional NetBIOS-based network, names are resolved to IP addresses using broadcast packets. Basically, a workstation yells on the wire, "Hey! I'm looking for a station named WS2—are you out there?" If WS2 is on the wire, it will respond with a packet that contains its IP address. Once again, though, because this process is broadcast-based, most routers will not forward the packets to other networks. In effect, this limits communication to the workstations within a single network segment.

The WINS server also provides a name-resolution service. Instead of using the broadcast method, clients send their request to the WINS server. The WINS server checks the requested name against its database of registered names. If the name is available, the WINS server will return the IP address to the requesting workstation. Once again, because this communication is performed using directed packets, rather than broadcast packets, routers do not interfere with the process. Figure 2.5 shows the name resolution process in a WINS environment, which occurs in the following steps:

1. The client queries the WINS server for the IP address assigned to a NetBIOS name.

2. The WINS server checks the database for a matching record.

3. The WINS server returns the requested information or an error indicating that the requested resource is unavailable.

Lastly, WINS clients send a notification to the WINS server when they are about to go offline. This notification tells the WINS server to remove the record corresponding to the client from its database. (If a client shuts down

FIGURE 2.5

WINS name resolution

without sending this notification, WINS has a mechanism that will delete the record automatically if it hasn't heard from the client in a specified period of time.) From an administrative perspective, this means that the WINS database is both built *and* maintained dynamically—without intervention from the network administrators.

Wherever possible, network directories should have mechanisms that automatically update and maintain the information that they contain.

WINS across a WAN

WINS includes one last mechanism that warrants discussion here. Imagine a WINS network that includes wide-area network (WAN) links, as shown in Figure 2.6. Because WINS uses directed, rather than broadcast-based, communication, the router can pass the requests across the WAN from City 2 to the WINS server in City 1.

While this configuration is possible, it might not be appropriate to send all of the WINS registration and resolution traffic across the WAN link. Bandwidth is usually limited (and expensive) across this kind of line. WINS includes the ability to set up a partnership between WINS servers, overcoming this limitation. With a configuration like the one in Figure 2.7, there is a lot less traffic across the WAN link.

When two WINS servers are configured as partners, they exchange their databases on a regular basis. They can be configured to exchange information based on the number of changes to the database or on a timed basis. In either case, there will be less traffic across the link, and the administrator has more control over when that traffic is generated.

FIGURE 2.6

WINS across a
WAN link

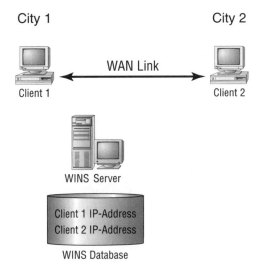

FIGURE 2.7

WINS partnership

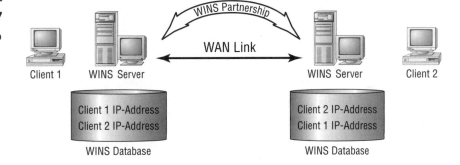

A network directory should include a mechanism that allows control over
the update traffic generated to keep the information current.

WINS in Short

WINS was Microsoft's first attempt at implementing an enterprise-capable
directory service. Considering this fact, WINS is surprisingly stable and efficient. Unfortunately, WINS alone cannot provide the level of service

demanded of a true network directory (although much of the WINS technology can be found in ADS). Microsoft learned a few valuable lessons from the design and implementation of WINS—and these lessons have added to the functionality of ADS.

Novell Directory Services (NDS)

With the release of NetWare version 4, Novell introduced what is arguably the most commercially successful network directory to date. NDS was intended to act as the central point of control for *all* network services in a NetWare environment. NDS is a fully functional, mature, and stable example of the kind of services that a network directory can provide. As such, it merits close examination here—if for no other reason than to serve as an example of a well-designed directory.

There have been numerous rumors concerning the demise of NetWare as a viable product. To paraphrase Mark Twain, the rumors of its death are greatly exaggerated! Case in point: Novell has recently released NetWare 5. NDS becomes more stable and provides more functionality with each release. Don't be surprised if the networks of the future are a mix of NDS and ADS working together to provide network services!

The NDS Structure

The NDS database is critical to the proper functioning of a NetWare network. NDS is queried each time a network resource is accessed. When a user attempts to log on to the network, for instance, the client software submits the user's name to NDS for authentication. Later, this user might try to access some resource, such as a printer, and NDS would again be queried: first to determine whether the user had the necessary permissions and then to find the physical location of the resource. NDS is accessed during all network functions.

The best way to understand NDS (or any network directory) is to think of it as a database. Many administrators are intimidated by the "network" functions of a directory and forget that a network directory is nothing more than a database. The NDS database contains records, or *objects,* that represent network resources. There are many different types, or *classes,* of resources that can be managed through the NDS database. The record type for each class of object has a different set of fields, or *properties.* You wouldn't, for example, need a logon name property for a printer object, because printers do not log on to the network.

Table 2.2 lists a few of the more common classes of objects that exist in an NDS database.

T A B L E 2.2 NDS Object Classes	Class	Description of Object
	User	Holds information specific to a user, such as logon name, password, account restrictions, telephone number, and address.
	Printer	Holds information about a network printer. This object class contains properties such as network address, name, and amount of printer memory.
	Group	Represents a set of users with similar resource needs. All members inherit permissions assigned to the group.
	Volume	Acts as a pointer to a discrete portion of storage space (hard disk, optical, CD-ROM, and so on). This object has properties that pertain to storage devices: network address, the server upon which it resides, and certain permission information.
	Print Queue	Represents a directory used to store print jobs until the system is ready to release them to a printer.
	Alias	Acts as a pointer to an object that exists elsewhere in the NDS structure.

There are many other classes of objects that can exist in the NDS database. NDS is also *extensible:* custom object classes can be created to store information specific to a particular environment. The definition of the object classes contained within a directory is known as its *schema.* The ability to extend the schema to include new or custom object classes is critical for any directory to remain viable in the future.

A network directory contains information about network resources. The definition of a directory's resource records is known as the schema. For a directory to be a viable long-term solution, it must be able to adapt to new technologies. In other words, it must be easily extended to include new object types.

Global Distributed Replicated Database

NDS is marketed as a "global distributed replicated database" used for the management of network resources on a NetWare network. While most marketing phrases are more hype than substance, this phrase actually does a fairly good job of describing how NDS works on a network. By breaking the phrase down into its components, we can understand the basic functionality of the directory.

Global   In earlier versions of NetWare, each server held its own "accounts database" known as the *bindery*. When a user accessed a given server, this bindery (a flat database) would be queried to determine if the username and password submitted were valid. From an administrative perspective, this meant that a user account had to be created at each server that the user might need to access. Users were often required to submit to the logon process multiple times as they accessed different resources on different servers.

One of the many functions of any network directory is to centralize control of network functions. In an NDS-based system, there are no bindery files. Instead, the NDS database is used for all authentication processes. Notice that this implies that there is only one database for the network—no matter how large or geographically dispersed the network. This is what is meant by the term *global database*. When user Wu in Tokyo logs on to the network, he accesses the same database as user Bob in Chicago.

Distributed   Given that an object represents each network resource and each object is really only a record in a database, the NDS database in a global environment could grow into a large file. The next logical question is, "Where is NDS stored?"

Since NDS is critical to most network functions, it might be best to place it in a central location, as shown in Figure 2.8. Placing the database in the middle of your environment seems to put it in the "fairest" location. This placement actually mirrors other kinds of corporate access—it always seems that the offices farthest from the center are the last to know anything.

F I G U R E 2.8

Centrally located NDS
database

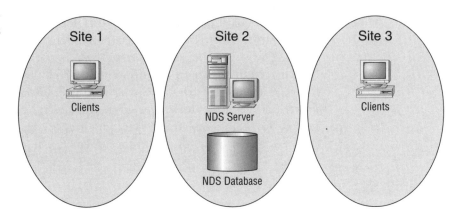

While this arrangement might look good on paper, what if Site 1 is in
Tokyo, Site 2 is in Chicago, and Site 3 is in London? Do we really want users
in Tokyo accessing a server in Chicago every time they need to utilize a network resource? Probably not! This configuration would not only be incon-
venient for the user (imagine how long it would take to log in across the
WAN link), it would also generate an unacceptable amount of traffic on
what is probably an expensive link.

Since a centrally located database is not a good idea, another design
would be to place the database on *all* servers in the network, as shown in
Figure 2.9.

F I G U R E 2.9

NDS on all servers in
the network

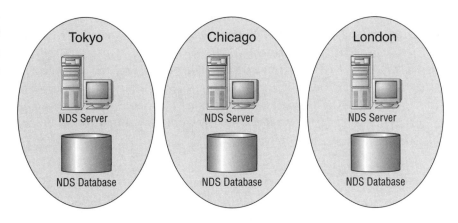

While this configuration would ensure local access to NDS for authentication, it is still not a viable solution. Imagine the traffic that would have to be generated to keep the multiple copies synchronized!

These two scenarios demonstrate the value of a distributed database. NDS can be divided into chunks—the technical term is actually *partitions*—that can be located on servers throughout the network, as shown in Figure 2.10. A good design would be to place the partition that contains records for Tokyo resources (including user accounts) on a server near those resources. This design has the added benefit of distributing the workload of maintaining the database across multiple servers so that no single server is overworked.

FIGURE 2.10

A distributed NDS database

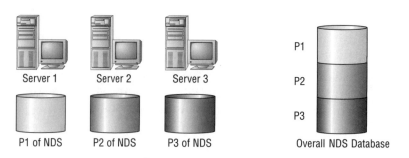

Server 1   Server 2   Server 3

P1 of NDS   P2 of NDS   P3 of NDS   Overall NDS Database

P1
P2
P3

Replicated   While the design shown in Figure 2.10 does solve the problem of where NDS should be located, it does not provide any fault tolerance for the critical information stored in the database. Suppose that Server 1 were to go offline. Since the server that contains her authentication information is not available, user Susan in Chicago would be unable to access *any network resources.*

To solve this "single point of failure" problem, each partition of the database can be copied, or *replicated,* to multiple servers, as shown in Figure 2.11. In the event that Server 1 becomes unavailable, the system can still authenticate user Susan, because her account information is still available on Server 2.

Scalability

Figure 2.11 shows another important feature of NDS. Notice that we now have complete fault tolerance of the database: Each partition exists on more than one server. To provide this fault tolerance, though, no server has to

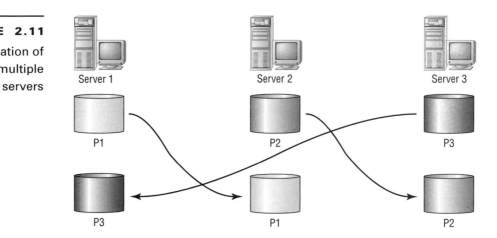

FIGURE 2.11

Replication of partitions to multiple servers

hold more than two-thirds of the database. As a network grows, each server will have to hold less and less of the database—and therefore spend less and less time managing NDS—but we will still have complete fault tolerance. This is known as *scalability*. As the number of servers increases, the amount of overhead placed on each server decreases. In other words, NDS becomes more efficient as the network becomes larger.

NDS in Short

NDS is a mature, stable, and efficient network directory. It can be used as the measuring stick for all other directories. The only real weakness of NDS is its proprietary nature. When NDS was released, there were no other viable directories on the market, thus no industry standards were in place to guide Novell's development team. This resulted in a directory that is not as accessible to non-Novell environments as administrators might like. Given the track record of Windows NT and Microsoft, in the long run it is more likely that developers will be working on ADS add-ons than NDS add-ons.

Since this is a book about a Microsoft product, I felt obliged to make that last statement. Actually, Novell has released a product known as NDS for NT that provides directory-based management of NT domains through Novell NDS. For more information, see *The Complete Guide to Novell Directory Services* by Dave Kearns and Brian Iverson (ISBN 0-7821-1823-2, Sybex, 1998).

In Short

Each of the solutions that we have discussed—DNS, WINS, and NDS—offers lessons in how a directory should be implemented (and in a couple of cases, how one should *not* function). The "wish list" can act as our yardstick as we compare ADS to these other directories:

- Any directory service *must* include a set of clearly defined, standard rules for naming the objects that it contains.

- A network directory should include the ability to split the database in order to distribute the maintenance and access overhead across multiple computers.

- A network directory should have the ability to dynamically confirm the validity of at least some of the information it contains.

- A network directory in a large environment must be completely fault tolerant. The loss of a single server should in no way affect network functionality.

- In a large environment, a directory service should have some mechanism for dynamically adding information to the database.

- Wherever possible, network directories should have mechanisms that automatically update and maintain the information the directories contain.

- A network directory should include a mechanism that allows control over the update traffic generated to keep the information current.

A network directory contains information about network resources. For a directory to be a viable long-term solution, it must be able to adapt to new technologies. In other words, it must be easily extended to include new object types.

In Chapter 3, we will discuss the ways that information can be organized within a database. Network directories serve a very specific function, so they use a very specific form of organization.

CHAPTER

3

The X.500
Recommendations

In the preceding chapters, we discussed network directories as repositories for network information. For this information to be of any use, it must be organized in a manner that makes it easy to access and secure. There are many different types of databases on the market and just as many different ways to organize them. For network directories, however, various design specifications preclude most of these.

A flat-file database, for instance, would not work for a large directory. Imagine how large the file would be in a global network. The size limitations would confine its usefulness to networks so small that they don't really need a directory. Beyond even the physical limits, imagine trying to define a record type that could manage everything from user accounts to router configuration.

A relational database also would not handle the needs of a full-fledged network directory. Given the diversity of the information that a network directory must store, the number of related files would grow so large that just the index of relationships would soon overwhelm even the fastest computers on the market.

Based on the specialized needs of a network directory, the industry has developed the X.500 recommendations for organizing directories. Microsoft has adopted these recommendations in its design of the ADS database. A firm understanding of these recommendations is necessary before any discussion of ADS can continue. Since X.500 is a recommendation and not a standard, incompatibilities exist between the implementations of X.500. For example, Microsoft's implementation differs from Novell's, but since the namespace is consistent, the information stored in the directory can be accessed from either implementation.

What Is X.500?

Before we discuss what X.500 *is,* we should define what it is *not.* X.500 does *not* define the implementation of network directories. X.500 is instead a model upon which vendors can build their own products. In this, it resembles the seven-layer OSI (Open Systems Interconnection) networking model, which simply defines the functions that must be performed by networking software at each layer, without defining direct implementation techniques.

The X.500 Recommendations

The X.500 specifications were originally developed in conjunction with the OSI networking model (the same seven-layer model that many of us learned, and then forgot, while studying for various networking certifications). The goal of the specification was to provide a mechanism that would allow products from different vendors the ability to access and share information. Exactly what type of information is not defined; that is left up to the implementation of the vendor. What *is* defined is a common method of organizing, naming, and accessing that information—in other words, a standard definition of the format that the directory will take to facilitate interoperability. Two international standards organizations—the ISO (International Standards Organization) and the IEC (International Electrotechnical Commission)—created a joint committee, the International Telecommunications Union (ITU), to oversee a set of technical documents with this goal in mind. The documents that make up the X.500 recommendations are listed below.

If you are overly curious or suffer from insomnia, the following nine documents make up the core of the X.500 technical suite. While most administrators will not need this level of expertise, these documents do give a wonderful feel for the goals of the international committee. It's interesting to note that if you read these documents and then work with any product on the market, you will have a firm understanding of the difference between compatible and compliant.

- ITU-T Recommendation X.500 (1993) ISO/IEC 9594-1:1993, *Information Technology—Open Systems Interconnection—The Directory: Overview of Concepts, Models, and Services.* This is probably the best read of the bunch. It provides a great overview of what a directory is all about.

- ITU-T Recommendation X.500 (1993) ISO/IEC 9594-2:1993, *Information Technology—Open Systems Interconnection—The Directory: Models.* Provides a series of models to be used in the other documents.

- ITU-T Recommendation X.500 (1993) ISO/IEC 9594-3:1993, *Information Technology—Open Systems Interconnection—The Directory: Abstract Service Definition.* Defines, in an abstract way, the externally visible services provided by a directory (such as Read or Write services to the data).

- ITU-T Recommendation X.500 (1993) ISO/IEC 9594-4:1993, *Information Technology—Open Systems Interconnection—The Directory: Procedures for Distributed Operations.* Specifies ways in which the distributed components of a directory can interoperate.

- ITU-T Recommendation X.500 (1993) ISO/IEC 9594-5:1993, *Information Technology—Open Systems Interconnection—The Directory: Protocol Specifications.* Defines various protocols used by or to access the directory.

- ITU-T Recommendation X.500 (1993) ISO/IEC 9594-6:1993, *Information Technology—Open Systems Interconnection—The Directory: Selected Attribute Types.* Defines various attributes for the data stored in a directory, such as the naming of objects.

- ITU-T Recommendation X.500 (1993) ISO/IEC 9594-7:1993, *Information Technology—Open Systems Interconnection—The Directory: Selected Object Classes.* Defines a series of common types of data that might be stored. These classes can act as the starting point for vendors when creating their products.

- ITU-T Recommendation X.500 (1993) ISO/IEC 9594-8:1993, *Information Technology—Open Systems Interconnection—The Directory: Authentication Framework.* Defines two methods of authentication:

  - Simple, in which passwords are exchanged

  - Strong, which can take advantage of credentials formed using cryptographic techniques

- ITU-T Recommendation X.500 (1993) ISO/IEC 9594-9:1993, *Information Technology—Open Systems Interconnection—The Directory: Replication*. Defines methods for replication of the data within the directory to various directory servers and provides for automatic updates.

Using the X.500 Recommendations

As a guideline (rather than a detailed specification), the X.500 recommendations act as a frame upon which vendors can build their own implementation. The members of the ITU agency (hereafter referred to as the X.500 committee) had no idea what the scope of such products would be, but to help focus their efforts they did make a few assumptions about the environments in which directories would be used:

- The networks would be large and subject to constant change. Think of a large network: How many resources are completely static? Users move from place to place, devices are added, removed, or moved on a regular basis, and the attributes of objects (passwords, telephone numbers, or even network addresses) are extremely variable.

- While the overall rate of change will be high, the useful lifetime of the information will not be short. Stated another way, the information stored in the directory will be accessed by users more often than it changes.

- Most network resources are identified by some "address" that is chosen for efficiency rather than user convenience.

The overall goal was to provide users (*users* can be either people or other computer programs) with information about network resources, while insulating them from the mechanics of the network. At the same time, the directory should allow for the maintenance, distribution, and security of that information. Network resources can be just about anything that can attach to a network—from users to computers to printers.

Since a primary goal of the directory is to insulate users from the mechanics of the network, the information stored must be presented in a user-friendly manner. Each resource must be given a user-friendly name and the interface should be intuitive (or at least as intuitive as possible). This name can be thought of as a pointer to the resource. Since the name is just a pointer, it can remain the same even if something has changed on the networking side. A printer named ColorLaser, for instance, can still be named ColorLaser even if it is upgraded to the latest model or moved to another area of the office. From the users' perspective, these changes have no bearing on their access to the resource.

Developing Uses for a Directory

During the creation of the recommendations, the X.500 committee envisioned three generic, practical uses for a directory. These generic examples were intended to inspire developers to more complex uses.

Interpersonal Communication   The directory can play a role in many forms of interpersonal communication (such as e-mail) by providing the information necessary for users (or their software-based agents) to communicate with their counterparts in another system. Imagine a worldwide directory that includes things like telephone numbers and addresses. A user would have a single point of access to all of that data.

Intersystem Communication   The directory could also be used to provide the information necessary for one service to talk to another. A prime example would be one mail server trying to deliver mail to another mail server. Today, we use another database (DNS) for this type of mail delivery across the Internet. As you saw in Chapter 2, DNS is a great tool, but it does have its limitations.

Authentication Services   The directory could also act as a primary source for identification and authentication of users to resources. By using passwords or some other form of identifier, the directory could act as a single point of control over access to information and services.

Designing a Directory

Designing any database is really more a logical exercise than a technical one. First you must decide the purpose of the database, then you decide on an overall structure. For an X.500-compliant network directory, such as ADS, these two steps are predetermined:

- Its purpose is to store information about network resources.
- Its structure is hierarchical.

With most databases, the next step would be to define records and fields. This is where the design of a network directory becomes a little more complicated than the access databases that most of us are comfortable with.

The Schema

One of the first tasks involved in designing any type of database is defining the types of records that exist within it and the information that each record will contain. Within an X.500 directory there can be many different types of records. A record is called an *object,* and each type of record is known as a *class.* Each class of object is made up of different fields known as *attributes.* A record for a user would be of the class "user," have various attributes (like telephone numbers or passwords), and be known as a user object. The definition of the object classes and attributes available for any given directory is known as its *schema.*

Since the X.500 recommendations are just a model and not an implementation, there are very few object classes predefined. There is, however, a well-documented set of rules for how objects and attributes should be created to allow for interoperability between various vendors' directories. While an in-depth discussion of this process is beyond the scope of this book, an overview can be helpful when implementing a directory on a network.

The X.500 committee assumed that certain types of information might be made available through the directory. These generic types include

- Information about people, such as e-mail addresses, telephone numbers, and public key certificates

- Information about servers and services, such as network port addresses

- Information about the directory itself, used to perform consistency checks and replication

You should note a couple of things about the list. First, it is extremely generic; there is very little detail provided about the class of objects that should exist. Second, the list is open to expansion should the need arise.

Determining the Scope

When designing a directory-based product, a vendor must first define the scope of the directory. That is, they must first decide the various classes of objects they wish to support. Basically, the vendor must decide which aspects of the physical world should exist in the directory database. The directory for a network operating system, for instance, would have to include things like user accounts, groups, servers, storage devices, printers—in other words, the various pieces of information that would be involved in a network. A manufacturer of network equipment, however, might have a completely different list. Here, it might be more appropriate to store things like routers, bridges, and gateways.

As you can see, deciding the scope determines what information will be available within the directory. The goal of the X.500 recommendations is that these different types of directories will be able to share information because they are based upon the same design framework.

Which Attributes?

Once a vendor has determined the scope, the next step is to decide what attributes should be stored for each class of object. The attributes are a second step because the format of the directory allows multiple classes of objects to use the same attribute definitions. The name attribute, for instance, would be used for all records regardless of class. An IP address attribute, however, might only be used by physical devices or user accounts (documenting where the user is logged on to the system). It would probably not be a necessary attribute for a group object.

After these decisions have been made, a vendor can begin the process of building the schema of the database. The schema holds the definition for the object classes in the database and their attributes. The first step in building a schema is to define the attributes for objects. Then the developers combine attributes to build object classes.

Creating a Directory

Microsoft has claimed that the ADS schema will be easily extensible; in other words, you will be able to define your own attributes and object classes. We're not going to get into the actual coding process, but it might be helpful to explore the thoughts behind building a schema.

Determining the Directory's Scope

Begin by determining the scope of your directory. Microsoft has an ambitious plan for ADS: It will probably contain records for users, routers, applications, printers, and just about everything else you might associate with your networks. For our purposes, let's keep your directory simple. You should design a few user-related object classes and leave the highly technical network components to the experts at Microsoft.

First, let's define the classes of objects to include the following:

User   Represents the network user to the system

Group   Represents a number of users for administrative purposes

Printer   Represents the physical device on the network

Storage Space   Represents some form of storage, such as hard drive, CD-ROM, or tape drive

Service   Represents some service provided to the network, such as e-mail, DHCP, or DNS

This list is not complete enough to act as an actual network directory, but it will suffice for our purposes.

The next step is to define the information that you would like to store for each object class—in other words, the attributes that will be needed for each object.

For a user object, you might want to store some of the following attributes:

- Name: A unique identifier
- Password
- Security certificate: A place to store advanced security certificates
- Telephone number
- E-mail address: Multiple forms for Exchange, SNMP, or other mail systems
- Mail stop
- Department
- Network address: Multiple values to hold current IP, MAC, or other network addresses

- Description: A text field to be used for any nonstandard information
- Class: The type of object
- Location: Physical location of the user

This list could go on and on. If your users do a lot of traveling, for instance, you might want to store things like frequent-flyer memberships, seating preferences, or rental car company preferences. Your Human Resources department might like your directory to store items such as benefits package options or dates of hire.

For the group object, your list might include:

- Name: A unique identifier
- E-mail address: Multiple forms for Exchange, SNMP, or other mail systems for all members
- Telephone number: Perhaps for the person responsible for the group's activities
- Description: A text field to be used for any nonstandard information
- Class: The type of object
- Member list: A list of all user accounts associated with this group
- Purpose: A text field used to describe the function of the group

Once again, this list could have numerous options. You might, for instance, want to store a pointer to a group Web page on your intranet server.

Things should be a little simpler for your printer object:

- Name
- Network address: The IP or MAC address of the device
- Make/Model: The manufacturer and model number for the device
- Serial number
- Date of purchase
- Warranty information: A text field describing any warranties in effect for the printer—perhaps you could even add a date option to alert you when the warranted time has expired

- Memory

- Fonts

- Client print drivers: Multiple drivers for various clients that might use this printer

Your storage device object should also be fairly straightforward:

- Name

- Network address

- File system: FAT, NTFS, CDFS, etc.

- Configuration: RAID, mirrored, etc.

- Date of purchase

- Warranty information

- Size

- Writable media: Yes/No

- Removable media: Yes/No

Finally, we come to your service object. This object might be a little more complex. There are so many network services that coming up with a standard format might not be possible, but you can add attributes as needed later. Here are some attributes to get you started:

- Name

- Network address

- Description

- Location

As you can see, planning the information that should be held within the directory can be a complex job. You have to include any critical information (how would you find a print device without some sort of address?), as well as any information that might reduce either the management or user-access overhead.

Defining Attributes

Once you have created your list of object classes and attributes, the X.500 recommendations determine how you should define these items. First, you should combine all of your attributes into one list and cross-reference those that can be used for more than one object class, as shown in Table 3.1.

T A B L E 3.1: Directory Attribute List

	User	Group	Printer	Storage Space	Service
Name	X	X	X	X	X
Password	X				
Security Certificate	X				
Telephone Number	X	X			
E-mail Address	X	X			
Mail Stop	X				
Department	X	X	X	X	X
Network Address	X		X	X	X
Description	X	X	X	X	X
Object Class	X	X	X	X	X
Location	X		X	X	X
Member List		X			X
Purpose		X			X
Make/Model			X	X	
Serial Number			X	X	
Date of Purchase			X	X	

T A B L E 3.1: Directory Attribute List *(continued)*

	User	Group	Printer	Storage Space	Service
Warranty Information			X	X	
Memory			X		
Fonts			X		
Print Drivers			X		
File System				X	
Configuration			X	X	X
Size				X	

By creating the attribute definitions first, developers can save themselves a lot of redundant work. Objects are "built" by adding various attributes to a frame, rather than by building each object from the ground up. There are certain attributes that will be common to all object classes. Each object needs a unique name, for example, so that it can be referenced as a separate entity. Each object will also have to be classified as a member of a class, so that the system can properly identify the resource or service to users.

Hierarchical Structures: X.500 and DOS

X.500 presents a method of organizing the data stored within a directory that is easy to manage and that also makes it easy for users to access the information they need. The recommendations define the model as a hierarchical structure, often referred to as the *directory tree*. For some reason, many experienced network administrators have a hard time with the concept of a directory tree structure. For years, networks have had a server-centric design: Each server was an island of services in a sea of connectivity.

The X.500 recommendations present a new paradigm for network management that can take some getting used to. While it *is* different, the concept is nothing new. Computer professionals have been working with a hierarchical system for quite some time—DOS! Since both DOS and an X.500

directory tree are based upon a hierarchical structure, the management of each is very similar. Let's review a few simple DOS basics before we look at the X.500 structure—basics that will help us understand a hierarchical network directory structure.

Default Directory

The first term to review is *default directory*. In DOS, the default directory is the directory in which you are currently working. Here's another way of looking at it: If you were to save a file (without specifying a path), it would be placed in your default directory. This is quite a bit different from Windows 98 and NT, which hold a default "save" location (usually a directory named My Documents) in the Registry. Because many DOS activities revolved around the default directory, we often configured our prompt to display the default directory. (Remember the C:\ prompt?) Figure 3.1 shows a common DOS directory structure. Let's review a few more basic DOS recommendations before we go on.

FIGURE 3.1

DOS directory
structure

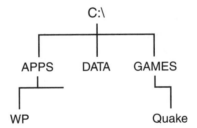

Naming DOS Files

First, let's review how DOS files are named. Most of us are probably used to simply typing in just the filename to start a program. In the example in Figure 3.1, for instance, we would probably start a game of Quake by typing **Quake**. In reality, though, that is not the full name of the file. The full name of the file includes the path back to the root of the drive: In this case, the full name of the file would be C:\games\quake\quake.exe. As a convenience, DOS includes the path function so that we don't have to type in the complete name to start a program.

The concept of a "complete" name will be very important when we start looking at X.500 directories.

Moving Around in DOS

In DOS, we use the CD (Change Directory) command to move around the structure. If your default directory were `C:\` and you wanted to move to the Quake directory, you would enter the following command:

```
CD games\quake
```

In the background, DOS would perform an append action, adding what you typed to your default directory to end up with your destination. If the named destination exists, you are moved there. If not, DOS will return an error.

If your default directory were `C:\apps\wp` and you wished to move to the `C:\data` directory, you would enter the following command:

```
CD \data
```

The backslash character (\) indicates the root in this command. DOS moves to the root and appends the path you have entered. Once again, if you have entered a correct path, you will be moved there.

For most of us, moving around a DOS file system is second nature. Luckily, this means that moving around an X.500 directory structure is also second nature!

The X.500 Hierarchical Structure

The structure of a directory specifies how the information within the directory will be organized. There are two main goals for the design of any network directory structure:

- Object identification

- Object organization

Both goals are critical to the proper functioning of any directory.

Object identification ensures that each object within the structure has some sort of unique identifier. Each unique identifier must map directly to some resource. Think of it this way: Without some unique name, you would be unable to ask for information about a particular resource. At best, you could ask for information about all similar objects. Imagine that you needed to print a document. Instead of identifying the printer near your desk, you would have to present a request for all "HP printers in my building," or some other, less specific grouping. In this case, you wouldn't know whether your job would print at the nearest printer or at some HP printer on another floor. The unique identifier allows you to specify a particular object within the directory database.

Object organization allows the data within the directory to be broken into subsets for administrative purposes. Suppose you wanted a local administrator at the Tampa office to be able to create new user objects within a certain area of your structure. Without some sort of organizational plan, it would be difficult to limit the access of the administrator.

The X.500 recommendations not only fulfill these two requirements quite well (as you'll see in a few pages) but actually exceed them. The X.500 structure defines a uniform way to uniquely name objects and provides a framework that can be used to organize those objects once they are created. It also provides for other necessary services: distribution of the database to multiple servers, replication of pieces of the database to more than one server, and various protocols to be used when accessing the directory.

The X.500 Tree

As I stated earlier, there are many similarities between the DOS file structure and the X.500 directory structure. In DOS, you organize your files by creating directories and subdirectories. In an X.500 structure, we have the equivalent of directories, called *containers*. Instead of using containers to organize files, you use them to organize the objects within your database.

You may have heard the DOS structure referred to as a "tree" because of the way subdirectories branch off from the root of the drive. Since the X.500 structure acts in much the same way, we refer to it as the *tree*. You use the tree to organize your objects for ease of management or ease of access (just as you'd use directories to organize files for the same reasons in DOS). In an X.500 tree, we refer to the objects as *leaves*. A leaf object can be defined as any object that does not contain any other object. This can get complicated, so let's start with the container objects and ignore leaf objects for now.

In DOS there is no real difference between a directory and a subdirectory, except that subdirectories are beneath some directory in the structure. Unlike DOS, the X.500 structure does define different types of container objects. Each has a specific purpose and certain limits on placement within the tree.

The types of containers are

Country   Represented as a C object. The highest container object in the schema as defined by the X.500 committee. It can only exist at the top, or root, of the tree.

Organization   Represented as an O object. These containers can only exist off the root of the tree or below a country.

Location   Represented as an L object. A grouping object that can exist at any level of the tree except directly below the root.

Organizational Unit   Represented as an OU object. Another grouping object. Basically, this is the equivalent of a subdirectory in DOS. OUs can exist under Os or other OUs.

Figure 3.2 presents a graphical representation of an X.500 structure for the company King Technologies. King Technologies has offices in Tampa, Florida and Berlin, Germany.

FIGURE 3.2

Directory tree structure for King Technologies

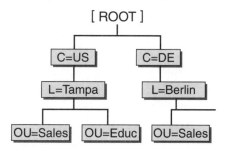

As with a DOS disk, there is no *right* way to organize a network directory. Many of the principles are the same, though. In DOS you create a directory for one of two reasons: to ease access or to ease management. The same holds true when creating containers in a network directory. Unnecessary levels only add to users' confusion and to management overhead.

Once you have planned the structure, the next step is to populate it with leaf objects. Within the directory, leaf objects are represented by CN, as shown in Figure 3.3.

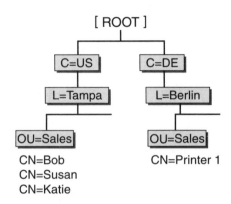

In Short

An X.500 network directory is nothing more than a complicated database. The database holds objects, which in turn have attributes (records and their fields). Because of the complicated nature of its job, the directory is organized in a hierarchical fashion. The structure is defined as a series of container objects connected in a tree-like manner.

There are numerous types of container objects and rules about their use, as you can see in Table 3.2.

T A B L E 3.2 Containers in an X.500 Directory	**Name**	**Representation**	**Valid Placement in the Tree**
	Country	C	Can exist only at the top, or root, of the tree
	Organization	O	Can exist only directly below the root or a country container
	Location	L	Can exist anywhere except directly off the root
	Organizational Unit	OU	Can exist only under an organization object or another organizational unit

In this chapter, we discussed how a directory is designed, the types of information it can hold, and how that information is organized. Once any directory has been populated with data (user accounts, groups, peripherals, and so on), it must be made accessible if it is to have any value. In the next chapter, we will discuss an industry standard set of protocols specifically designed to access information stored in a directory database.

CHAPTER
4

Accessing the Directory

So far, we have concentrated on the structure of directory databases. Once you have defined the schema, the next step is to populate the database with objects. The mechanics of creating objects and filling the database with data will be discussed in detail in later chapters. For the moment, let's assume that you have created your environment. Now you can just sit back and relax, right? Hardly! You have entered a lot of useful information—the next step is making that information available to the right people. After all, why did you spend hours typing in addresses, phone numbers, and locations if that information was never going to be used?

Making Information Available

At first, your users will not even be aware of the directory. Of course, if not for the splash screens of modern operating systems, many users wouldn't even know they were working on a network (until it goes down). They will log on to the network, access necessary resources, and fulfill their job functions without giving a second thought to the underlying mechanism of the network.

In the early days of networks, administrators tried to hide the "plumbing" of networks so that users could do their jobs without having to be concerned with the mechanics of networking. The highest compliment an administrator could receive was a user's unwitting question, "Network, what network?" Of course, with today's operating systems this goal is impossible—it seems that users are constantly being presented with splash screens advertising the network software.

As time passes, users will begin to see the directory as a source of useful information, asking "What's Joe's phone number?" or "What's the mailing address of the marketing department?" or even "I need to e-mail the receptionist in the sales group—what is his name?" The answers to all of these questions can be stored within your directory and made available to users. Not only can you make the information available, you will be able to control access to specific attributes. Perhaps everyone should be able to access the e-mail addresses, but only managers should be able to access home telephone numbers.

Accessing the Data

The fact that this information *can* be made available implies that there must be some mechanism used for access. The design and capabilities of the directory itself will influence the methods used to access the data it contains. Certain aspects of a network directory must be taken into account when choosing an access method.

An X.500 directory follows a hierarchical structure. Hierarchical databases organize data much differently than standard databases. In a flat-file or relational database, each record has some unique field (or combination of fields) that differentiates it from every other record in the database. In a hierarchical database, each object is identified by its place in the structure. The tools used to access information from an X.500-compliant database must understand the structure of the schema and must format requests appropriately.

Presentation Scheme

A directory's *presentation scheme* defines the methods that can be used for accessing information stored in the directory. Without a well-defined presentation scheme, the data would be inaccessible. The X.500 specifications provide a standard set of access capabilities for presenting directory information to users. Access is accomplished through the use of a *Directory User Agent* (DUA) built into an application designed for directory access. The DUA interacts with a *Directory Service Agent* (DSA) at the directory server, as shown in Figure 4.1.

FIGURE 4.1

Client access to the
directory

DAP and LDAP

Two protocols are available for use in accessing the directory:

- Directory Access Protocol (DAP)

- Lightweight Directory Access Protocol (LDAP)

DAP was defined as a part of the X.500 specification. LDAP, on the other hand, was defined independently of X.500 as a method for accessing both X.500 and non-X.500 directories. Each has its strengths and weaknesses, but LDAP has become the preferred method of access because of its less proprietary nature and lower overhead on the client. LDAP clients with the proper permissions can search, add, delete, and modify objects and attributes within a directory. LDAP functionality consists of 16 calls, used for directory management.

Directory Access Protocol (DAP)

During the development of the X.500 recommendations, the X.500 committee spent time considering the ultimate use of the directory. There are certain functions that are standard with *any* database and other uses that would be specific to the function of the directory. Users of any database need to be able to perform the following tasks:

Lookup   This is the basic information retrieval used by users. Users request specific information about a known resource (such as "What is Bill's phone number?").

Searching and filtering   A user can use information associated with resources to locate individual resources (such as "List all users in the Sales department").

Browsing   An LDAP call can be used to present information in some sort of list from which users can choose specific resources. ("I don't remember the name of the object, but I will recognize it when I see it.")

Other tasks will be more directory oriented. These tasks are not *normal* database functions—they are applicable only to the purpose of a network directory:

Name Resolution   Resources can be located based upon easily remembered names. This can be thought of as a special case of lookup. (The corporate standard for user accounts is last name, first initial. Knowing this standard, and knowing the name of the person I'm looking for, allows me to easily find his object in the directory.)

Authentication   Authentication involves some type of security system used to positively identify a user in order to determine permissible access to resources. (A user proves her identity by providing a password. Resource access can be based upon this "proven" identity.)

The five tasks just listed—lookup, searching and filtering, browsing, name resolution, and authentication—are the end result of some action taken by the client software. They all revolve around the ability to interrogate the directory. DAP provides five functions that a client can initiate when accessing the database for information:

Read   A request aimed at a specific object. This action will return the values of some or all of the attributes of the object in question. If a limited set of attributes is to be returned, the client software (DUA) supplies the list of desired attributes to the server (DSA). A client might, for instance, request the phone number attribute of a particular user object.

Compare   This is a request aimed at a particular attribute of a particular object. In some implementations, a user might be able to compare an attribute without having the ability to actually read it. An example of this functionality might be security software that checks for the existence of a password without being able to read the passwords themselves.

List   This action will return a list of objects in the directory. A user might, for instance, request a list of all printers within (or below) the Tampa container in the directory tree.

Search   This action returns a list of objects where a certain attribute matches a supplied filter. A user might, for example, want a list of all users where the telephone number attribute begins with the 727 area code.

Abandon   This action informs the directory to stop an action requested by a user. If a user is performing a search on a large directory, for instance, the desired information might be presented before the entire search has been completed, or the search is taking too long and has been terminated by the client, or the search has timed out. Issuing an Abandon request would cause the DSA to stop the search.

Client software will use these five basic functions to make the information stored within a directory available to users or network services. Users, for example, can search the database for the telephone numbers stored within it, basically eliminating the need for a special-purpose database for this task (or worse—a paper-based solution that is never up to date). Network services can query the database as part of their function. An e-mail package might query the database to determine whether a user is currently connected to the network, and if so, to find the address of the user's station. Once the database is made accessible, its uses are limitless!

Modifying the Directory

Reading the information is only half the story, though. While some of the information within the directory will be automatically maintained, much of the information must still be entered and maintained manually. This implies that there must be another set of functions that provide the ability to modify the directory. DAP defines four specific functions for modifying the directory:

Add entry   This request adds a new object to the directory.

Remove entry   This request deletes an object from the directory.

Modify entry   This request is used to change an existing object. This function is used to change attributes such as telephone numbers or addresses.

Modify distinguished name   This request is used to rename objects within the directory (as well as any subordinate objects).

As you can see from the descriptions, these four functions allow complete management of the directory. Objects can be created, deleted, and manipulated using the DAP protocol and an appropriate tool.

Providing Access to the Directory

Once you have implemented a directory, it can become critical to the proper functioning of your network. Since it can be used to authenticate users during the logon process, for instance, there can be absolutely no question about the integrity of the information that the directory stores. Each DAP request can be configured so that security mechanisms can be included in the process.

To put it another way, consider that the directory can contain information that is either confidential (such as user passwords or other security certificates) or critical to network functionality (such as the address of a network printer). Clearly, you want to protect such information against inappropriate access or manipulation. Each of the requests defined in the DAP specifications can include security information that can be used to determine whether the requesting user is allowed to perform the function. Normal users, for instance, would not have the rights required to change the database—this ability would be reserved for administrative personnel.

Network directories must have some sort of internal security that can be used to limit access to the information they contain.

In a typical scenario, the directory will be used to authenticate the user during the logon process. The user will have supplied some unique fact, such as a password, that ensures his identity. Passwords are the most common method of authentication used today, but other methods are on the horizon. There are numerous hardware- or software-based tools that can use much more specific information to identify a user. Some of the options available either today or in the near future include:

- Hardware that accepts a magnetic ID card (much like a credit card) that contains a user's identification credentials

- Hardware that can scan a user's fingerprints or retinal patterns and match them against a stored value

- Software that uses a camera to "sense" a user's face and matches it against a stored picture

- Certificate software that uses a series of encrypted values to ensure identity (much like the software used to secure Web-based transactions)

Whatever the method used for identification, an X.500 directory can be used to store the unique information necessary for authentication. During the logon process, the security subsystem can compare a value submitted by the user's client software against this particular attribute of the user account, as shown in Figure 4.2.

1. The user supplies identification information to the logon software (this can be a password, a certificate, or some other, more sophisticated identifier).

2. The client software then submits this information to a directory server.

3. The directory server finds the user's object and compares the information against the value of a security attribute.

FIGURE 4.2

User authentication

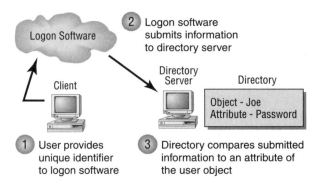

Once the user has been properly identified, this identification can control access to information within the directory. Each attribute of each object can contain a list of the users who are allowed to read or manipulate its value. DAP requests can pass the user's identity to the directory service with each request.

What's the Cost?

Any time you add another service to your network, it costs money. First there is the cost in person-hours. You will need to be trained in the capabilities and tools of any new technology. Users will also need training if they are going to see any benefit from the implementation. All of this training adds up to lost person-hours for your company. The hope is that the cost will be offset by higher productivity in the future. Such costs are hard to quantify and therefore hard to justify. They are also (thankfully) beyond the scope of this material. There are also, however, tangible costs associated with new services; these costs *are* within the scope of this book.

As anyone who has ever had to work with a large, complex database can confirm, performing complex searches can eat up server resources. The larger the database and the more complex the queries, the better your hardware will have to be to provide adequate performance. ADS is no different from any other large database in this respect. DAP has defined a set of standard capabilities to help with this issue.

DAP is defined as a client-intensive protocol. Most of the "up-front" work is performed at the client computer. The client software is responsible for the proper formatting of any requests, which means that any client software must have a complete understanding of the directory it is designed to query. Moving these functions to the *client* reduces the overhead at the server, but it does have a few drawbacks.

Client Overhead

Because the client must fully understand the directory, the programs tend to be large and resource-intensive. The more complex the directory becomes, the more complex the client software must be to access it.

Client overhead might seem like an unimportant issue given the power of today's computers. Actually, it is critical to industry acceptance of X.500 directories. DAP was developed to allow remote access to the information stored within a directory. DAP works fine if a user is sitting at his Pentium II desktop computer, but it might not work so well for a user who is away from her desk. Consider the type of information stored in the directory: User names and addresses, phone numbers, e-mail addresses—exactly the kinds of things stored in most electronic Rolodexes or palmtop computers. It would be great if a user could access the directory from his Palm Pilot! Unfortunately, most of these types of components have limited resources—usually not enough to handle the overhead of DAP client software.

Proprietary Software

Since any client software must understand the directory that it will query and since the X.500 standards are a model, not an implementation, vendors will need to produce proprietary client software to access their directory. In effect, this will either limit networks to a single-vendor solution or force users to master multiple programs to access the information in different brands of directories.

Limiting Use of Resources

As well as moving much of the work to the client, DAP also includes the ability to limit the server resources used by any request. Users can set limits for the actions they take, as in the following examples:

Time limits DAP client software can set a limit on the length of time to be spent on a given request. In a large database, this can prevent a client from performing a search that "spans the globe." If a request exceeds its time limit, the server will abandon the action.

Limits on the size of the results DAP client software can also limit the size of the returned information set. If a user inadvertently asks for all "User" accounts, for instance, this could restrict the amount of information returned.

Limits on the scope of the request These limits allow a user to configure the query so that only a portion of the directory is searched. When asking for a "Printer" object, for example, the user could limit the search to the local portion of the directory tree.

Setting priority DAP client software can be configured so that certain requests have a lower priority than others. For example, looking up a telephone number should not have the same priority as finding the address of the nearest WINS server.

These limits can be implemented in various ways. During the installation of the client software, default maximum values for each limit could be set—thereby limiting any user who performs a query from that computer. The directory itself could easily hold limits on an individual or group level. Using the directory to hold limits would mean that users would have their default maximums set *any* time they perform a query (the directory would check the "query limits" attributes of a user when she accessed the database). Another option would be to limit queries on a server-by-server basis. This option would allow administrators the option of reducing the workload on servers that are already overworked.

DAP in Short

In an effort to standardize the methods used to access an X.500 directory, the X.500 committee created a protocol specifically designed for this purpose: the Directory Access Protocol. DAP defines the methods used to both read and modify the directory database.

DAP has a few built-in design features that merit discussion. Knowing that a directory must contain internal security, each DAP function is capable of including security information in its requests. This security can be as simple as using the logon credentials of the user's account (in other words, trusting the directory to have properly identified the user at first access using some sort of password-security scheme) or as complex as including various industry-standard security certificates.

Since the X.500 directory recommendations allow for many types of security (simple password authentication, X.509 certificates, or even more complex identification like fingerprint or retinal matches), DAP is extensible so that it can take advantage of any of these security procedures.

DAP was specifically designed to reduce the workload at directory servers by moving much of the functionality to the client computer. While this design benefits the directory, it does mean that client computers must have the necessary horsepower to perform these functions. Another feature is the ability to limit resource usage at the server. User queries can be limited in the time, size, scope, or priority of the searches they perform.

All in all, the DAP specifications achieve their goal—defining a standard method of accessing an X.500 directory. As you will see in the next section, however, the weaknesses of DAP have forced the development of another protocol—one that is better designed for real-world applications.

Lightweight Directory Access Protocol (LDAP)

While the Directory Access Protocol (DAP) is the access protocol defined within the X.500 specifications, it is not the access method that is getting the most press. That honor goes to the Lightweight Directory Access Protocol (LDAP), a protocol that is *not* defined within the X.500 recommendations. LDAP developed in direct response to the major weaknesses of DAP:

- Using DAP-based software places a tremendous amount of overhead on the client computer. Many client machines, especially PCs or Macintosh-based computers, lack the resources necessary to support any DAP services.

- DAP was designed specifically to communicate with X.500 directories. This means that many vendor-specific products will not be accessible using DAP-enabled software.

These two limitations of the DAP protocol have hindered the implementation of X.500 directories on production systems. While the X.500 specifications are a great model, they are limited by the fact that they *are* only a model. Most commercial products will be X.500 compatible, but will not conform 100 percent to the model set forth by the standard. In effect, this lack of a multivendor access protocol has made X.500 directories an interesting theory but not a real-world solution. Combine this with the fact that even if you take a chance and implement an X.500 directory, many of your client computers will lack the necessary horsepower to access the database—and you end up with a great idea whose time has not yet arrived!

LDAP was developed to overcome these limitations. Rather than becoming part of the X.500 recommendations, LDAP has been developed through a series of RFCs (Requests For Comment). This ensures that the protocol is developed as an open standard, available to anyone wishing to develop a directory-based product.

How LDAP Differs from DAP

The major difference between DAP and LDAP is that LDAP is not a client-based service. Yes, clients will use LDAP-enabled client software to communicate with a directory server, but they will communicate with an LDAP service on a server instead of directly with the DSA (Directory Service Agent) of the network directory. The LDAP service will interpret a client request and pass it along to the DSA.

In effect, this means that a vendor can build into its directory software an LDAP service that can accept standard LDAP requests and convert them into whatever format is necessary for the vendor's product. It also means that one client software package will be able to access information from the directories of multiple vendors. We'll talk about the specific services in a little bit, but you can see the basic process in Figure 4.3.

1. The client sends a Read request to the LDAP service on a network server. This service can be running on a directory server or on any server that can connect to a directory server.

2. If necessary, the LDAP server can authenticate the user to whatever operating system is in use. This allows the user access to cross-vendor directories. (LDAP can even query the directory for authentication.)

3. The LDAP service then converts the request into a format appropriate to the directory being accessed. If the directory were X.500 compliant, for example, the LDAP service would convert the request into a DAP request.

4. The LDAP service submits the request to the DUA at the directory server.

5. The directory server returns the requested information to the LDAP service.

6. The LDAP service returns the requested information to the client.

F I G U R E   4.3

The LDAP communication process

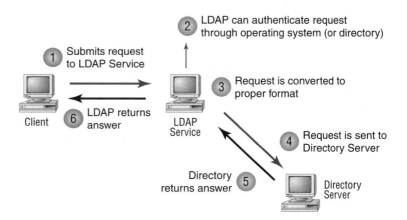

Cross-vendor support is not the only benefit of an LDAP implementation. Take another look at Figure 4.3 and notice that the overhead has been moved from the client to whatever server is supporting the LDAP service. This allows users with limited resources access to the information within the directory. Don't be surprised to see palmtop computers with the capability to access a directory remotely through use of an LDAP solution.

Directory-Enabled Applications

Actually, the reduction in client-side resource use opens up a slew of possibilities for directory-based applications. One of the more basic uses might be the set-top box for a cable company. The cable company could easily configure a directory-based application that would provide current schedules or authenticate users to view special programming, as shown in Figure 4.4. For example, this would allow the cable company to demand authentication for a viewer to watch shows intended for mature audiences. The user account could store the birth dates of everyone in your household. When you chose a program to watch, the cable's directory server could compare your age against the age requirements of the program.

F I G U R E   4.4

LDAP set-top cable implementation

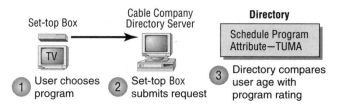

Why stop at the obvious—how about a directory-enabled refrigerator? Imagine a refrigerator that could scan the bar codes on the products it held and build a shopping list for you. Using LDAP, that list could then be sent to a directory at your market and your weekly groceries could be waiting for you when you arrived at the store. I'm not sure I'd want a refrigerator that is quite so intrusive, but the possibility is interesting!

These types of directory-enabled applications are available only because of the low demands that LDAP places on the client device. LDAP can be used by just about any device that can hold a microprocessor.

LDAP and DAP: The Similarities

While the methods of their implementations differ, LDAP is really nothing more than a subset of the functions available in DAP. The development of LDAP centered around five design considerations to reduce the load on the client device:

- Implementing only a subset of the functions provided by DAP
- Offloading the complex operations necessary to locate resources in a distributed environment
- Simplifying the encoding of attribute types and values
- Using ordinary strings to represent data
- Using standard communication protocols (such as TCP), instead of complex, function-specific protocols

Whereas DAP has five "Read" functions defined, LDAP only defines three actions:

Compare   Works just like the DAP Compare function. The client can compare object attributes for a match to given criteria.

Search   Works just like the DAP Search capability. The client can search all or some of the directory for objects that have attributes matching a given set of values. LDAP also uses the Search function to emulate the DAP Read and List functions. (Basically, the "search" is conducted using predefined search conditions.)

Abandon   Works just like the DAP Abandon function. The client can use this request to inform the LDAP service that it no longer needs to continue the query.

LDAP also defines functions that can be used to modify the database:

Modify   This is the equivalent of the DAP Modify request. LDAP simplifies the language involved by supporting three operations:

- Add values
- Delete values
- Replace values

Add   This request is used to add a new entry to the database.

Delete   This function allows the deletion of an entry from the database.

Modify RDN   This function requests that the name of an object be changed.

While LDAP defines a more modest list of functions than DAP, it has sufficient functionality to satisfy most user or administrative needs. LDAP is probably going to be the access protocol of choice for most directories on the market.

In Short

LDAP provides most of the functionality of DAP while avoiding its weaknesses. First, LDAP puts a lot less overhead on the client device. This allows almost anything with a microprocessor the opportunity to access and use the information in a directory. Second, by making LDAP a more server-centric service, it is possible to use this standard to communicate with vendor-specific directories.

These two facets of LDAP (less client overhead and multivendor support) have made it the rising star of the directory industry. Most, if not all, directories on the market include an LDAP service as part of the basic package. Using LDAP-enabled software, a client could easily pull information from an ADS server, as well as from most other directory services available.

Part One of this book has given you a non-vendor-specific overview of network directories—in other words, a view of the technology without reference to specific Microsoft solutions or products. The Microsoft marketing department has already begun the process of flooding the market with ADS product propaganda. As you weed through the press releases on Windows 2000 Server and ADS, this background should help you separate the sales pitch from the technical information. (Not always an easy task!)

Part Two will discuss the Microsoft-specific directory service—ADS. We'll look at how ADS will change the way NT networks are accessed, managed, and designed. We'll also take a peek at the new tools and techniques used in a Windows 2000 Server environment based upon Active Directory Services.

PART

II

Microsoft Active
Directory Services

CHAPTER

5

Microsoft NT
without ADS

Now that we have discussed the theories behind directories, we can begin our discussion of Microsoft's Active Directory Service. Microsoft has utilized many of the time-tested methods used in current directory technologies. You will find pieces of DNS, WINS, and even NDS in ADS. You will also find that Microsoft has taken great pains to remain open to industry standards. ADS is modeled after the X.500 directory recommendations, is accessible using industry standard protocols, and has the ability to incorporate complex authentication technologies.

Given Microsoft's position in the computer industry, ADS will probably become a *de facto* standard within a short period of time. The extensible nature of the schema, combined with a large base of NT-based application developers, should produce new tools and techniques that will benefit the entire networking industry.

Microsoft Windows NT has been a major network operating system for quite some time. Before the release of ADS, NT used a domain-based solution for network management. While domains were nothing new, they did provide solutions to many of the problems inherent in server-based operating systems. Three major benefits that NT's domain structure provided were as follows:

- Single login capability for users

- Central management of users, groups, and network resources

- Universal access to resources

NT's domain structure was often difficult to manage, especially on larger networks, but it did (and does) support some very large networks. The success of earlier versions of NT has had an influence on the design of Windows 2000 Server. First, Microsoft needed to provide a level of backward compatibility so that existing clients could leverage their current investment in Microsoft technologies. Second, those components that *did* work well have not been discarded—they have carried over into the latest version. Some of these components are now "new and improved," but others have come across unchanged.

To fully appreciate Windows 2000 Server—and especially Active Directory Services—it is important to understand the strengths and weaknesses of earlier versions of NT. If you are an NT expert, this chapter will be a review. If you are a newcomer to the NT world, this chapter should prepare you for some of the topics we will discuss later.

What Is a Domain?

Microsoft has defined a *domain* as a logical grouping of users and computers. Unfortunately, this definition can also be applied to workgroup (or peer-to-peer) networks. A better definition would be:

> A domain is a logical grouping of users and computers *managed through a central shared accounts database.*

The idea of a centrally located management database is the key to understanding domains and their functions. In older technologies, each computer that provided a service to the network had its own database of accounts. As you can see in Figures 5.1 and 5.2, this could result in a single user having accounts located on several computers.

FIGURE 5.1

Typical user needs

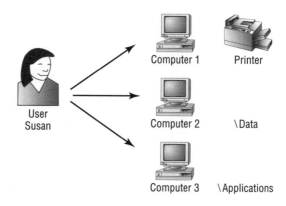

Susan needs access to the printer attached to Computer 1, the data located on Computer 2, and the shared applications located on Computer 3.

FIGURE 5.2

Accounts databases

Susan needs to have an account created on each computer that contains resources she must access. For Susan, this might mean remembering multiple passwords and logging on numerous times. For the system administrator, this means that "Susan" must be managed in multiple locations. The bottom line is that this arrangement mandates redundant work for both the user and the administrator.

In a domain, the accounts database is located on a central server. This server, known as a *domain controller*, handles all logon attempts, authentication to resources, and management tasks. Remember the three big benefits of a domain?

- Single login capability for users

- Universal access to resources

- Central management of users, groups, and network resources

The central location of the accounts database is the key to these functions, as shown in Figures 5.3, 5.4, and 5.5.

FIGURE 5.3

Single logon for users

When Susan wants to log on to the network, her workstation (or whatever computer she is sitting at) sends the authentication request to a domain controller. The domain controller checks its accounts database to determine whether Susan has a valid account and, if she does, whether there are any restrictions placed on her account that would prevent her from logging in at this time or from this location. The domain controller then returns a yes/no answer to her workstation. If the answer is yes, Susan is allowed access to the network using this single logon procedure.

FIGURE 5.4

Universal access to resources

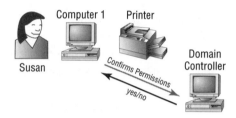

When Susan attempts to print to the shared printer attached to Computer 1, as shown in Figure 5.4, her request is authenticated using information from the accounts database located on a domain controller. Computer 1 permits or denies access based on this authentication process.

Actually, this description simplifies the authentication process. We'll expand upon the process a little later in this chapter.

FIGURE 5.5

Central management

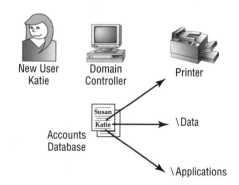

Account administration is managed through the central accounts database stored on a domain controller. When a new employee is hired, such as Katie in Figure 5.5, her account is created at a domain controller. This account is then granted permissions to use resources throughout the network.

Authenticating in NT 4 and Earlier

As a user logs on to the network, the authentication request is forwarded to a domain controller. The domain controller determines whether the logon request is valid (checking passwords, time restrictions, station restrictions, and other items that might limit a user's access to the network). If the request is valid, the domain controller gathers that user's system identifier (SID) and the SIDs of any groups that the user belongs to, and passes them back to the client computer as a *security token*. This token is used during authentication to network resources.

During the authentication process, the user's security token is compared to the access control list (ACL) of the resource. The ACL contains the SIDs of all users and groups that have been assigned permissions to the resource. If this comparison of the SIDs in the user's security token with the SIDs in the object's ACL produces a match, the user is granted the appropriate level of access. Hence the name access control list.

As you can see, our earlier description of the domain's ability to provide universal access was an oversimplification. The domain controller is not consulted each time a user attempts to use a network resource. Instead, the domain controller is consulted only during the initial logon process. It provides the user with a "set of keys" that can open the door to a distinct group of resources.

It is important to understand this distinction because it highlights a weakness of a domain-based environment. Users are only authenticated to a resource during logon. If a user's permissions are changed while that user is logged on, the change will not take effect until the next time he logs on to the network. The following dialog represents a common exchange between users and administrators:

User: I need to change the data in the XYZ data area.

Administrator: Okay, I'll make sure you've got the rights to do that.

User (*five minutes later*): I still can't get at that data I called about.

Administrator: Oh, did you try restarting your computer?

The user could have just logged on again, but most administrators simply give the first rule of NT—restart the computer—rather than explaining the process of logging back in.

One of the nice things about a directory service is that it is used for multiple purposes. Not only does it contain the user's SID, but it also is used by the user's computer to locate the resource. Since ADS is being accessed to find the physical location, why not do an authentication process as well? This means that changes to security are indeed effective immediately.

Primary and Backup Domain Controllers

There are three types of servers in an NT network:

- Primary domain controllers (PDCs)
- Backup domain controllers (BDCs)
- Member servers

Each type of server has a function in the overall design of the network. Administrators must decide what type of server a particular computer will be during the installation of the NT Server operating system. After installation, domain controllers can switch roles (a BDC becoming a PDC, for example). Member servers cannot become domain controllers without reinstalling the operating system. Member servers can, however, move from one domain to another, while domain controllers cannot.

Member Servers

Member servers are computers using NT Server as their operating system that do not contain a copy of the domain accounts database. There are many reasons why a server might be configured in this manner. Perhaps the server will be dedicated to a task that places a heavy load on the device (such as an e-mail application). In this case, you would not want to burden the server with the additional overhead of user authentication.

Also, you might already have enough domain controllers for your environment. Each copy of the domain accounts database that exists adds overhead to your network. Keeping a backup domain controller synchronized with the primary domain controller produces network traffic and, once again, adds overhead to your system. In any event, member servers are really irrelevant to our purpose. Since they do not hold account information, they do not need to be discussed in this context.

How PDCs and BDCs Work

The copies of the domain accounts database for an NT domain are organized in a *single-master environment*. By this, I mean that changes to the database can occur at only one of the copies: the copy held by the PDC. All other domain controllers are BDCs. BDCs receive updated information from the PDC for their domain. In other words, there is one, and only one, *master* copy of the database, as you can see in Figure 5.6.

FIGURE 5.6

Single-master
environment

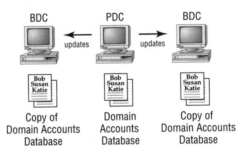

I'll discuss the single-master domain model in detail later in this chapter.

One drawback to the single-master environment is that it creates a single point of failure. Since there can be only one master copy, and it resides on the PDC, this implies that there can be only one PDC for each domain. In the event of the PDC going offline, no changes can be made to the domain accounts database, as shown in Figure 5.7. While it is easy to promote a BDC to the status of PDC, it is not an automatic process. In other words, the promotion requires administrative intervention.

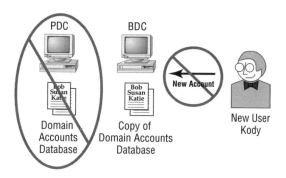

FIGURE 5.7

Results of a PDC going
offline

On the plus side, though, a single-master environment does make synchronization of the backup copies fairly straightforward. Since only one copy of the database can be changed, all updates originate from this copy.

The Synchronization Process

Keeping the domain accounts database synchronized across multiple locations can consume a lot of processing power and produce a lot of network traffic. While limiting changes to the copy stored on the PDC does simplify the process, any procedure that is both automatic and occurring across a network is going to be complex.

To understand the process used to synchronize the BDCs, we must delve a little deeper into the structure of the domain accounts database and its supporting files. One attribute of each object in the database is known as the *version ID*. Think of this value as an overall "change counter" for the database. Each time a change is made, the version ID is incremented.

The PDC also creates a log file that documents the version ID for each change made to the database. This process is shown in Figure 5.8.

FIGURE 5.8

Version ID

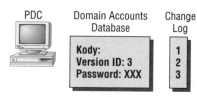

If a new user is added to the domain, the information is placed in the database. The system's version ID is incremented, and this value is placed in the version ID attribute of the new user. The change log is also updated with a record of the change.

The PDC keeps a record of the value of the system version ID at the time of last update for each BDC. Every five minutes, the PDC checks the database to see if any changes have been made. If any have, it then checks the value of the version ID for each BDC against its last update, as shown in Table 5.1.

TABLE 5.1 Version IDs for Each BDC	Server	Version ID at Last Synchronization
	BDC1	2
	BDC2	3
	BDC3	1

In our example, the current version ID is 3. Any BDC with a value of less than three would not have received this change to the database. These servers will be notified that changes exist. The PDC only notifies 10 BDCs at a time to avoid saturating the network with synchronization traffic.

Changes are documented only at the record level—not at the field level. This means that if user Bob changes only his password, then Bob's entire record will be sent to each BDC.

The change log is of a fixed size. By default, it can hold about 2,000 changes. When the change log fills, the system will begin writing over the oldest records in the log file. This can lead to a situation where the PDC is not sure which changes have occurred since the last update of a BDC. As an example, look at Figure 5.9.

As changes occur, the system increments the value of the version ID. If a BDC was last updated when the system version ID was 27, the PDC could not be sure how many changes had been overwritten in the change log. When this occurs, the BDC will be sent the entire database. This is known as a *full synchronization*.

FIGURE 5.9

Full change log

The bottom line is that the synchronization process generates overhead on many components of a network. The PDC must check for changes, notify the BDCs of any changes, and then update the BDCs. The BDCs must process the incoming changes on a regular basis. This can affect network bandwidth, especially in an environment with frequent changes.

Trusts between Domains

Microsoft has defined a *domain* as a "logical grouping of users and computers organized for administrative purposes." Unfortunately, this is also the phrase Microsoft uses to define the term *workgroup*.

Let's take the definition to the next level. The major difference between a workgroup and a domain is where users are authenticated to the resources they wish to access. In a workgroup, user accounts are defined on the machine that holds the resource. In a domain, user accounts are defined and managed in a central database. This database, called the *Security Accounts Manager (SAM)*, is managed by NT's Directory Services. So a more accurate definition of an NT domain would be *an administrative grouping of users and computers, defined and managed through a single database*.

The SAM is a secure database that contains information about the users, computers, global groups, and local groups defined in a domain. Each of these is called an *object* in the database. The maximum number of objects that can be organized in a single SAM is 40,000. The SAM is stored on an NT server, which plays the role of *domain controller* for your network. A domain controller is an NT server that contains the domain accounts database. Domain controllers are responsible for the authentication of users—in other words, for the logon process.

Although the accounts database can support up to 40,000 objects, a system might be designed with multiple domains (accounts databases) for various reasons. These reasons include the following:

- Having more than 40,000 objects consisting of users, computers, and groups

- Wanting to group users or resources for management purposes

- Wanting to reduce the number of objects viewed in management tools (Yes, it's great to have all users in one place, but do you *really* want to scroll through a list of 40,000 objects every time you need to manage an account?)

Partitioning the Database

The act of splitting the users and resources into multiple domains is called *partitioning the database*. There are two main benefits to this type of design:

- You can delegate administration for each domain. This gives each department or location the ability to manage its own resources.

- It reduces the length of the list you have to scroll through to find a given object.

Establishing Trust

By default, each domain is a separate entity. By this I mean that domains do not share information, nor are resources from one domain made available to users defined in another domain. To allow users to access resources in another domain, a *trust* must be established between the domains. A trust can be defined as a communications link between two domains. There are two domains involved in a trust:

- One that contains the user accounts that should have access to resources

- Another that contains those resources

The domain with the user accounts is called the *trusted* domain; the domain with the resources is called the *trusting* domain.

Deciding which domain should be the trusted domain and which should be the trusting domain can sometimes be confusing. Think of it this way: You never hear the phrase "trusted computer," but most companies do have "trusted employees." The domain where the employees are defined is always the "trusted" domain.

Trust Isn't Always a Two-Way Street

When you are documenting your system, you should represent trusts with arrows. The arrows should point to the trusted domain. When one domain trusts another, this is known as a *one-way trust*, and you can see this in Figure 5.10.

FIGURE 5.10

One-way trust

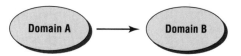

When each domain has users who need to access resources in the other domain, you will create a *two-way trust*. As you can see in Figure 5.11, a two-way trust is really just two one-way trusts.

FIGURE 5.11

Two-way trust

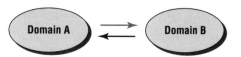

NT 4.*x* trusts are *non-transitive*. This means that trusts are never *inherited* from one domain to another. If Domain A trusts Domain B, and Domain B trusts Domain C, this does not imply that Domain A trusts Domain C. This trust would have to be created manually.

Let's say you are going on vacation. You give your house keys to Harry, a friend from work. In this scenario, you have made Harry a trusted friend (and, as you'll find out, you are maybe just a bit too "trusting"). When you get back from vacation, you find that Harry let his friends Tom and Dick use your keys. You'd probably be angry, right? You didn't expect that Tom, Dick, and Harry would have access to your house! Giving your keys to Harry was a non-transitive trust. You trusted Harry—not all his wild friends!

AGLP is an acronym that describes the fundamental process for granting permissions to resources across trusts: Accounts go into Global groups, which go into Local groups, which are then granted Permissions.

The steps for granting these permissions are shown in Figure 5.12.

FIGURE 5.12

AGLP

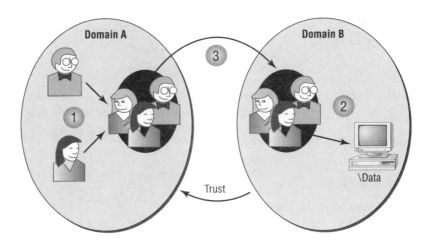

Here's what the figure illustrates:

1. In the domain where the users are defined (Domain A), either use an existing or create a new global group and make the appropriate users members of this group.

2. In the domain that contains the resource (Domain B), create a local group with the necessary permissions.

3. Make the global group from Domain A a member of the local group in Domain B.

The Four Domain Models

How you design your NT environment can have a big impact on its performance. A *domain model* defines how you will use directory services in your environment. There are four basic domain models; each has some definite advantages and disadvantages. The four models are as follows:

- Single domain
- Single master
- Multiple master
- Complete trust

Single Domain Model

The *single domain model* is the easiest of the four models to implement. In it, all users and computers are defined in a single domain, as shown in Figure 5.13. The single domain model is most appropriate when there are fewer than 40,000 objects and you require central administration of the domain environment.

F I G U R E   5.13

The single domain model

Since all resources are defined in a single accounts database, no trusts need to be established. Users have access to all resources to which they have been granted permissions.

Advantages and Disadvantages

The advantages and disadvantages associated with the single domain model are listed in Table 5.2.

T A B L E 5.2	**Advantages**	**Disadvantages**
Advantages and Disadvantages of the Single Domain Model	Simple to implement and manage.	Performance can degrade as the number of resources increases.
	Central control of user accounts.	All users are defined in the same database: no grouping by location or function.
	Central control of all resources.	All resources are defined in the same database: no grouping by location or function.
	No trusts are necessary.	Browser performance will slow with large numbers of servers.

Single-Master Domain Model

A *single-master domain model* consists of at least two domains. In it, all user accounts are defined in a master domain. The other domains are used to manage physical resources, as you can see in Figure 5.14. This design is most appropriate when you want central control of user accounts, but local administrators are responsible for departmental or geographic control of physical resources.

The single-master domain model is also appropriate when the number of objects defined in the database would exceed the maximum of 40,000. In this case, moving the computer accounts to another domain would spread the object records over multiple domains. (Although in a company of this size, you would probably start with the next model: multiple-master domains.)

If you think your company might grow into multiple locations or might grow past the 40,000-object limit, it is best to start with the single-master domain design. This offers more growth options than the single domain model.

FIGURE 5.14

The single-master domain model

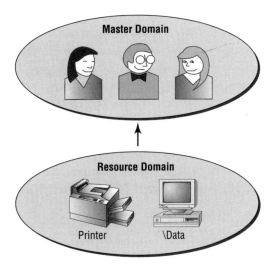

In this model, each resource domain establishes a one-way trust with the master domain.

Assigning Rights

Use the AGLP process to assign users in the master domain permissions to the resources defined in the resource domains, as demonstrated in Figure 5.15.

1. Create a global group in the master domain with the appropriate members.

2. In the resource domain, create a local group and assign it the necessary permissions.

3. Next, make the global group from the master domain a member of the local group from the resource domain.

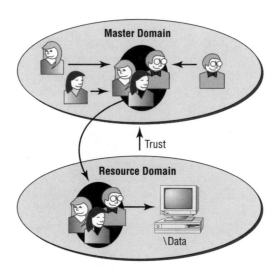

FIGURE 5.15

Groups in a single-
master domain model

Advantages and Disadvantages

You can see the advantages and disadvantages associated with the single-master domain model in Table 5.3.

TABLE 5.3	**Advantages**	**Disadvantages**
Advantages and Disadvantages of the Single-Master Domain Model	Best choice if resources need to be managed by different groups.	Performance can degrade as the number of users defined in the master domain increases.
	User accounts are centrally located.	Local groups must be defined in each resource domain.
	Resources are grouped logically (either by department or by geographic location).	Administrators of resource domains must "trust" the administrator of the master domain to set up global groups correctly.
	Global groups must be created only once.	

Multiple-Master Domain Model

The *multiple-master domain model* is shown in Figure 5.16. It is the most scalable of the four models. It looks quite a bit like the single-master model, except that there is more than one domain where user accounts are defined. There are various reasons why you might choose this model:

- The accounts database is limited to a maximum of 40,000 objects (users, groups, and computer accounts). If your environment were large enough, you might be forced to partition the database just to stay within the defined limits.

- Your company's management strategy might also lead to this model. If each location or department wants to manage its own user accounts, you might want to create separate domains for management purposes.

- You might also create multiple master domains for ease of administration. Let's face it—just because the accounts database *will* hold 40,000 accounts doesn't mean that you are going to like paging through such a large list to find stuff.

- In a WAN (wide-area network) environment, you might make multiple domains in an effort to reduce the amount of network traffic that crosses the wide-area links.

FIGURE 5.16

The multiple-master domain model

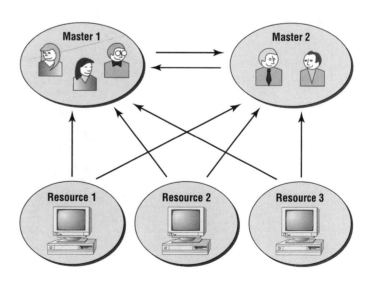

Master domains have two-way trusts between themselves, and each resource domain has a one-way trust to each master containing users who might have to access its resources. You can determine the number of trusts in a multiple master structure by using this formula: $M \times (M - 1) + (R \times M)$, where M is the number of master domains and R is the number of resource domains. (This assumes that each resource domain will have to trust each master domain.)

Assigning Rights

Assigning rights in a multiple-master domain environment is a bit more confusing than in the preceding models. You still use the AGLP method, but you might have to create the global groups in each of the master domains, as shown in Figure 5.17.

F I G U R E 5.17

The use of groups in a multiple-master domain model

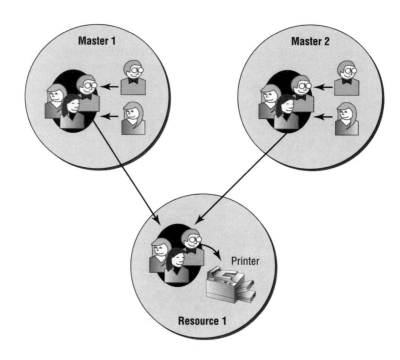

Advantages and Disadvantages

The advantages and disadvantages of the multiple-master domain model are listed in Table 5.4.

T A B L E 5.4	Advantages	Disadvantages
Advantages and Disadvantages of the Multiple-Master Domain Model	Best model for large environment with central MIS department.	Both local and global groups might have to be defined in multiple domains.
	Scales to any size network.	Large number of trusts to manage.
	Each domain can have a separate administrator.	Not all user accounts are in one domain database.

Complete Trust Model

The *complete trust model* takes full advantage of directory services. In the complete trust model, each domain has both user accounts and resources. Each domain must trust all other domains. This model, as shown in Figure 5.18, is perfect for a company where each department or location wants control over both its physical resources and user accounts.

The reality is that most complete trust environments happen by accident. First, each department or location installs NT for its own use. Somewhere down the line, they realize that it would be nice if they could share resources. At that point there are only two options: back up all data on all domain controllers and start from scratch with one of the other domain models, or implement a complete trust model and deal with the large number of trusts to manage.

FIGURE 5.18

The complete trust
model

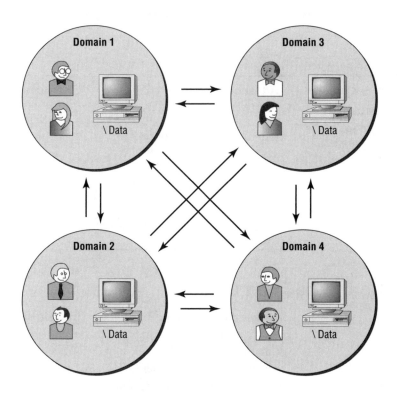

 In a complete trust model, all domains trust all other domains. Determine the number of trusts with the following formula: $D \times (D - 1)$, where D is the number of domains in the network.

Assigning Rights

Assigning rights in a complete trust environment can be extremely confusing. In this model, you must create both local and global groups in every domain, as shown in Figure 5.19.

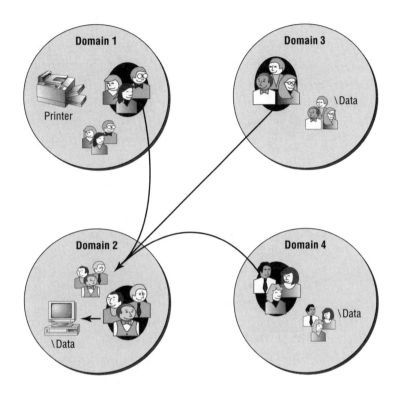

F I G U R E 5.19

Groups in a complete
trust domain
environment

Advantages and Disadvantages

The advantages and disadvantages of the complete trust domain model are
listed in Table 5.5.

T A B L E 5.5	**Advantages**	**Disadvantages**
Advantages and Disadvantages of the Complete Trust Domain Model	Works for companies with no central MIS department.	Large number of trusts to manage.
	Scales to any number of users.	More domains mean more points of management.
	Each domain can have its own administrator.	Each administrator must trust that all other administrators know what they are doing.
	Resources and user accounts are grouped into management units.	

Supporting a Single Logon Account

In a traditional server-based network, each server maintained its own list of users who could access its resources. Since there were multiple lists of users (one for each server), users often had to remember several user account names and passwords. This could be confusing for the users. From an administrative perspective, having users defined in multiple places added complexity and redundant management.

As an example, let's imagine a small manufacturing firm in St. Paul, Minnesota. This firm has two servers—one for engineering tasks and the other for accounting—each using a traditional server-based operating system. If I were hired as the Head of Engineering, with both design and financial responsibilities, the LAN administrator would have to create a user account for me on each server, and I would have to remember both user account names and passwords.

This is clearly unacceptable in anything other than a small network. Microsoft Windows NT lets you use a single user account to access resources on the entire network.

Pass-Through Authentication

A process called *pass-through authentication* makes it possible for users to log on from computers or domains on which they have no account. When a user sits down at a computer defined in a domain that trusts her "home" domain, she will have the option of choosing her domain from a drop-down list.

The NT server in the computer's domain will then use the trust relationship to pass the authentication request to the user's home domain. For example, if user Bob from Domain 1 attempts to log on at a machine in Domain 2, the logon process will use the procedure depicted in Figure 5.20.

F I G U R E   5.20

Pass-through authentication

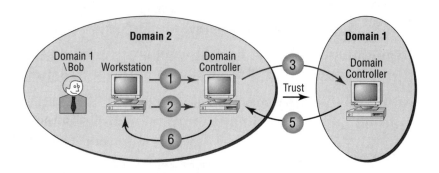

Here's what happens:

1. When the Windows NT machine boots, its NETLOGON service locates a domain controller in Domain 2. As part of this process, the computer receives a list of all trusted domains to present in the logon screen.

2. When the user identifies himself as Bob from Domain 1, the NET-LOGON process passes the request to a domain controller in Domain 2.

3. The domain controller in Domain 2 recognizes that the request is for a user defined in a trusted domain, so it passes the request to a domain controller in Domain 1.

4. The domain controller in Domain 1 checks its accounts database to ensure that the username is valid and the right password has been entered.

5. If the request to log on is valid, the domain controller in Domain 1 passes the user's SID and group information to the domain controller in Domain 2.

6. The domain controller in Domain 2 trusts that the authentication was done properly, so it passes the information about user Bob back to the NT machine where Bob is trying to log on, completing the logon process.

Allowing Users to Access Resources in Different Domains

To grant a user rights to a resource in a trusting domain, follow these steps:

1. Create a global group in the user's home domain.

2. Create a local group in the trusting domain. Grant the local group permission to the appropriate resource.

3. Make the global group a member of the local group.

I always picture the trust as a highway between the two accounts. You can't use a highway to travel unless you have a vehicle. When using a trust, the global group is the vehicle; user accounts are the passengers.

In Short

Earlier versions of NT, based upon a domain environment, provided three main benefits over earlier network operating systems:

- Single logon for users

- Central management for administrators

- Universal resource access through pass-through authentication

Before NT and the domain environment, most network operating systems were server-based, meaning that each server was managed as a separate entity. This type of management scheme resulted in redundant management and increased workload for both users and administrators.

The NT domain environment was Microsoft's first foray into enterprise networking. While it does alleviate many of the headaches of earlier network operating systems, it also introduces its own problems to the network:

- The overhead of synchronizing multiple copies of an accounts database can overwhelm servers and saturate network segments.

- The single-master synchronization scheme creates a single point of failure in the PDC.

- Managing multidomain environments was basically the same as managing server-based networks—each domain was seen as a separate entity.

- Trusts added administrative overhead and security risks to the network.

When all is said and done, Microsoft Windows NT versions 4 and earlier represented an attempt to overcome the limitations of a flat-file accounts database. While they accomplished much of this goal, the performance, security, and management capabilities left much to be desired.

Unfortunately, much of ADS has been designed to be backward compatible with domain-based networks. While most of these capabilities can be turned off or ignored, mixed environments will be very common for quite some time. A mixed environment will not show ADS in its best light—a fact that might slow down its acceptance.

Now that we've taken a look at NT *without* ADS (most of this chapter was probably a review for you), we can begin to look at NT *with* ADS. In Chapter 6, we'll discuss how ADS overcomes the limitations inherent in a domain-based environment. We'll also look at how ADS fits into the overall Microsoft product line and how ADS has been added to the architecture of NT. Once we've discussed how ADS is supposed to work, in later chapters we can look at how it actually does work.

CHAPTER
6

Microsoft NT with ADS

Just as NT was originally designed to overcome the weaknesses of server-based network operating systems, Windows 2000 Server with ADS was designed to overcome the weaknesses of a domain-based environment. While Microsoft is loath to admit it, domains create as many problems as they fix, especially in larger networks.

How Networks Develop

Very few networks are installed all at once, especially in medium to small companies. Most networks grow over time—almost like a fungus! First the accounting department installs a server. They get it configured properly (this *can* take some time) and start bragging it up around the company. The folks in the production department see what the accountants are doing and decide to install their own server, creating their own domain in the process. The sales department staff suddenly wants Internet mail, so they bring in a consultant and have their own server installed, creating yet another domain. Before you know it the company is NT-based, but there are no connections between the various departments.

The next step in the development of the network is sharing resources between departments. First someone in sales needs access to the quarterly accounting reports. Then someone in production decides she wants to look over the marketing materials in order to stock inventory based upon what the company is advertising. Departmental administrators start creating local accounts and trusts between domains to allow for this unplanned resource-sharing. Before you know it, a complete trust domain structure is born!

Remember the three big benefits of domains over older, server-based networks?

- Single logon
- Universal resource access
- Central administration

The "network on the fly" scenario described above has the potential to provide all three. The question is, do the benefits outweigh the costs? Management of a larger domain-based network with lots of trusts can be overwhelming! In a complete trust design, the number of trusts is $D \times (D - 1)$, where D is the number of domains involved. This doesn't seem like a lot—until you do the math for a few networks, as shown in Table 6.1.

	Number of Domains	Number of Trusts
T A B L E 6.1 Trusts in a Complete Trust Network	2	2
	3	6
	4	12
	5	20
	6	30
	7	42
	8	56
	9	72
	10	90

As you can see, even a small company with five or six departments (or sites) will generate a relatively large number of trusts. This is compounded by the fact that most small companies either have no staff administrators or have an administrator without a lot of experience.

Of course, there's really not a lot of management involved with trust relationships once they are created—it is the global groups, local groups, global accounts, and local accounts that will turn you in circles. As an example, look at the environment shown in Figure 6.1. Jim works in the Seattle office, but he needs access to resources in Tampa.

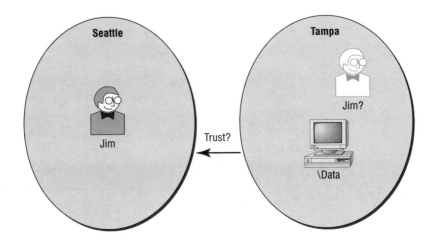

FIGURE 6.1

Jim's dilemma

In a domain-based system, there are two possible solutions:

- Connect the two domains by a trust relationship.
- Create a local account for Jim in the Tampa domain.

In either event, the administrators have to decide which is the appropriate method. If they choose to create the trust, they will have to remember that the Tampa domain now trusts the entire Seattle domain. While NT's inherent security should protect against the abuse of this trust, that risk is still a consideration. If the administrators decide to create an account for Jim in the Tampa domain, they will have to train Jim in the skills necessary to connect to resources in Tampa. Either way, they will have increased the potential amount of management required on their system.

The General Goals of ADS

The overall goal of Microsoft Windows 2000 Server and Active Directory Services can be stated simply:

> Reduce both the user and administrative overhead
> associated with computer networks.

As a proposal, it's fairly simple. As an implementation, it becomes much more difficult. This has been the goal of most network operating systems since networking began. The biggest problem is that this "goal" is really made up of two areas:

- User access

- Network administration

Often these two goals are at odds: Making a network easier for the user ends up creating more administrative overhead. Conversely, giving more responsibility to users usually means less work for the administrators. Placing higher demands upon system users is not a realistic expectation. Given the complex nature of today's networks, users cannot be expected to understand many of the necessary technologies.

The result is that the complexity of networks has forced both end-users and administrative personnel to become more network literate. Users are becoming more and more aware of the network, and administrators are being forced to master more and more complex technologies. At some juncture, this spiral will reach a point of diminishing returns. Users will be forced to master technology at the expense of their ability to perform their job functions (in other words, users will spend more time worrying about the network and less time being productive). Network administrators will spend such a large amount of time managing existing systems that no time will be left for improvement or optimization.

Since technological advances do not appear to be slowing (much to the relief of those of us who make our living writing about them) and these advances have the potential to increase the productivity of end-users, something must be done to avoid that point of "diminishing returns." Network directories in general, and Active Directory specifically, attempt to accomplish this by providing a simpler, more intuitive interface to the increasing complexities of a network. ADS attempts to provide two things:

- A common interface to network resources

- An intuitive interface to network resources

At first glance, these two goals might appear to be identical. The truth is, however, that we have intuitive interfaces in many of today's technologies. Almost every vendor realizes that easing access and management—through GUI interfaces, online help systems, and the like—is critical to success. The problem is that there is not a "standard" method of presenting information to end-users, administrators, or even other vendors.

Enterprise Management

ADS aims to allow you to manage your entire network (and all of its associated resources) in a consistent manner: more specifically, through a series of tools used to access configuration information stored within the ADS database. At first glance, this might not seem like such a revolutionary change to network management. If you stop and think about it, though, a *single* tool to manage *all* network resources—users, printers, servers, routers, switches—is indeed a lofty goal. If successful, accomplishing this goal could change the way that network administrators approach their current responsibilities.

Three prerequisites must be met before this goal can be reached:

- Design of an industry-standard method for storing and accessing configuration information

- Acceptance of this standard by third-party vendors of hardware and software

- Customer buy-in to the products created (and brought to market) by these vendors

An Industry Standard

ADS is the embodiment of the first of these three prerequisites. In ADS, Microsoft provides the framework for an industry-standard method of storing, accessing, and using configuration information for network resources. Through ADS, Microsoft defines how information should be formatted. By embracing industry recommendations and standards, such as X.500 and LDAP, Microsoft makes ADS accessible to any vendor who wishes to take advantage of it. More important, by creating a system for easily extending the schema of the ADS database, Microsoft creates an environment that all vendors can take advantage of.

I cannot overstress the importance of an open environment. By creating a directory service that is easy to access and utilize, Microsoft brings the first truly "open" directory service to the networking industry. While there have been other commercially successful directories (Novell's NDS, for example), none has been as easily accessible or extensible as ADS. Developers can use simple tools to extend the capabilities of ADS to meet their needs. This openness is the first step in fulfilling the second of our three prerequisites.

Vendor Acceptance

With an open environment, backed by Microsoft, the stage is set for the completion of the second prerequisite: acceptance of a standard by product vendors. Given the clout that Microsoft wields in the industry, it would seem that this is a foregone conclusion. In reality, however, ADS must provide some added value (over older, proven technologies) before products will be written to take advantage of ADS.

At a recent trade show, it was rumored that Microsoft offered incentives to any vendor that would fly an "ADS-ready" flag on its booth. While many booths had this logo, most were demonstrating products that did nothing more than trust ADS to perform user authentication. In other words, most of the products were not, in fact, ADS-based; rather, they were ADS-friendly. A large difference!

At first, this added value will probably consist of products that utilize ADS services to authenticate users to control access, use information stored in ADS, or perhaps automatically add data to standard attributes of an object class. For instance, consider the following:

- Most so-called ADS products will accept the identity of a user once authenticated through the ADS database. This information can then be used to control access to specific features of the product.

- Other products might access the information stored within the directory. A simple example would be a company directory (phone book) that gathers its information dynamically from user attributes and provides a user-friendly interface to LDAP queries of that data.

- Some products might actually make the jump to placing data in the ADS database. The installation software for a printer, for instance, might automatically fill in the make, model, and serial number attributes of a printer object in the directory.

While each of these applications would be an improvement over non-ADS-enabled products, none of them is really revolutionary in design. Before ADS can become the industry standard, Microsoft must entice developers to create products in which ADS is an integral component. Such products would depend upon ADS for a portion of their functionality. A few examples might include

- Devices that store their configuration in the directory database rather than in a local file. These devices will have to include firmware that can find an ADS server so that this information can be gathered as they initialize.

- Software that stores a user's preferences (things like default fonts, colors, or even the location of stored data) in ADS. By moving this information to a central database, a user's preferences will be available to her no matter where she is on the network.

- Software that knows where other copies of itself are located. If a server becomes unavailable, a user can be routed to another copy of the software—without any interruption of normal network services.

Given the strength of a directory service, these few suggestions are just the tip of the iceberg. The big question is, "What will Microsoft do to justify the costs involved in reengineering products to be ADS-aware?" Without this justification, third-party providers will not take a chance on this new technology. Three aspects of ADS will provide this justification:

- Microsoft's large market share in both the desktop and networking arenas. Developers are confident that any Microsoft product will be successful—and a large installed base increases their own odds of success.

- Microsoft has made programming ADS applications as easy as possible. ADS applications can be created using most of today's prevalent tools, including Microsoft Visual Basic and C++.

- Microsoft has made ADS easy to access through the use of industry-standard protocols such as LDAP.

User Acceptance

The last of the prerequisites to the success of ADS is user acceptance. There are two types of users that must be considered:

- End-users
- Administrators

Each type will have its own criteria for accepting any product.

End-Users

A common maxim of older networks has always been "The best networks are those of which the user is unaware." In a nutshell, this credo of network administration refers to the fact that end-users should not have to be concerned with the mechanics of networking. Users should see their computer as just another tool—no different from a screwdriver—for doing their jobs.

With Windows 2000 Server and Active Directory Services, this credo might be changed to "The best networks are those that intuitively guide users to the resources they need." As I mentioned earlier, networks (and the resources they provide) have become much more sophisticated over the last few years. Networks provide many more services than they used to, and this increase in service has pushed users into becoming more computer (and network) savvy. Typical office workers are now required to understand both the specific applications they use to manipulate information *and* the networks that connect them. The argument over whether or not this is a good trend will probably continue for years. The simple truth is that users must have a basic understanding of networks to survive in today's business world.

From an end-user perspective, some of the most basic aspects of ADS might be the best selling points. ADS promises the following benefits to users:

- A single logon for *all* network resources. Many users are faced with multiple logons to access the varied resources on their networks—one for the LAN, another for the mainframe, and yet another for some legacy system down the hall. With ADS, the user will be authenticated to the Windows 2000 network, and this authentication should be valid across multiple environments.

- Dynamic mapping to network resources. Users are often overwhelmed by the task of remembering the locations and names of resources throughout a large network. Using ADS to represent resources, such as applications, printers, and shared data, makes the process of accessing resources as easy as clicking an icon.

- A consistent set of services on the network. Users are often confused by changes to their environment. By providing a central database to store all of a user's preferences, policies, and other unique configuration information, ADS can re-create a user's environment—no matter where he logs on to the network.

For ADS to become successful, Microsoft must make the information that the directory database holds easily (and readily) available to end-users. Moving to a graphical interface is a first step. The simple fact that Microsoft owns the most popular end-user operating systems (Windows 9*x* and Windows NT) gives ADS a leg up on the competition. Almost every end-user will understand the process of using a Windows-based application.

The next step is to design the killer application—in other words, some application that becomes indispensable to the average end-user. We've discussed quite a few applications for directory services, everything from an employee telephone directory to automatic configuration of network devices. None of these examples, however, is really indispensable to the average end-user. What is needed is a new application that insinuates itself so thoroughly into business that it becomes as commonplace as the calculator and as indispensable as the fax machine. While I'm sure that this application will be developed, there is no telling at this point what its purpose will be.

Administrative Users

While ADS can provide numerous services to end-users, its primary function is that of network resource management. As such, ADS will first and foremost have to be sold to network administrators—administrators who have little time or patience for new technologies that promise the world but do not deliver! As a group, network administrators are mostly overworked and underappreciated (until an information emergency, that is) but are fascinated by the possibilities of technology. If ADS fulfills its promise, it should be an easy sell to these individuals. For administrative personnel, ADS can provide the following:

- A single point of management for each user. Administrators will no longer have to create multiple accounts for a user who needs to access multiple environments. The same account information (or at least the same account object within the database) can be used to access many different types of systems: NT servers, Novell NetWare servers, mainframe systems, and even UNIX boxes.

- A single interface for managing products from multiple vendors. Since ADS can be extended to hold the configuration information for any type of object, a single set of tools should be able to manage any resource that can be represented by an object within the database.

- The ability to provide a uniform configuration for a like set of resources. ADS provides the ability to *copy* objects. From an administrative perspective, this means that like objects (for instance, two routers) should have to be configured only once; the second can be configured by copying the configuration of the first.

- The ability to provide a standard set of policies across an entire network. For resources that are so enabled, administrators can use ADS tools to create policies of use. Such resources will accept the identity of the user (as confirmed by the NT network) to enable or disable services. A router, for example, might limit access to a particular route (the Internet, perhaps) based on membership in an ADS-defined group.

- The ability to selectively delegate administrative responsibility based on an object's location in the tree structure. Earlier we discussed the concept of containers within an X.500-compliant directory structure. In ADS, each container can act as a security boundary. In other words, if you have created a users container, you can delegate the administrative tasks for the objects it contains. This allows you to limit the areas in which a particular user might have administrative powers.

- The ability to selectively delegate administrative responsibility based on an object's attributes. You can, for instance, allow all members of the Help desk group to change passwords for all user objects, without allowing them any other administrative privileges.

- The ability to distribute printer drivers from a central location. ADS will store the drivers necessary for a client to use a particular printer. When a user attempts to print, the driver can be automatically installed (or upgraded) on her computer.

This ability is not new—both NT 4 and Novell NetWare also have this capability.

All in all, what administrators need is an environment where new technologies mesh easily with old technologies, where management tasks do not consume every waking hour, and that can be customized to fit the specific needs of the business. In other words, what administrators need is ADS! Active Directory includes many tools that bring it close to achieving these lofty goals.

Extensibility   One of the major features of the Active Directory database is that it can be extended to include *any* information that might be necessary in a particular environment. Suppose, for instance, that Company XYZ is in a business that forces employees to travel on a regular basis. In this type of company, each office would probably have one person who was responsible for arranging travel—flights, hotels, auto rentals, perhaps even tickets to activities like plays or ballgames.

If user Carrie was based in Grand Rapids, Michigan, the local travel personnel would probably know all about Carrie and her travel preferences. They would know whether she likes window or aisle seats, nonsmoking or smoking rooms. They'd be aware of the appropriate type of automobile for her—e.g., whether she needs a van to carry equipment or whether a compact car would cover her needs. When Carrie needed to travel, she would just call the local person and give her destination and travel dates and everything would be arranged for her.

If Carrie is away from home, though, this scenario changes a bit. Either Carrie calls her office to arrange travel (which means faxing itineraries, and lots of phone time) or she talks to the travel person at the branch nearest her. The problem is that this travel person won't know all of Carrie's preferences. He would either have to ask Carrie—who is busy working on her project—or call her office and have the material faxed to him (okay—he would probably be able to do this through e-mail). Either way, information that should be readily available, based upon the type of company we have described, is not!

In an ADS-based environment, this scenario changes quite a bit. After analyzing the business needs of the company, the administrators decided that the ADS database should store travel preferences as properties of the user account. Using fairly straightforward tools, they extended that property list of user accounts to include things like airline of choice, frequent flyer identification, smoking/nonsmoking, special diet needs, and perhaps even hobbies (so that entertainment arrangements can be made or suggested). Now, wherever Carrie travels, her preferences are available to the local staff. If her plans change, they can make arrangements easily. If she's doing a really great job, they can check her entertainment preferences and arrange tickets to a ballgame. In other words, the data that is needed is readily available.

The process of changing or adding to the properties of objects is known as *extending* the schema of the database. Extensibility ensures that ADS can be customized to fit the needs of any size or type of business.

Integration with DHCP (Dynamic Host Configuration Protocol)   Since TCP/IP is the protocol of choice for Windows 2000 networks, and is mandatory for Active Directory Services, many of the traditional TCP/IP tools have been improved upon in Windows 2000. One of the most basic, yet critical, tools is that of DHCP. DHCP is used to dynamically configure the TCP/IP protocol stack on clients—automatically as they boot rather than manually at each computer.

Traditionally, as DHCP clients initialize they broadcast a packet on the network requesting the services of a DHCP server. This DHCP server responds with an offer that includes all of the pertinent TCP/IP configuration parameters. The DHCP server keeps a database of available IP addresses and is responsible for ensuring that no duplicate addresses are given out.

In Windows 2000, DHCP services have been integrated with ADS. First, the DHCP database of IP addresses has been moved into the Active Directory database. This allows central control of all DHCP services; more important, it also negates the necessity to implement DHCP relay agents or configure routers to pass BootP broadcast packets.

Another benefit of integrating DHCP into the Active Directory database is that the IP addressing information is moved to a more accessible forum. We'll see the benefit of this in the next section.

Integration with DNS (Domain Name System)   As we discussed in Chapter 2, DNS is used to resolve user-friendly names, such as www.royal-tech.com, into the IP address of a resource. The biggest drawback to DNS was its static nature—each entry had to be created manually for each resource or service. This limitation meant that while DNS was great for some resources (e-mail servers, Web servers, and the like), it wasn't all that great as an all-around resource locator. (This was why WINS was created.) For Windows 2000, Microsoft has integrated a new version of DNS—Dynamic Domain Name System (DDNS)—into Active Directory. With DDNS, a resource can dynamically register itself in the DNS database. The bottom line here is that the resource records can be created on the fly as each resource initializes. This turns DNS into a dynamically maintained database of active resources—in other words, it replaces the DNS/WINS combination that was used in earlier versions of Microsoft networking.

Global Catalog Server   We've discussed the various protocols used to access the data in the Active Directory database—DAP and LDAP. We've also discussed the various uses that this information can be put to—the company phone book, holding parts of the Registry so that user preferences are available from multiple locations, even checking the settings on various types of hardware. What we haven't talked about is the network traffic generated by these types of queries. Think about it: If I use the Active Directory database to find phone numbers for users around the globe, the traffic generated could outweigh the benefit of the central database.

In order to reduce this network overhead, Windows 2000 includes a component known as the Global Catalog. This service is installed by default on the first domain controller in your forest.

The Global Catalog contains a partial replica of every object defined in every domain in your forest—in other words, here is a list of everything in your environment, but with only part of the actual data. Only selected properties of each object are stored in the Global Catalog, specifically those properties that are most likely to be searched upon.

Let's take my company phone book as an example. If my company's network spanned the globe, I would probably have created multiple domains. Remember that each domain represents a partition of the overall Active Directory database. As such, if I were to search my local partition (domain database) for the phone number of a fellow employee whose account resides in another domain, the information would not be available (at least not from my local server). Without any additional components, my local server would have to access a domain controller at the remote domain and perform the query on my behalf, ultimately returning the information that I requested. The problem here is that my request has now traveled across the WAN links that connect my network. The amount of traffic generated for a single query would probably not affect the performance of my network, but if we extrapolate that traffic for 1,000 users—well, suddenly we have a problem.

The Global Catalog acts as a reference point for these types of queries. In the scenario above, my local server would forward my query to the Global Catalog server. There, we would hope, the requested information would be found. The best part of this entire process is that I have complete control over which properties are stored in the Global Catalog and who can access the information.

I can also designate multiple servers to hold the Global Catalog, thus ensuring that a catalog is available locally to all of my users. (Of course, the more Global Catalog servers I have, the more traffic is generated to keep the replicas up to date.)

Policy-Based Administration   Earlier versions of Windows NT had the ability to create policy files to control certain aspects of a user's environment. While this capability was useful, it was limited in scope—you could create policies only for users, groups, or computers. The level of control was also limited to a very select set of parameters, things like access to the display options on a computer or ability to disable the "Run" option on the Startup menu. All in all, administrators had more control than was available with earlier operating systems, but the capabilities were too limited.

In Windows 2000, policies have been expanded so that they can apply across a site, domain, or *organizational unit (OU)* as defined in the Active Directory database. The controls available have also been expanded so that administrators can now control just about every aspect of a user's environment.

Policies now include options that allow central administration of items like operating system updates, installation of applications (either mandatory or user-controlled), user profiles, and the traditional Desktop.

Single Namespace

Within the realm of networks and network applications, there are numerous ways to identify resources. Within a single environment, administrators and users are often forced to understand (and use) multiple methods for naming and finding the resources they need.

One common method of naming servers and share points is to use *UNC (Uniform Naming Convention)* names. UNC names adhere to the following format:

```
\\<server name>\<share point>\<path to resource>
```

where

- *<server name>* refers to the name of the device that holds the resource

- *<share point>* refers to the name given to the shared data area

- *<path to resource>* refers to the logical directory structure used to find the requested information

The acronym UNC is also interpreted as Universal Naming Convention in many current texts. Since UNC is a Microsoft term and this book is about Microsoft technology, I've decided to go with the original.

While users have grown accustomed to this format, it is not necessarily either intuitive or convenient. Users must know the entire UNC name to use an object on their network. This is one of the reasons why graphical interfaces are so popular: Users can click to an object rather than having to remember its name.

Another confusing environment can be that of messaging systems. Exchange Server, for instance, generates multiple names for each recipient created. These names follow the format of various standards and foreign mail systems (thus allowing mail to be routed to and from other environments). A typical recipient will have names matching the following standards:

- Distinguished names (or X.500 names)

- X.400 names

- Lotus cc:Mail names

- Microsoft Mail names

For our purposes, we do not need to examine each of the naming standards in detail. Besides, most of this is done behind the scenes, meaning that the mail administrator doesn't necessarily have to understand each naming standard. There are, however, times when such knowledge is critical to troubleshooting a message delivery problem. The problem with this type of system is that no one can be expected to have detailed knowledge of all of these standards (especially not for systems one has never worked with).

With Windows 2000 Server and ADS, each object in the directory has one unique name that can be used to reference it. ADS uses X.500 names to represent each of the objects that it contains. In an X.500 environment, the complete, or *distinguished,* name of any object is a complete path to the top of the tree structure, as shown in Figure 6.2. From an administrative perspective, this means that there is only one naming format in use on a network.

FIGURE 6.2

Distinguished object names

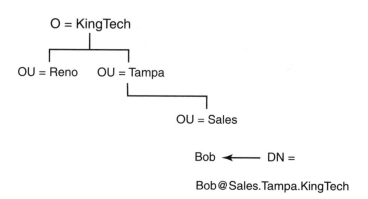

As you can see in Figure 6.2, there are certain similarities to all objects named within a particular ADS tree. At the very least, every object share's name includes the name of the root object, much as all members of a family share a common last name. Just as you can refer to my family as "the King family," you can refer to an ADS tree by its topmost object (the root).

Namespace

The root object of a tree defines the beginning of a *namespace*. The concept of a namespace is critical to understanding ADS. A namespace is a structure in which a name (in this case, the name of the root object of the ADS database) is applied to all of the objects it contains.

> In other words, a namespace is any specific context in which a name can be resolved to a resource.

Name Resolution

Name resolution is the process that uses the name of an object to find some information about that object. Probably the most common name resolution process is using the telephone book. With a telephone book, you use a name to find a telephone number or address.

In ADS you can use the name, or even just a portion of the name, of an object to find the value of its attributes, as shown in Figure 6.3. Susan is looking for the mail-stop of a user named Bob in the sales department. She uses a tool to submit a query, and ADS returns the resources that match her criteria. This is the process of name resolution.

F I G U R E   6.3

Name resolution

Susan

Query: Show me all Bobs in
the Sales Department

Result: Bob.Sales.Tampa.KingTech
Bob.Sales.Reno.KingTech
BobP.Sales.Tampa.KingTech

When you create the tree structure for an ADS tree, its contents are organized in a hierarchical (and, ideally, logical) manner. Each department, workgroup, or object class can be given its own container. These containers relate back to the original Active Directory namespace, as shown in Figure 6.4.

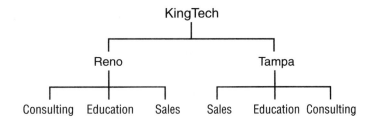

The King Technologies tree has two regional containers, or organizational units:

- Tampa.KingTech
- Reno.KingTech

Each region is divided into three departmental OUs. For the Reno office, these are Sales.Reno.KingTech, Education.Reno.KingTech, and Consulting.Reno.KingTech. In our previous example, if Susan had known which office Bob worked in, she could have limited her search to the appropriate area of the ADS structure by specifying the Sales.Reno.KingTech container. This shows the hierarchical nature of the ADS tree structure. It also demonstrates the concept of namespace: Each object in the context KingTech can be resolved to a unique name.

Active Directory Names

In an ADS directory, each object has a unique name within the structure. There are three different types of name used depending upon the function being performed:

- Distinguished names
- Relative names
- User principal names

I know that I said there was a single naming standard; as we discuss each of the three name types, you will find that they are all derived from the same single namespace.

Distinguished Names

The *distinguished name (DN)* of any object identifies the entire path through the ADS structure to find that object. Every object within an ADS tree has a DN. For example, Katie King, who works in the Reno sales department of King Technologies, would have the following DN:

`Katie King@Sales.Reno.KingTech.com`

- `Katie King` is the actual name given to the object in the ADS database.

- `Sales` is an OU within the `Reno` container.

- `Reno` is an OU within the `KingTech` container.

- `KingTech` is the organization at the top of the structure.

- `com` represents the container in which the `KingTech` namespace is defined on the Internet.

A distinguished name is the most complete and accurate way to represent any object within the ADS tree. DNs can, however, be cumbersome to use in a productive manner—can you imagine typing Katie's entire DN each time you wanted to send her an e-mail or manage her object? Luckily, there are a few shortcut naming standards that can reduce the length of names used to access resources.

Relative Names

A *relative name (RN)* is made up of the parts of an object's DN that are attributes of the object itself. For Katie, her RN would be `Katie King` because this is the only part of her DN that is specific to her object. The rest of her name is made up of RNs of the containers used to make up her DN. `Sales`, for instance, is the RN of her parent container.

The term *parent* is used to describe any object above another in an ADS tree.

User Principal Names

The *user principal name (UPN)* is the name a user uses to log on to the network. Katie *could* use her DN—`Katie King@Sales.Reno.KingTech.com`—but this could be confusing for her. The UPN is a shortcut made up of her RN and the DNS name of the container in which she resides: `Katie King@KingTech.com`.

We'll discuss DNS naming in more detail in Chapter 9.

A major goal of ADS is to simplify the process of finding information about resources on a network. By using a standard set of rules to create DNs, RNs, and UPNs for objects, Microsoft begins the process of removing multiple naming formats from large environments. This can help to reduce both user and administrative confusion, easing the process of resolving names to resources.

Active Directory in the Windows 2000 Server Architecture

When reading (or writing) a book about Active Directory, one tends to forget that ADS is just one small piece of the overall Windows 2000 Server environment—although a critical small piece! Before we begin our discussion on the specifics of ADS, we need to see how ADS fits into the overall architecture of Windows 2000 Server.

As you can see in Figure 6.5, the Active Directory subsystem is contained within the security subsystem of NT—more specifically, within the *Local Security Authority (LSA)* subsystem of the security environment. The specific module that contains Active Directory within the LSA is the *Directory Service module.* Understanding how these modules are organized can help when designing your ADS network for optimal efficiency and performance.

The modular design of Windows 2000 Server means that each component is a separate and distinct piece that is responsible for a particular function. These components work together to perform operating system tasks. Active Directory is a part of the component called the security subsystem, which runs in *user mode.* User mode is a separate section of memory in which applications are executed. Applications running in user mode do not have direct access to the operating system or hardware; each request for resources must be passed through various components to determine whether the request is valid. One such component is the security subsystem. *Access control lists*

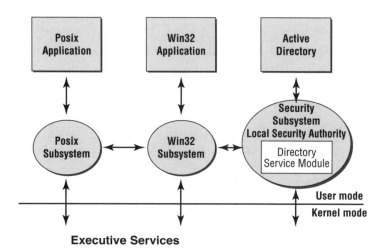

(ACLs) protect objects in the Active Directory structure. ACLs list who or what has been given permission to access the resource. Any attempt to gain access to an ADS object or attribute is validated against the ACL by Windows 2000 Server access validation functions.

The Windows 2000 Server security infrastructure has four primary functions:

- It stores security policies and account information.

- It implements and enforces security models for all objects.

- It authenticates access requests to ADS objects.

- It stores trust information.

The security subsystem for Windows NT is a mature, stable component. Using this subsystem to manage ADS ensures that the information stored within the ADS database will be secure against unauthorized access.

There have been a few changes to the overall NT architecture with Windows 2000 Server: the addition of Plug-and-Play and power management modules; the addition of Quality of Service (QOS), asynchronous transfer mode (ATM), and other drivers to the I/O manager; and some low-level changes to the operating system kernel.

The Security Subsystem

Active Directory is a subcomponent of the LSA, which is in turn a subcomponent of the security subsystem. The LSA is a protected module that maintains the security of the local computer. It ensures that users have system access permissions. The LSA has four primary functions:

- It generates tokens that contain user and group information, as well as the security privileges for that particular user.

- It manages the local security policy.

- It provides the interactive processes for user logon.

- It manages auditing.

The LSA itself is made up of various components, each of which is responsible for a specific function. These components are shown in Figure 6.6.

FIGURE 6.6

LSA components

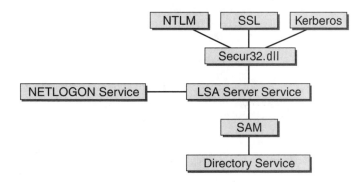

`Netlogon.dll`   Maintains the secure connection to a domain controller. It passes the user's credentials to a domain controller and returns the domain security identifiers and user rights for that user. (In Windows 2000 Server, the NETLOGON service uses DNS to locate the domain controller.) In the event that the environment is a mix of NT 4 and Windows 2000 servers, the NETLOGON service also controls the replication process between the PDC and BDCs.

`Msv1_0.dll`   The Windows NT LAN Manager (NTLM) authentication protocol.

`Schannel.dll`   The Secure Sockets Layer (SSL) authentication protocol.

`Kerberos.dll` The Kerberos v5 authentication protocol.

`Lsasrv.dll` The LSA server service, which enforces security policies.

`Samsrv.dll` The Security Accounts Manager (SAM), which enforces stored policies.

`Ntdsa.dll` The Directory Service module, which supports LDAP queries and manages partitions of data.

`Secur32.dll` The multiple authentication provider, which manages the rest of the components.

The Directory Service Module

The Directory Service module is itself made up of multiple components that work together to provide directory services. These modules are arranged in three layers, as you can see in Figure 6.7. These layers are

- Agents layer
- Directory System Agent layer
- Database layer

These three layers control access to the actual database itself, which is known as the *Extensible Storage Engine (ESE)*.

FIGURE 6.7

Directory Service components

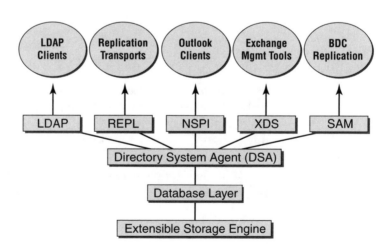

Agents Layer

There are five interface agents that gain access to the directory through internal functions:

- Lightweight Directory Access Protocol (LDAP)
- Intersite and intrasite replication (REPL)
- Name Service Provider Interface (NSPI)
- Exchange Directory Service (XDS)
- Security Accounts Manager (SAM)

Each of these interfaces uses a different method to access the information stored within the database.

Directory System Agent (DSA) Layer

The DSA is responsible for creating a hierarchical tree-like namespace from an existing flat namespace. This allows you to view objects in a more logical manner, rather than as a flat list. The database itself is not really a "tree"— the DSA uses the information found for containers to create the logical structure that we see in the various management tools. The DSA has the following responsibilities:

- Enforce all Directory Service semantics.
- Process transactions.
- Enforce the common schema.
- Support replication between ADS servers.
- Provide Global Catalogue services.
- Propagate security descriptors.

Database Layer

The database layer provides the functionality needed to access and search the directory database. All database access is routed through the database layer. It controls the ways in which the data is viewed.

Extensible Storage Engine

The ESE is the actual database used to store the Active Directory database. It is a modified version of the JET database used in Microsoft Exchange versions 4 and 5. The ESE enables you to create a 17-terabyte database that (theoretically) can hold up to 10 million objects.

The JET database engine has been used for Microsoft Exchange Server for quite some time. The version used by ADS comes with a predefined schema (the definition of object classes and their attributes). ESE reserves storage only for the space actually used. If you create a user object, for example, which *could* have 50 predefined attributes, but you only give values to four of them, then ESE will only use as much storage space as needed for the four attributes. As you add values to other attributes for that user, ESE will dynamically allocate space for the growth in record size. ESE can also store multiple values for a single attribute (such as telephone numbers). It will allocate space as needed for each telephone number added to a user object.

The Internal Architecture of the Active Directory Module

The rootDSA object is inside the DSA in the Directory Service module. It is the top of the logical namespace defined by the ADS database and therefore at the top of the LDAP search tree, as shown in Figure 6.8.

FIGURE 6.8

ADS internal architecture

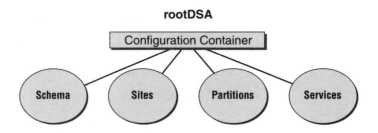

The rootDSA object contains a configuration container, which in turn holds data about the entire ADS network. The information stored in the configuration container provides the data necessary to replicate the directory database, how this server relates to the overall namespace, and how the database is partitioned. This information is known as the *name context* for the various types of information. The four name contexts described under the configuration container are

Schema   Contains the definitions of all object classes and their attributes.

Sites   Contains information on all of the sites in the Enterprise network, the domain controllers in those sites, and the replication topology.

Partitions   Holds pointers to all of the partitions of the directory database.

Services   Holds the configuration information for networkwide services such as Remote Access Service, system volumes, and DNS.

In Short

Microsoft Active Directory Services is intended to tie together all of the diverse aspects of network management within a single database, which can be accessed using a single set of tools. Once implemented, ADS should ease the administrative burdens placed upon network administrators.

Now that we've looked at the goals and the architecture of ADS, we can turn our attention to specific pieces of ADS. In the next chapter, we'll take a closer look at how domains exist in a Windows 2000 Server environment and how ADS implements backward compatibility with older NT systems.

CHAPTER

7

Alphabet Soup: ADS,
TCP/IP, DNS, WINS

While Microsoft Windows 2000 Server is capable of utilizing many different communication protocols, ADS depends on TCP/IP. Before you can begin to install and configure an ADS environment, you must have a strong foundation in TCP/IP and the various TCP/IP tools and techniques. We'll begin by discussing some basic elements of the TCP/IP suite, move to a section on IP subnetting as it relates to Windows 2000 Server and ADS, and then go on to a few of the TCP/IP tools you'll need to understand to implement ADS.

TCP/IP Basics

TCP/IP (Transmission Control Protocol/Internet Protocol) is a suite of protocols specifically designed to fulfill two goals:

- Allow communication across WAN (wide-area network) links

- Allow communication between diverse environments

Understanding the roots of these protocols leads to an understanding of their importance in today's networks.

The History of TCP/IP

In the late 1960s and early 1970s, the U.S. Department of Defense Advanced Research Projects Agency (DARPA) conducted a series of tests with packet-switching networks. These tests had two goals:

- The development of a network that would allow research facilities to share information (at the time, DARPA discovered that numerous universities were conducting the exact same research but did not have the ability to share their results)

- The development of a network that would act as a link between defense sites in the event of a nuclear attack

The second of these goals might sound kind of silly in light of today's global political situation, but at the time, the threat of "nuclear holocaust" was a fact of life. Many of today's most important technologies were developed with the Cold War in mind.

These experiments developed through numerous stages until they finally came together in what we now call the Internet. The TCP/IP suite was developed as part of these experiments. The TCP/IP suite itself is still developing to meet the needs of changing technology.

The development of TCP/IP is overseen by the Internet Society. The Internet Society is responsible for the internetworking technologies and applications used on the Internet. The Internet Architecture Board (IAB) is an advisory group of the Internet Society that is responsible for setting Internet standards. Internet technologies are defined through a series of articles known as RFCs: Requests for Comments.

If a member of the IAB believes that she has a new technology for the Internet or an improvement to an existing technology, she would write a Request for Comments that outlines her idea. This RFC is submitted to the IAB and posted for discussion. (Hence the name Request for *Comments*.) If the idea has merit, it might eventually become part of the standard definition of the TCP/IP suite. Having each proposed change posted on a public forum for discussion fosters an environment of cooperative development. This process also helps to ensure that any change is well thought out and tested before implementation.

Common TCP/IP Protocols and Tools

Over the years, many RFCs have been added to the standard definition of the TCP/IP suite. TCP/IP has developed into a rich, if somewhat complex, set of protocols perfectly suited to the task of managing a complex network. The mature status of most of the technologies is one reason that Microsoft has selected TCP/IP as its protocol of choice for Windows NT networks. Table 7.1 lists some of the more common TCP/IP protocols and the purpose of each.

T A B L E 7.1 TCP/IP Protocols	**Protocol**	**Purpose**
	Simple Network Management Protocol (SNMP)	A protocol designed to be used by network management software. Specifically designed to allow remote management of network devices. This definition has been expanded to include the management of just about any network resource.
	Transmission Control Protocol (TCP)	A communication protocol that is connection-oriented and provides guaranteed delivery services.
	User Datagram Protocol (UDP)	A communication protocol that uses a connectionless delivery scheme to deliver packets. This is a non-guaranteed delivery protocol.
	Internet Control Message Protocol (ICMP)	A protocol used for special communication between hosts, usually protocol management messages (errors and reports).
	Internet Protocol (IP)	A protocol that performs addressing and routing functions.
	Address Resolution Protocol (ARP)	A protocol used to resolve IP addresses into hardware addresses.
	Simple Mail Transfer Protocol (SMTP)	A protocol specifically designed to handle the delivery of electronic mail.
	File Transfer Protocol (FTP)	A protocol used to transfer files from one host to another.

While this is not a complete list of the various protocols that make up the TCP/IP suite, it shows some of the more important protocols in use. As we add complexity to our networks, so must we add complexity to the protocols that provide network functionality.

There is also a standard set of TCP/IP-based tools that every network administrator should be aware of. Table 7.2 lists a few of the more common utilities and their functions.

TABLE 7.2 Common TCP/IP Utilities	Utility	Function
	File Transfer Protocol	This was listed as a protocol in Table 7.1, but it is also considered a critical TCP/IP utility. FTP can be used to test the transfer of files to and from hosts.
	Telnet	Provides terminal emulation to a host running Telnet server software.
	Packet Internet Groper (Ping)	Used to test TCP/IP configurations and connections.
	IPCONFIG	Verifies the TCP/IP configuration on the local host.
	NSLOOKUP	A command-line tool used to read records in the DNS database.
	TRACERT	Used to display the route taken between two hosts.

You will need to be proficient with each of these tools in order to set up and troubleshoot an ADS environment.

TCP/IP Addressing

In a TCP/IP environment, each network host (any device that uses TCP/IP to communicate) needs a unique identifier. This identifier is known as its *IP address*. IP addressing is well beyond the scope of this book, but we will cover the basics just to ensure that we are speaking the same language.

Without getting into too much detail (I'll suggest some additional reading at the end of this chapter), here's an overview. Each IP address is made up of 32 bits. Since computers use a binary system to represent information, each of those bits has one of two values: 0 or 1. The arrangement of those bits must be unique against all computers on any network that a host can communicate with. A typical IP address would look something like this:

```
10000011.01101011.00000010.11001000
```

Notice that the 32 bits are divided into 4 *octets* (an octet is a grouping of 8 bits). Each octet is one byte of data. While this is actually what the computer "sees," it is not how humans think (or at least most of us don't think in binary). Rather than using the binary value, IP addresses are converted into their decimal equivalent. We see IP addresses in a format known as *dotted decimal*. The dotted decimal representation of the address shown above is

```
131.107.2.200
```

An IP address has two parts:

- The network address
- The host address

The *network address* is used to route information to the correct network segment, and the *host address* identifies a particular device within that segment. This is really no different from the street addresses used by the U.S. Postal Service, as you can see in Figure 7.1.

The address line on a letter contains both the house number and the street name. This allows the post office to sort the mail (using the street name) so that the appropriate carrier receives it and can identify which house it should be delivered to. The same process is used with IP addresses: The network portion allows routers to deliver packets to the correct network, and the host portion identifies which host should receive them.

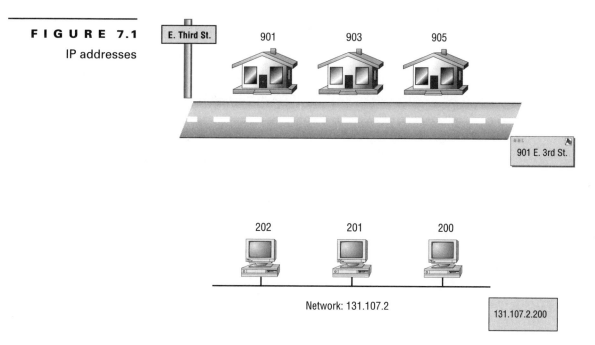

F I G U R E 7.1

IP addresses

IP Subnetting

IP addressing is a little more complex than I just described. When a company receives a network address (either from the Internet authorities or from an Internet Service Provider), the company is given a range of possible addresses. There are three main classes of addresses available: A, B, and C.

There are actually more than three classes of IP network addresses, but we will stick with the more common classes here.

The ABCs of IP Addresses

Class A addresses begin with a first octet value between 1 and 126. In other words, there are only 126 class A networks available on the entire Internet. (Needless to say, there are no more class A addresses available.) The first octet is the network portion of the IP address and the last three octets represent the host portion. Each class A network can support over 16 million hosts. Now you can see why only a few of these addresses are needed—not many companies have that number of hosts on their networks.

How do you calculate the number of hosts a network can support? On a class A network, only the first octet represents the network. This means that 3 octets—or 24 bits—are used to provide the host portion. In a binary system, you can determine the number of unique combinations by raising 2 to the number of bits available. In this case, 2 raised to the 24th power equals 16,777,214—more than 16 million available combinations. Without going into the binary math involved, two of the possible combinations are illegal, so really there are 16,777,212 hosts available on a class A network.

Class B networks begin with a first octet value between 128 and 191. In a class B network, the first two octets represent the network and the last two represent the node portion of an IP address. This means that there are only 65,534 class B networks available, each of which can support 65,534 nodes (2^{16}-2).

Finally, class C networks begin with a first octet value between 192 and 223. On a class C network, the first three octets represent the network and the last octet represents the host portion. This means that there are a little over 16 million class C network addresses available, but each can only support a maximum of 254 hosts.

Subnetting IP Addresses

The problem with the standard address classes is that they assume no routers between the various hosts on the network. In other words, if you were given a class B network address, it is assumed that you have somewhere in the neighborhood of 65,000 hosts on a single network. In reality, this situation would be intolerable. Even if you could find a topology that would support it, the amount of traffic on such a network would slow performance to a crawl.

To overcome this limitation, IP network addresses can be *subnetted*. The process of subnetting can be extremely confusing (especially since this is not something you consider every day), but the theory is fairly straightforward.

When a company is given a network address, it is given the *network portion* of each valid IP address for the network. In other words, if a company is given a class B address of 131.107.0.0, each IP address on its network *must* begin with 131.107. This is the portion of the address used by network devices to route packets to the network.

Another way to look at this is to see the network portion as mandated by some external entity (the Internet, for instance). The local administrator owns the host portion, such as the last two octets in our example. He can do what he likes with them. This means that with a class B license, the local administrator has 16 bits to use as he sees fit. In order to control traffic, the local administrator might choose to use some of these bits to represent local network addresses. While this *does* make the process of assigning IP addresses much more complex, it offers a few advantages that cannot be ignored:

- Since internal routers will direct traffic to the appropriate local network, congestion is reduced. Each network segment will carry only traffic intended for local hosts.

- Each topology has limitations on the number of hosts that can be physically attached to a single network wire. Subnetting allows the administrator to control how many hosts are on each internal network.

- Later we will see that we can define ADS *sites* that are used to control directory database replication. These sites are based upon IP subnet addresses.

As you can see, TCP/IP addressing can be a complex subject, well beyond the scope of this material. For more information, I would suggest you read one of the books recommended at the end of this chapter.

Now that we've taken a look at some of the basic principles of TCP/IP, we can examine a few of the utilities designed to make managing a network easier.

Dynamic Host Configuration Protocol (DHCP)

Each host on a typical routed IP network must have certain parameters set correctly in order to communicate. The three most common parameters are

IP address   Used to uniquely identify the host

Subnet mask   Used to determine which portion of the IP address represents the network address

Default gateway   Used to represent the IP address of the router to which all non-local traffic will be directed

Traditionally these parameters were configured manually on each device on the network. From a management perspective, this meant that an administrator had to visit each device to configure its IP parameters. Entering this information manually took a lot of time and was prone to error. While there is a better way to accomplish this task, you can still opt for manual configuration of a Windows 2000 Server computer if you desire.

TCP/IP addresses are configured in much the same way as they were in NT 4. There are, however, a few changes to the interface. To access the configuration window, click the My Computer icon on the Desktop. From there, you will be presented with the window shown in Figure 7.2.

FIGURE 7.2

My Computer options

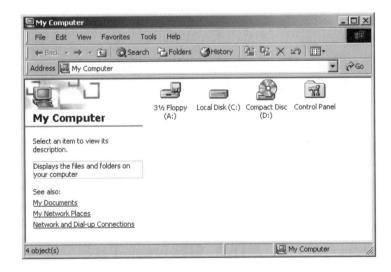

Choosing the Network and Dial-up Connections link will bring you to the window shown in Figure 7.3.

From this window, right-click the Local Area Connection icon and choose Properties. Highlight the Internet Protocol (TCP/IP) option and again choose Properties. At this point, you will be presented with the window shown in Figure 7.4. Check the box labeled "Use the following IP address," and enter your parameters.

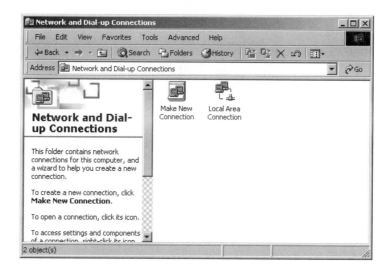

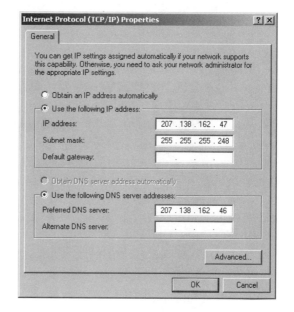

Our discussion of how to manually configure the IP parameters on a Windows 2000 Server computer is mostly academic. You will use this method mostly to configure static IP addresses for special-case devices. Microsoft's preferred method for configuring IP hosts is to use *Dynamic Host Configuration Protocol (DHCP)*, which we'll turn to next.

Installing DHCP Service

DHCP uses the BootP protocol to automatically configure TCP/IP clients as they join the network. DHCP services must be installed on an NT server. The basic premise of DHCP services is that clients can be configured automatically as they join the network, rather than manually as the computer is installed. Since configuration occurs each time the client computer attaches to the network, changes to the configuration are dynamically updated on the client.

The DHCP installation process has been modified from the NT 4 process, so let's take a good look at it.

To install DHCP services on your Windows 2000 server, open your Control Panel (by choosing Start ➢ Settings ➢ Control Panel) and click Add/Remove Programs. You will be presented with a new interface, as shown in Figure 7.5.

FIGURE 7.5

Add/Remove Programs in Windows 2000 Server

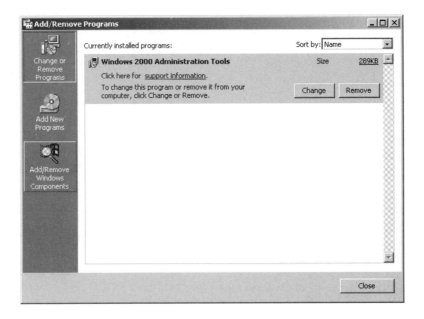

Click the Add/Remove Windows Components button. The Windows Components Wizard will appear, as shown in Figure 7.6. This window displays the various NT components that you can install on your server. The DHCP service is part of the Networking Services selection. Make sure that Networking Services is chosen and click Details. You will notice that there are numerous components to this option; make sure that only the items you want installed at this time are chosen. Then click OK and press the Next button, then the Finished button to complete the installation.

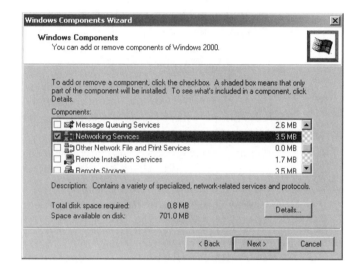

FIGURE 7.6

The Windows Components Wizard

Once DHCP services have been installed, you will find a new tool in your Administrative Tools group: DHCP Server Management.

How Does DHCP Work?

There are two processes to consider when looking at DHCP services:

- Configuring the DHCP server
- Configuring clients as they attach to the network

The next couple of sections discuss these processes.

Configuring the DHCP Server

When configured properly, DHCP servers provide an important service to the network. As with most important functions, though, an incorrectly configured (or worse, unplanned) DHCP server can wreak havoc on your orderly world. Remember the major task of DHCP servers: to give IP addresses and other configuration parameters to clients as they join the network. If a DHCP server is incorrectly configured, it could conceivably hand out IP addresses that are either invalid or—worse—already in use on your network. For this reason, each DHCP server must be authorized before it can function in an Active Directory environment.

Each server in an Active Directory environment will function in one of three roles: domain controller, member server, or stand-alone server.

Domain controllers contain a copy of the Active Directory database and perform account management for domain members.

Member servers do not maintain a replica of the Active Directory database, but they have joined a domain and have an associated record in the ADS database.

Stand-alone servers do not hold a replica of the ADS database and are not members of any domain. Basically, stand-alone servers announce their presence as a member of a workgroup.

Only domain controllers and member servers can act as DHCP servers in an ADS environment. By mandating that all DHCP servers be verified as legal, Windows 2000 provides a level of security that was unavailable in earlier operating systems. Not only does this protect against "industrial espionage" (I've always wanted to use that phrase in a book—of course, I had a spy novel in mind), but it also epitomizes one of the biggest advantages of a directory service: central control. The central Information Services department no longer has to worry about some hotshot in Cleveland installing a DHCP server without understanding IP addressing or subnetting.

Authorizing a DHCP Server

To authorize a server to act as a DHCP server, first install DHCP services as described earlier. Then open the DHCP management tool located in the Administrative Tools group. You will be presented with a screen similar to the one shown in Figure 7.7.

DHCP management
tool

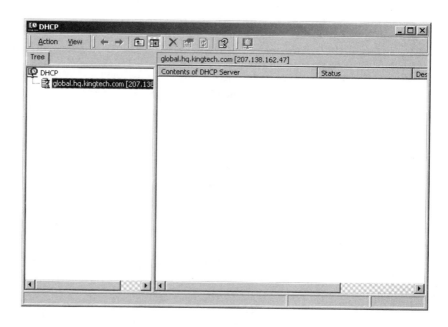

From the opening screen, choose Manage Authorized Servers from the Action menu. You will be presented with the screen shown in Figure 7.8.

F I G U R E   7.8

Authorizing DHCP
servers

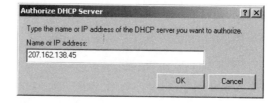

Type in the name or IP address of the server that you wish to add to the authorized DHCP servers list.

Creating a Scope

At the server a *scope* must be created. A scope is a database of the parameters that the DHCP server will pass to clients as they initialize. The DHCP server can provide more than just an IP address, subnet mask, and default gateway—there are numerous TCP/IP parameters that might need to be configured on any given client, and DHCP can designate all of them!

To create a scope, open the DHCP management tool located in the Administrative Tools group. There are two ways to complete most tasks: manually or with the aid of a *Wizard*. (A Wizard is just a script that walks you through the steps involved in configuring an item.) Personally, I like the Wizards—even though I'm fairly comfortable with most items, Wizards ensure that I don't inadvertently forget something. To start the New Scope Wizard, first highlight the server you wish to add the scope to, then from the "Action" menu choose "New," then "Scope." The opening screen is the standard "Welcome to our wizard" message. Click Next and you will be presented with the window shown in Figure 7.9. Here you will give your scope a name and perhaps add a few comments to document your system.

FIGURE 7.9

New scope name and comments

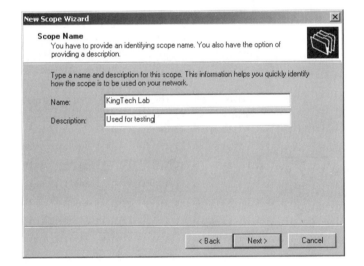

The scope name should be something that will remind you of the purpose of the scope, such as "KingTech Test Lab." You can also add an administrative comment, such as "IP addresses not valid on the Internet."

The first technical configuration option is on the next page of the Wizard, shown in Figure 7.10. Here you will be asked to give a range of addresses that should be given out by the DHCP server when using this scope. (This is where knowledge of the IP addressing scheme discussed earlier will come in handy!) You should also configure the subnet mask for this network.

FIGURE 7.10

Defining the range of addresses

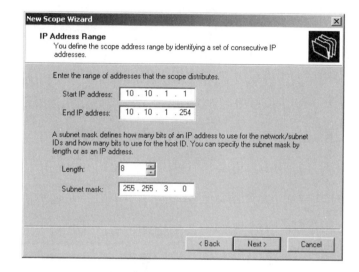

You will then be asked for a list of any IP addresses that should be excluded from the range, as shown in Figure 7.11. You might need to exclude addresses if you have devices that are manually configured with an address from your range.

Manually configured addresses are also known as static addresses because they should never change.

The next screen, shown in Figure 7.12, will ask you for the duration of IP address leases. When a client receives an IP address from the DHCP server, the client "leases" it for this amount of time (the default is three days). This allows the DHCP server to free up the address if the computer goes offline for an extended period of time.

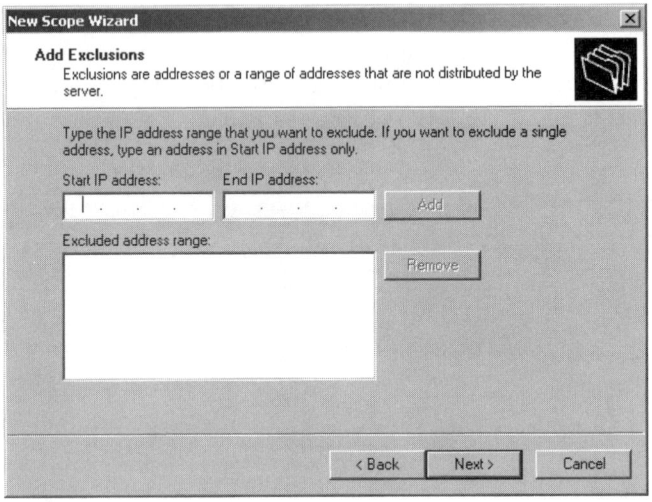

FIGURE 7.11

Excluding IP
addresses

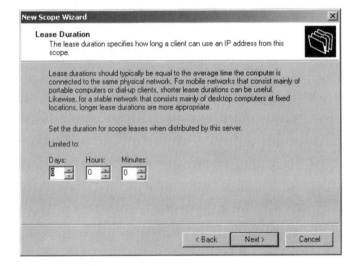

FIGURE 7.11

Excluding IP
addresses

FIGURE 7.12

Setting lease duration

The last screen of the Wizard reminds you that you will still have to configure any additional parameters that should be passed to clients by the
DHCP server and that you will have to activate, or turn on, the scope before
it will function. By selecting the appropriate button as shown in Figure 7.13,
you can choose either to configure these options now or to do so later.

FIGURE 7.13

Additional options

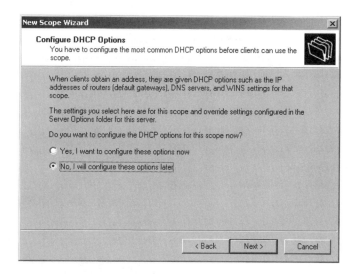

There are numerous options that can be added to a DHCP scope for inclusion in the configuration of clients. Once you have finished creating the scope, it will be added to your view in the DHCP management tool, as shown in Figure 7.14.

FIGURE 7.14

KingTech Lab scope

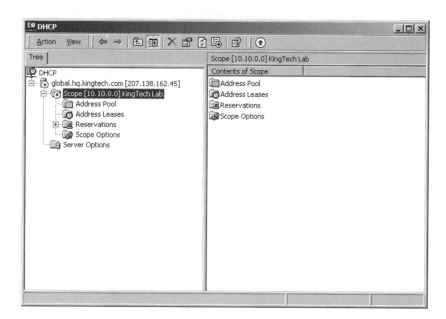

To configure additional parameters, right-click Scope Options and choose Configure Options. The window shown in Figure 7.15 will appear. A complete discussion of the options available is beyond our purposes, but you should be aware that no scope is complete without a few additional options. As an example, you will probably want to configure the default gateway option for most clients.

FIGURE 7.15

DHCP options

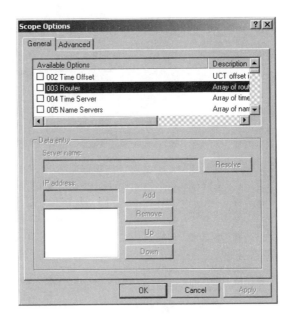

DHCP Auditing

While DHCP is an established and reliable process, there might be circumstances where you need to track the DHCP actions taken on a server. Perhaps you suspect that unauthorized computers are being placed on your network or you want to track who is utilizing your services. (Tracking who uses your services can be used to "charge back" to other departments or to justify an increase in the IS budget.) For these and other reasons, the version of DHCP services included with Windows 2000 includes the ability to audit its services.

Once enabled, DHCP logging will create comma-delineated text files that document the actions taken by the DHCP service. Administrators have quite a bit of control over the placement, size, and use of DHCP auditing. You can set the following parameters for DHCP auditing:

- Placement of the log files.

- Maximum size limit (in megabytes) for all DHCP log files.

- How often the DHCP service checks for available disk space before writing new records to a log file. (This one is useful for limiting the overhead on your server.)

- Minimum available space restriction that will be used to determine if there is enough disk space available to continue logging. This prevents the DHCP auditing service from filling your hard disks.

To enable DHCP auditing, open the DHCP management tool, click the appropriate DHCP server, and choose Properties on the Action menu. You will be presented with the window shown in Figure 7.16. Make sure that the "Enable DHCP audit logging" option is selected.

F I G U R E 7.16

Enabling DHCP audit logging

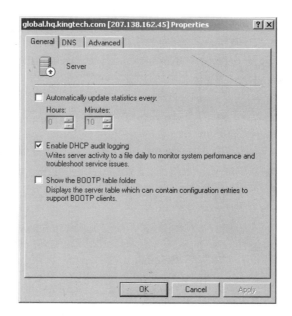

On the Advanced tab, you will be able to set the path to the audit files. This allows you to place them on a partition that has enough available disk space.

Once logging has been available, you will want to check the audit files on a regular basis. Below is the output from a sample log file:

```
Microsoft DHCP Service Activity Log

ID Date,Time,Description,IP Address,Host Name,MAC Address
00,11/26/99,13:34:12,Started,,,
55,11/26/99,13:34:43,Authorized(servicing),,WORKGROUP,
01,11/26/99,13:51:10,Stopped,,,
```

As you can see, each entry provides an event code that identifies the action taken, the date, the time, and a short description. Notice the trailing commas in our sample—these represent other fields that will be available when appropriate: IP address, Host name, and MAC address. Our sample is a very simple example of a DHCP log file. There are numerous event codes that you will want to be familiar with. I've listed a few of the more important ones in Table 7.3.

T A B L E 7.3 DHCP Log File Event Codes	Event ID	Name	Description
	00	Start	The log was started.
	01	Stop	The log was stopped.
	02	Pause	The log was paused due to insufficient disk space.
	10	Lease	A new IP address was leased to a client.
	11	Renew	A lease was renewed for a client.
	12	Release	A client has released its IP address.
	13	Duplicate	An IP address was found in use on the network.
	14	Out of addresses	A lease request was denied because the DHCP server had no available addresses.

TABLE 7.3 (cont.) DHCP Log File Event Codes	Event ID	Name	Description
	15	Denied	A lease request was denied.
	50	Unreachable domain	The server was unable to find the domain in which it is configured (probably followed by more events).
	51	Authorization succeeded	The service was authenticated and started.
	52	Upgraded to Windows 2000	The service was recently upgraded to Windows 2000 so unauthorized DHCP server detection was disabled.
	53	Cached authorization	The server was unable to contact ADS, but used cached information to start.
	54	Authorization failed	(Usually followed by more event records to explain the problem.)
	55	Authorization (servicing)	Successful authorization occurred.
	56	Authorization failure, stopped servicing	The attempt to authenticate failed so DHCP services were stopped.
	59	Network failure	The system is unable to communicate on the network, services stopped.

While this is not a complete list of the available event codes (more can be found in both the DHCP help file and the Windows 2000 resource kits), it includes the more commonly seen events.

DHCP and Clustering

In this book, we are concentrating on "Mastering" one very specific topic—Active Directory. Windows 2000 includes many other new technologies, tools, and advances to make your computing environment more efficient, easier to manage, and more reliable. We can only touch on a few of those in this book. One noteworthy new technology is *clustering*. Clustering, available only with Windows 2000 Advanced Server, allows a group of independent computers, known as *nodes*, to work together as a single unit. There are many advantages to a clustering environment: the ability to manage a group of servers as a single entity, improvement in workload distribution, and failover in the event of hardware failure.

A basic cluster is made up of two or more computers attached to one or more storage systems. Each of the nodes runs software that allows it to monitor the status of the other nodes in the cluster. In the event of a failure, the cluster can be configured to restart the affected computer's critical services or applications on other computers in the cluster. The system can also be configured to spread the workload of an application or service across multiple machines.

 A complete discussion of clustering technology is beyond the scope of this text. For more information, see *Mastering Windows 2000 Server,* 2nd ed., by Mark Minasi, Christa Anderson, Brian M. Smith, and Doug Toombs (ISBN 0-7821-2774-6, Sybex, 2000).

The DHCP service can be configured to take advantage of a clustered environment. This configuration allows you to ensure that DHCP services will be constantly available through cluster fail-over. This type of fault-tolerance is critical in today's high-volume, constant-use, mission-critical networks.

To configure DHCP to take advantage of clustering, certain prerequisites must be met. The cluster itself must have a shared disk resource configured and working. You must then create an IP address resource (to act as the IP address of the DHCP service) and a name resource (to represent the DHCP service).

The IP address cluster resource represents the IP address that will be assigned to the DHCP service (as opposed to a specific host). This "virtual IP address" must be statically configured and must be valid on your network. The DHCP service will bind to the virtual IP address instead of the address of a physical device.

Each node in the cluster must also be configured with its own IP address. The DHCP named cluster resource is then configured with the IP address of the preferred node and the IP addresses of any node that should take over in the event of failure. Since the cluster shares a disk subsystem, the DHCP database is available even though the original DHCP server might be unavailable. In the event of a failure, the clustering software will start the DHCP service on another node, and service will continue normally.

The DHCP Client Configuration Process

There are four packets involved in the configuration of a DHCP client:

- Discover
- Offer
- Request
- Acknowledgment

The process is as follows:

1. As a DHCP client initializes, one of the first things it does is send a *discover packet* out on the wire. This packet is a broadcast, so all computers on the local network will pick it up to determine whether they need to respond.

2. Any DHCP server that receives the broadcast discover packet will respond. Each such server first checks its scope to determine whether it has an IP address available. If so, it marks an address as temporarily in use and sends an *offer packet* to the client. The offer also uses a broadcast packet because the client is not yet configured with an address.

3. The client accepts the first offer that it receives (there might be more than one DHCP server that responds). It broadcasts a *request packet* on the wire. The client uses a broadcast for two reasons:

- The client still has no IP address, so broadcasts are mandated.
- This informs all other DHCP servers that the client has made a selection.

4. Finally, the DHCP server broadcasts an *acknowledgment packet* and marks the client's IP address as being in use. Any other DHCP server that responded also receives the broadcast and can free up the address that it had temporarily marked as unavailable.

There are many different types of clients that can take advantage of the DHCP service—all of the modern Microsoft operating systems (Windows 9*x*, Windows NT 4, Windows 2000), of course, plus various other local operating systems currently on the market (e.g., various flavors of Unix, LAN Manager). Each local operating system will be configured to act as a DHCP client in a slightly different manner. Most, however, will have certain things in common. For instance, most will be configured in the same way as other network-related options (text files, some applications, or perhaps as part of the OS installation). Microsoft products, for example, are configured in the same place as the TCP/IP protocol is configured.

While DHCP does reduce administrative overhead by centralizing control over IP configurations, there are a few problems with the traditional implementation. First and foremost, DHCP is a broadcast-based technology. Most administrators tend to avoid broadcast-based technologies for two reasons:

- Broadcast packets place unwanted overhead on the network. Every computer that receives a broadcast packet must open it up to look inside and determine whether it needs to respond. In effect, broadcast packets use processing power on every computer that receives these packets.

- More important, most modern routers are configured to prevent broadcast packets from being forwarded to other networks. This means that broadcast packets are limited to the home network of the originating computer. With DHCP, this means you must have a DHCP server on each segment or you must manage some other solution (either configuring your routers to forward broadcasts or installing a DHCP proxy).

Microsoft has integrated ADS, DHCP, and DNS to solve these problems, as you'll see later in this chapter.

Domain Name Server (DNS)

As we discussed earlier, DNS is the directory used by traditional TCP/IP environments (like the Internet) to resolve user-friendly names into IP addresses. DNS is a group of name servers linked together to create a single namespace.

Remember that a namespace is just a system in which all resources share a common trait. In the case of the Internet DNS, the common trait is the Root object.

The namespace defined by the DNS system is logical in nature—in other words, it presents a group of text files as a single entity. The servers that hold these data files are known as *name servers*. Clients that query the name servers for name resolution are known as *resolvers*.

The DNS namespace itself is presented graphically as a hierarchical system, much like the system of folders and subfolders that makes up a file system. In DNS, each folder would be considered a DNS *domain* (not to be confused with an NT domain). Any domain that contains subdomains would be considered the *parent* of those domains, and the subdomains would be considered *child domains*. (A domain can be both a child of one domain and the parent of another.) Each domain has one, and only one, parent domain. At the top of the structure is the *root domain;* this is the only domain that has no parent. Planning the structure of domains and subdomains is a large part of planning any DNS installation.

Domains are named by the complete path to the root domain. In Figure 7.17, the complete name of the Royal-Tech domain would be royal-tech.com.

Notice that the root domain is not included as part of the complete name. It is assumed that every DNS name ends with the root domain.

FIGURE 7.17

Royal-tech.com

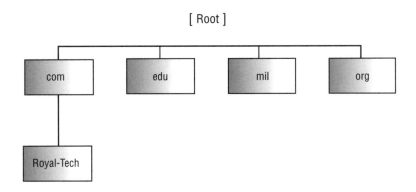

DNS is critical to an ADS environment because ADS uses DNS to resolve host names into IP addresses for internal functions, such as the replication of the directory database. Without a properly functioning DNS system, ADS will not function correctly. In other words, DNS is something that you will have to be very familiar with in order to properly plan your ADS-based network.

So What Exactly Is a DNS Domain?

There are two ways to look at DNS domains:

- Physically
- Logically

You will need to understand both views in order to properly install and configure the DNS service on your Windows 2000 server.

Physically, a DNS domain is really a piece, or partition, of a large distributed database. It exists as a text file stored on a server that is running DNS services. The file that holds the records for a domain is often called the *zone file*. The syntax used in the zone file is arcane—remember, the same people who designed the original Unix interface created this technology. Luckily, Microsoft's implementation of DNS uses a graphical interface to create the records in the zone file.

We'll look at the DNS Manager tool a little later in this chapter.

Logically, a DNS domain represents a boundary of responsibility. Whoever controls the server on which the zone file is located is responsible for the maintenance of the records within the file. Think of this in terms of the Internet. If there were one big DNS file located on a server somewhere, whoever was responsible for that server would also have to maintain the DNS records for all of the resources on the Internet—a big job, to say the least!

Breaking the DNS namespace into domains allows for a *distributed database*. A distributed database allows for delegation of responsibility. Even if your company is not connected to the Internet, you can still use these principles to distribute both the overhead on your DNS servers and the administrative tasks.

Planning DNS Naming

When planning your DNS naming structure, you must answer a series of questions:

- Will this system be attached to the Internet?
- How heavily will DNS be used?
- How can the system best be organized to provide an intuitive environment for end-users?

We'll look at each question in turn.

Will This System Be Attached to the Internet?

If your system will be attached to the Internet, certain aspects of the DNS namespace will be mandated for you. You will need to register a domain with the Internet Society and follow certain rules governing your configuration. More information about this process can be found at http://rs.internic.net.

If you are not connecting to the Internet, the same rules will apply, but you will have a little more freedom in naming your domain. Just remember that the name must be unique if you are ever going to connect.

How Heavily Will DNS Be Used?

If you expect your DNS system to be heavily utilized, you might want to consider setting up multiple DNS servers. DNS has the ability to replicate zone files from a master DNS server to secondary servers. While changes can be made only to the primary copy, the secondary servers can act both as a fault-tolerant copy of the zone file and as another name server to split the workload of resolving names. This consideration is not applicable if you decide to implement DNS as a portion of ADS, a choice we'll discuss in a bit.

How Can the System Best Be Organized to Provide an Intuitive Environment for End-Users?

This is probably the hardest part of designing a DNS system. Creating multiple subdomains can ease the overhead on each DNS server (since each server holds less of the database), but this can be confusing for your users. Microsoft recommends that the DNS structure not be more than three to five layers deep and that you keep names as short as possible. This reduces the users' learning curve considerably. Table 7.4 lists the common steps involved in designing a DNS domain structure.

T A B L E 7.4 Planning Your DNS Domain Structure	**Level**	**Example**	**Considerations**
	Top	.com	This level will usually be mandated by the Internet Society. There are certain top-level names associated with different types of businesses: .com for commercial, .org for nonprofit organizations, .edu for educational facilities, and so on.
	Top of local domain	royal-tech	This should be descriptive of your company, such as its name, product, or function. This is the domain name you register on the Internet, and it is often not exactly what you want. (My company's name is King Technologies, but the closest I could get was Royal-Tech.)
	Child domains	Sales.royal-tech.com	The entire purpose of creating child domains is to be able to delegate responsibility for administration of the zone file. Usually these names will indicate the department or organization that is responsible for each.

Integrating DNS with Active Directory

When you deploy Microsoft DNS services in an ADS environment, you have two choices:

- Use traditional, text-based zone files.
- Integrate the zone information with Active Directory.

Microsoft suggests the latter option! When you integrate DNS with ADS, all zone information is stored in the ADS database: a distributed, replicated, fault-tolerant database, which is then stored on all of the ADS servers within your organization.

ADS can store one or more DNS zones. All domain controllers can then receive dynamic DNS information sent from other Windows 2000 computers. Each Active Directory server can also act as a fully functional DNS authority, updating the DNS information stored on all of your ADS servers.

In other words, once DNS has been integrated with ADS, every ADS server acts as a primary DNS server for all zones. In fact, all zones stored by ADS must be primary—if you need to implement old-fashioned secondary zones (perhaps in a mixed DNS environment) you will have to stick with the old-fashioned text-file-based DNS.

In addition to integration with Active Directory, the Microsoft implementation of DNS provides the following functionality:

SRV resource records   These are a new type of record (defined in RFC 2052) that identifies the location of a service rather than a device.

Dynamic update   Microsoft DNS is more properly called DDNS: *Dynamic* Domain Name Server. It is capable of allowing hosts to dynamically register their names with the zone, thereby reducing administrative overhead.

Secure dynamic update   Windows 2000 Server security is used to authenticate hosts that attempt to dynamically register themselves within the zone.

Incremental zone transfer   Only changed data is replicated to other ADS servers.

Interoperability with DHCP   A server running DHCP services can register host names on behalf of its clients. This allows non-DDNS clients to dynamically register with the zone.

Active Directory uses DNS to locate domains and domain controllers during the logon process. This is made possible by the inclusion of SRV-type records in the DNS database. Each Windows 2000 domain controller dynamically registers an SRV record in the zone. This record represents the domain NET-LOGON service on that server. When a client attempts to log on, it will query its DNS server for the address of a domain controller. The bottom line here is that even if you are not going to use DNS for anything else, you will have to install and configure it for the logon process to work properly. Let me stress this one more time—DNS is critical to an ADS environment!

Installing and Configuring DNS on an ADS Domain Controller

If you are upgrading an existing NT 4 server that has DNS installed and configured, the installation of ADS will automatically upgrade DNS for you. If not, you will have to install DNS as a separate step (part of the Networking Services you installed with DHCP services).

If you have to configure a new DNS server, you will use the DNS Manager tool located in the Administrative Tools group. Here you will see your server listed, as shown in Figure 7.18.

FIGURE 7.18

DNS Manager

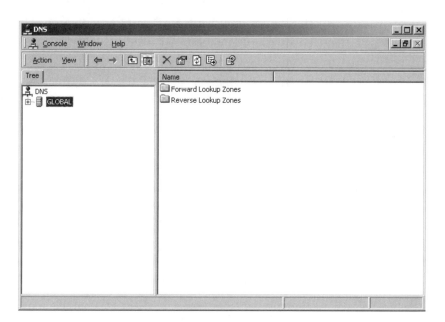

To create a new zone, right-click your server and choose Create a New Zone. A Wizard will start that will walk you through the steps involved. You will first be asked whether you would like to have a traditional DNS system (stored in text files) or have DNS integrated into ADS as shown in Figure 7.19.

FIGURE 7.19

New Zone Wizard

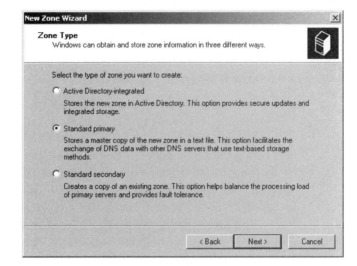

If you are going to create a reverse lookup zone, you will be asked for its network address, as shown in Figure 7.20; otherwise you will only have to provide the name for the new domain.

FIGURE 7.20

Configuring a reverse
lookup zone

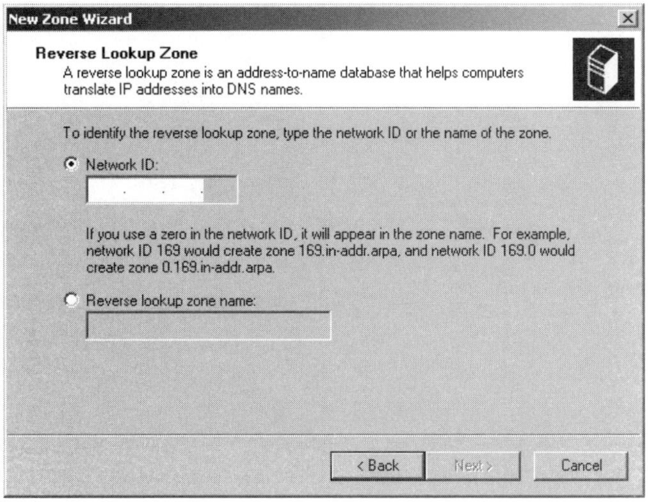

For more information about the specifics of DNS (like reverse lookup zones), I would suggest reading *MCSE: TCP/IP for NT Server 4 Study Guide,* 4th ed., by Todd Lammle with Monica Lammle and James Chellis (ISBN 0-7821-2725-8, Sybex, 2000).

DNS and Dynamic Updates

One of the most exciting new features of Windows 2000 DNS is the ability to configure the system to accept dynamic updates from clients. This allows clients to register and dynamically update their DNS records as they boot or as their configuration changes. In older systems, especially those where computers were frequently moved or reconfigured, keeping the DNS files up to date was a full-time job. Windows 2000 clients and server support dynamic updates as defined in RFC 2136—in other words, through an industry standard method.

In Windows 2000 DNS servers, dynamic updates can be enabled or disabled on a zone-by-zone basis. By default, all Windows 2000 clients will attempt to dynamically register themselves with DNS as they boot or as changes occur. Enabling or disabling dynamic updates is a fairly simple process. In the DNS manager, right-click the zone, choose Properties, and on the General tab configure the "Allow dynamic updates?" option as shown in Figure 7.21.

FIGURE 7.21

Allowing dynamic updates

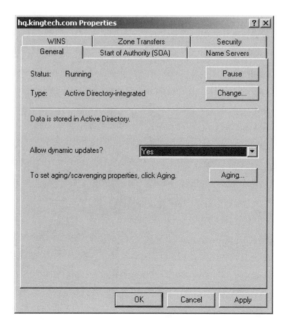

Clients will register themselves using their FQDN (Fully Qualified Domain Name). The FQDN is the NetBIOS computer name followed by the text placed in the "Primary DNS Suffix of this Computer" configuration parameter. This parameter can be found in the Network Identification tab of the System applet in Control Panel as shown in Figure 7.22. (Notice that the computer in the graphic is a domain controller, so this parameter cannot be changed.)

FIGURE 7.22

Fully Qualified Domain Name

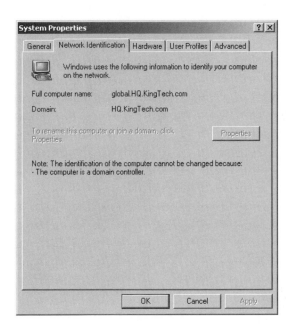

In Short

A basic level of TCP/IP knowledge is mandatory when configuring ADS. Our discussion has been limited to an overview. For a more detailed explanation of the technologies presented, I would suggest you read one or more of the following titles, available from Sybex:

- *MCSE Exam Notes: TCP/IP for NT Server 4* by Gary Govanus (ISBN 0-7821-2307-4, 1998)

- *MCSE: TCP/IP for NT Server 4 Study Guide,* 4th ed., by Todd Lammle with Monica Lammle and James Chellis (ISBN 0-7821-2725-8, 2000)

- *Mastering TCP/IP for NT Server* by Mark Minasi and Todd Lammle (ISBN 0-7821-2123-3, 1997)

In the next chapter, we will take a look at NT domains in an ADS environment: why they exist, their function in today's networks, and how to manage them.

CHAPTER

8

Building the Active
Directory Tree

In this chapter, we will look at both the theory and the mechanics of building your ADS tree structure. Of the two topics, the theory is probably the more important; the "mechanics" is just knowing where to click your mouse. (And Microsoft is always changing the interface, anyway!) Knowing the theory allows you to build a stable structure that does not place undue stress on any single point of your network. Creating an ADS tree without knowing the theory is a crapshoot—you *might* produce a design that is stable, but then again, you might not.

What Is a Domain?

You might recall the definition of a *domain* from earlier versions of NT: a logical grouping of computers and users managed through a central security accounts database. According to this definition, a domain was:

- Logically, an organizational grouping of resources allowing central management of those resources

- Physically, a database containing information about those resources

Combining the logical with the physical gave you a management or security boundary: Administrators for a domain could manage all resources in that domain by default.

The definition of a domain has not changed in Windows 2000 Server. The only real change is that we now have to work this definition into a bigger picture—that of the entire network. In earlier versions of NT, we tied domains together by establishing trust relationships between them. In Windows 2000 Server, trusts still exist, but they are established by default and function quite differently than before.

In Windows 2000 Server, domains act as the building blocks for an ADS tree structure. The first domain created becomes the *root domain*. The root domain acts as the top of the structure and determines the beginning of the ADS namespace. The name of this domain *must* match the top level of your desired namespace. After the first domain is created, each subsequent domain is added to the tree somewhere beneath it. In other words, additional domains are always children (although not necessarily children of the root domain), whereas the root domain has no parent. This concept is illustrated in Figure 8.1.

FIGURE 8.1

The root domain

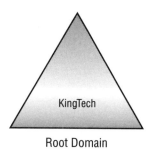

Root Domain

In Figure 8.1, the first domain for the company King Technologies has been named `KingTech`. As the first domain added to the tree, it becomes the root domain. All subsequent domains will follow the naming pattern of `<something>.KingTech`, as shown in Figure 8.2.

Figure 8.2 demonstrates the principle of *hierarchical naming*. Each subsequent domain adds the names of all domains above it together to create a distinguished name.

DNS Domains and NT Domains

In Chapter 7 we discussed DNS (Domain Name System) domains. A DNS domain represents a piece of the overall DNS namespace. DNS is a service used to find resources: A process submits a host name and DNS attempts to find a record that matches. If a match is found, DNS returns the appropriate IP address to the requestor. As such, we could define a DNS domain as *a bounded portion of a DNS namespace used to find IP host information.*

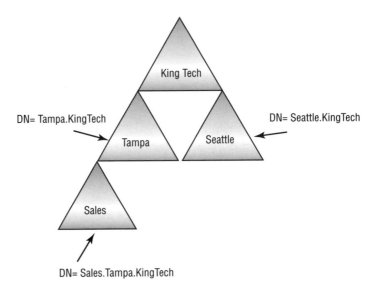

In this chapter, we will discuss NT domains, concentrating on how they relate to Active Directory. For our purposes, we can define an NT domain as *a bounded area of an ADS namespace used to organize network resources.* Comparing the two definitions, we can make two generalizations:

- DNS domains are for finding resources.

- ADS domains are for organizing resources.

I know that we have said that the Active Directory database is used to "find" resources, so let me clarify. While ADS holds information about resources on the network, it uses DNS to find and resolve distinguished names into IP addresses. In other words, ADS and DNS work together to return connection information to users or to other processes that request such information, as you can see in Figure 8.3.

In Figure 8.3, Susan uses the ADS database to find a share point. Here is what happens:

1. Susan browses the directory and clicks the \Data resource.

2. The client software sends a request to an ADS server.

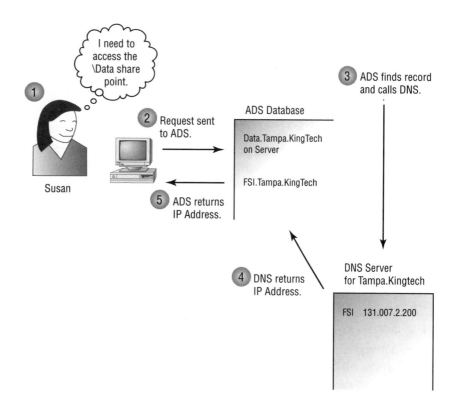

FIGURE 8.3

ADS and DNS work together to provide services.

3. The ADS server searches the directory database for the resource record. In the record, it finds the DNS name of the server on which the share point is located. ADS queries DNS for the IP address of the appropriate server.

4. DNS searches its database for the record for server FS1.Tampa.KingTech. Once it finds this record, DNS returns the IP address to ADS.

5. ADS returns the IP address of server FS1.Tampa.KingTech to the client.

At this point, the client software can establish a connection with the server using the appropriate TCP/IP technologies.

DNS is a critical piece of the ADS puzzle. Without DNS, ADS cannot resolve user requests into IP addresses of resources. For this reason, you must have a good grounding in DNS before installing and configuring Active Directory.

Partitioning the Database

In large environments, the ADS directory database can become quite large. As we saw earlier, the X.500 recommendations specify a method of breaking the database into smaller pieces, known as *partitions*, and distributing them across multiple servers. The X.500 recommendations also include a methodology for replicating changes to multiple copies of the same partition.

For the Active Directory database, domains act as the boundaries of partitions. In other words, each domain represents a partition of the overall directory database, as shown in Figure 8.4.

FIGURE 8.4

Each domain is a partition of the ADS database.

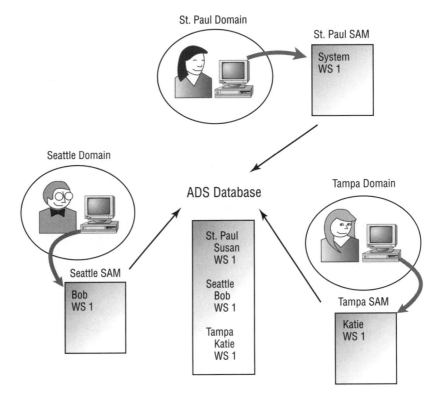

Breaking the database into smaller pieces places less overhead on each Active Directory server. It also grants the administrator more control over the amount and route of traffic generated by the database replication process. Consider the environment depicted in Figure 8.5. Since there is only one domain defined, each ADS server holds records for every resource in the enterprise. If a new printer is installed in Seattle, information about that printer will have to be updated on every ADS server in the entire company. The same holds true for *every* change made to the database. If user Katie in Tampa changes her password, that change will have to be replicated to every ADS server across the entire network. While this design is functional, it is probably not the best design possible for the network.

F I G U R E 8.5

Company XYZ domain structure

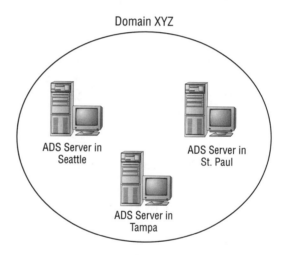

The KingTech Company has come up with a much better design, as you can see in Figure 8.6. In this design, each server contains records only for objects that are in its own geographic area. Notice that this design has two benefits:

- It limits the amount of traffic generated between the two locations.

- It ensures that no server is overburdened by holding records that are of no real value to its purpose.

We'll look at various design strategies in more detail later in this chapter.

FIGURE 8.6

KingTech domain
structure

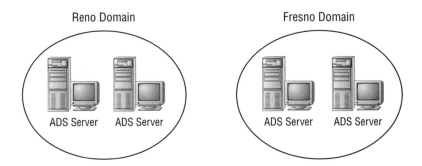

Trusts between Domains

Domains not only act as partition boundaries for the database; they also act
as boundaries for various administrative functions. In our review of NT 4
domains, we discussed the concept of *trusts* between domains. Put simply,
a trust is a secure connection between two domains. Without some sort of
trust, domains will not communicate and cannot share resources. This is
also true in Windows 2000 Server—except that trusts are created automatically and they work a little differently.

Trusts in NT 4 and Earlier

As a quick review, let's take a look at how trusts worked in NT 4. In version
4 there were two types of trusts: one-way and two-way. In Figure 8.7, the
Tampa domain trusts the Reno domain. In effect, this means that accounts
that exist in the Reno domain can be granted permissions to access resources
in the Tampa domain. *But not vice versa!* A one-way trust implies that only
one of the domains is trusted and only the trusted domain can access
resources in the other.

FIGURE 8.7

One-way trust

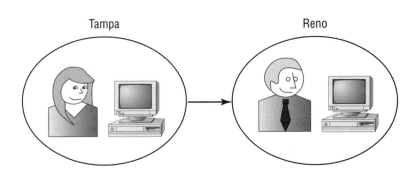

In Figure 8.8, a two-way trust has been established between the Tampa and Reno domains. In this configuration, accounts from both domains can be granted permissions in either domain.

FIGURE 8.8

Two-way trust

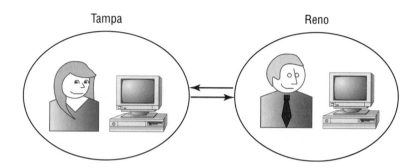

In NT 4 and earlier, trusts were non-transitive. This meant that trusts had to be explicitly defined between any two domains. As an example, look at Figure 8.9. In this figure

- The Tampa domain trusts the Reno domain.

- The Reno domain trusts the St. Paul domain.

- The Tampa domain does not trust the St. Paul domain.

To put it simply, if A trusts B, and B trusts C, this does not imply that A trusts C.

Trusts in Windows 2000 Server

In Windows 2000 Server, trusts have changed quite a bit from what we've just seen. First, in earlier versions of NT no trusts were defined automatically. All trusts had to be set up manually. In Windows 2000 Server, a two-way trust is established between every domain and its parent domain in the tree, as shown in Figure 8.10.

The second (and probably more significant) change in trust relationships in Windows 2000 Server is that trusts are now transitive. To put it another way, if A trusts B, and B trusts C, then A trusts C. Take another look at Figure 8.10.

FIGURE 8.9

Non-transitive trusts in NT 4

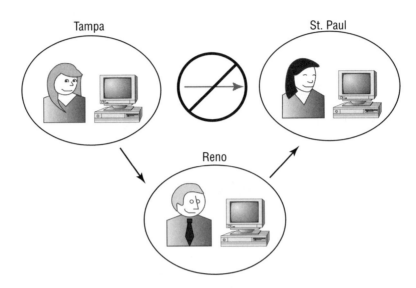

Tampa

St. Paul

Reno

FIGURE 8.10

Windows 2000 Server's default trust configuration

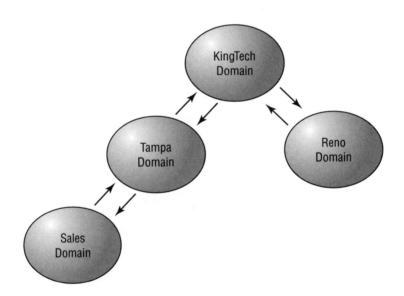

KingTech Domain

Tampa Domain

Reno Domain

Sales Domain

With transitive trusts, every domain in the tree trusts every other domain by default.

The result of these changes is that every domain within the tree trusts every other domain. This rids administrators of the headache of designing and manually configuring an environment in which users can be given permissions to all resources within the enterprise.

Administrative Boundaries

Domains act as administrative boundaries: It is easy to give one administrator control over all resources within a domain. In many cases, though, using domains as the boundary for administrative privileges does not offer enough granularity of management. Administrators would often like to be able to limit an assistant's power to a particular group of users or geographic area. For these needs, ADS includes the Organizational Unit (OU) object class.

 As you might recall from Chapter 3, the OU object is a container object used to organize the resources in your directory.

Organizational Units

OUs form logical administrative units that can be used to delegate administrative privileges within a domain. Rather than add another domain to an existing structure, it is often more advantageous to just create another OU to organize objects.

Organizational units can contain the following types of objects:

- Users
- Computers
- Groups
- Printers
- Applications
- Security policies
- File shares
- Other OUs

Remember that the ADS schema is extensible, so the preceding list might change if you change the schema of your tree.

There is only one type of object that an OU cannot contain, and that is any object from another domain.

Easier Access, Easier Management

You could define an OU as a container object designed to allow organization of a domain's resources. An OU is used in much the same way as a subdirectory in a file system. There is an old adage about creating subdirectories in DOS:

> There are only two reasons to create a subdirectory: to ease access or to ease management.

You might, for instance, create the DOS structure shown in Figure 8.11. Most of us would find this type of layout comfortable (and familiar). If you take the time to analyze why this structure works so well, you'll find that all subdirectories were created for one of two reasons: management or access.

FIGURE 8.11

Typical file structure

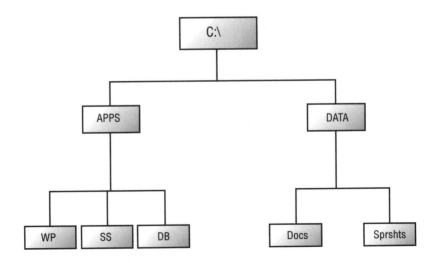

APPS Naming a directory APPS lets a user know exactly where to find applications, making access easier. It also lets an administrator know where to place any applications stored in the file system, making management easier.

DATA Again, the name helps both access and management. Placing both the APPS and DATA directories directly off the root of the drive makes navigation easier for users. Separating the data from the applications also simplifies setting up backup programs (you can back up everything under DATA rather than all .doc files in \apps\wp and all .xls files in \apps\ss, and so on).

The same reasoning applies to every directory in the file structure shown in Figure 8.11. This philosophy also works when designing the structure of your ADS tree. OUs should reflect the business structure of your company. Do not create containers for political reasons or just for the sake of structure.

The bottom line is: If you can't justify a container for either management or user convenience, then you probably don't need that OU.

Creating Containers

With that said, there are a few good business reasons why you *should* create containers:

- To delegate administrative control, allowing an individual the ability to add, delete, or modify objects in a limited portion of the tree.

- To ease management by grouping like objects. You might, for instance, create a container to hold users with similar security requirements.

- To control the visibility of objects.

- To make administration more straightforward, assigning permissions once to the OU rather than multiple times for each object.

- To make administration easier by limiting the number of objects in a single container. Even though the limit on the number of objects within a single container is large (well over a million), no one wants to page through a huge list every time they need to manage one object.

- To control policy application. We'll discuss changes to the system policy process later, but for now just be aware that policies can be set at the OU level.

- To be used as a holding container for other OUs. This would be the same as the APPS directory in our DOS example. The APPS directory does not really hold any files; it just acts as an organizer for other directories.

- To replace NT 4 domains. In earlier versions of NT, delegation of administration was achieved by creating multiple domains.

When to Use a New Domain

A Windows 2000 domain can grow to one million objects, or until the partition takes more than 17 terabytes of storage space. This means that most companies will not be forced into a multiple-domain configuration by the limitations of the directory. Multiple domains will be used to facilitate solutions to common network problems. Here are the primary reasons for creating an additional domain (rather than an OU):

- When there is a need for decentralized management of users or resources where administrators do not want to share control of a domain

- When you want to make delegation easier in cases of diverse environments, such as a network in which different languages are spoken

- If unique domain-level security policies are mandated

- When you want to control directory replication traffic (for instance, across a WAN link with limited bandwidth)

- If you will have over one million objects in the database

- When you are upgrading from an earlier version of NT that was configured as a multidomain environment

- If you have autonomous divisions that require unique namespaces

- When you are preparing for future changes to the company

- If the default trust relationships do not meet your needs

To be truthful, new domains will usually be created to control network traffic. A prime concern in most wide-area networks is bandwidth limitations on the wide-area links. Controlling the traffic placed on these links is the driving force behind most directory designs. Once this consideration is taken into account, the administrator is left with the task of designing the OU model for each domain.

Designing the OU Model

Organizational units provide structure within a domain. This structure is hierarchical in nature, just like the structure built by adding domains together. Each OU acts as a subdirectory to help administrators organize the various resources described within the directory. This structure must be meaningful to users and administrators alike for it to be of any value to the network. A structure designed without people in mind can be of more harm than good, as demonstrated in Figure 8.12.

FIGURE 8.12

Bad OU structure

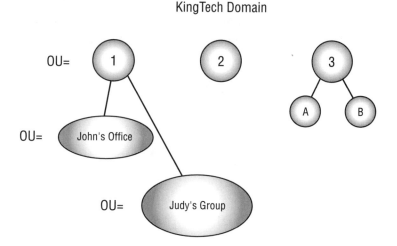

KingTech Domain

There are a couple of problems inherent in this design:

- Many of the OU names are not user friendly. A name of 1 might mean something to the administrator who created it, but it will probably mean nothing to the system's users.

- Naming containers after people *might* make things easier for a while, but as soon as there is a change in personnel or business structure, all such containers will need to be renamed.

What Makes a Good OU Model?

There are various *models* of good OU structures. A model defines categories of OUs and the relationships between them. The model you create for your tree should follow the business practices of your company. More than in any other form of network, a directory-based network demands that administrators understand the business practices and workflow of their company before designing the system.

Creating an OU model can be a difficult task—especially on your first attempt. Since a good design makes your life (and the lives of your users) easier in the long run, you would like to come up with a good, stable design the first time! With this in mind, some "cookie-cutter" models have been designed to act as guides during the planning stage of your own design.

Microsoft suggests seven different basic models for OU structures:

- Geographic

- Object-based

- Cost center

- Project-based

- Division or business unit

- Administration

- Hybrid or mixed

In the sections that follow, we will take a look at the advantages and disadvantages of each design model.

Geographic Model

A geographic model structures its OUs by geographic location, as shown in Figure 8.13. The KingTech Corporation has created a first level of OUs to represent continents and a second level to represent countries. This type of configuration is helpful if each country has its own administrator; you can easily grant administrative privileges to a local user account.

F I G U R E 8.13

Geographic model

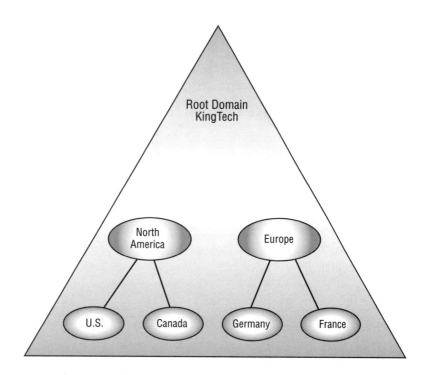

A geographic model offers a number of advantages:

- OUs will be fairly stable: Most companies sometimes reorganize internal resources, but the locations of their offices are usually stable.

- Corporate headquarters can easily dictate domain-wide policies.

- It is easy to determine where resources are physically located.

- A geographic naming standard is easy for both users and administrators to understand.

A geographic model also has some disadvantages:

- This design does not mirror the business practices of KingTech in any way.

- The entire structure is one large partition (single domain). This means that *all* changes to all objects must be replicated to all ADS servers worldwide.

In most cases, the replication traffic on the wide-area links will outweigh any of the benefits of using this model.

Object-Based Model

The design of an OU structure can also be based on object types, as illustrated in Figure 8.14. A first-level container would be created for each class of object that exists in the tree. Below this first level, a geographic layout might make administration easier.

FIGURE 8.14

Object-based model

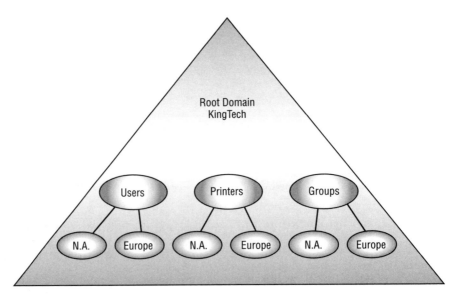

Here are some advantages of the object-based model:

- Resource administration is easier because each OU represents a specific class of object.

- Permissions are based upon OUs. It's easy to create OU-wide permissions, such as "All users should be able to use all printers."

- Administration can easily be delegated by resource type. For example, you can create a Printer Administrator who has permissions to add, delete, and modify all printers in the enterprise.

- A company reorganization should have little effect on the design. The same resources (with the possible exception of users) should exist no matter how the company is organized.

- Distinguished names are consistent for all objects in a class.

- It resembles the DNS structure, so it may lessen the learning curve for some administrators.

Disadvantages of the object-based model include the following:

- It is harder to define OU-based policies because all users are in the same containers.

- This flat structure will have to be created in each domain.

- There are too many top-level OUs. This can make navigating the administrative tools more difficult.

- If the schema is extended to accept new object types, new OUs will have to be created.

I've been working with directory-based networking for quite some time and I've never liked the object-based design. It offers the administrator little opportunity for customizing the environment to meet a particular business need. I might, for instance, have a printer that should be visible only to a particular group of users. While this goal is possible with the object-based model, accomplishing it is more work than it might be in other models.

Cost Center Model

A company may decide that the OUs within its ADS tree should reflect its cost centers, as shown in Figure 8.15. This model might be used in a company where budgetary concerns outweigh other considerations. A nonprofit organization, for example, might have separately defined divisions, each of which is responsible for its own management and cost controls.

FIGURE 8.15

Cost center model

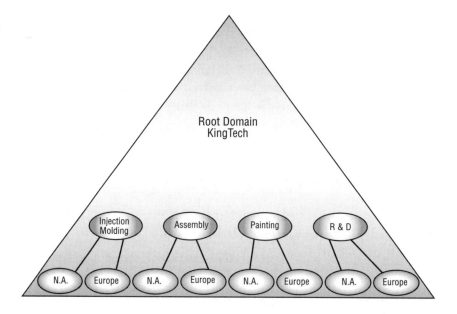

The cost center model has one main advantage: Each division or business group manages its own resources.

This model also has some disadvantages:

- Users might not be grouped together in a way that reflects their resource usage. A color printer, for instance, might belong to one department but might also be used by other departments as needed.

- Delegation of administrative privileges can be confusing.

The cost center design does not really take full advantage of the power of Active Directory. Most companies have departments, and each department might have its own budget—but there is usually some overlap of resources.

Project-Based Model

Some companies might prefer an OU structure that is based on current project teams. A manufacturing firm, for instance, might want to create an

OU for each resource group in a shop floor manufacturing process. The project-based model is shown in Figure 8.16.

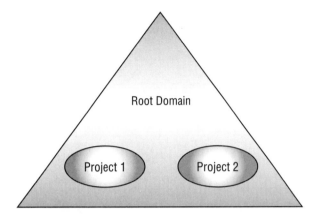

For certain environments, the project-based model offers some definite advantages:

- This model works well in an environment where resources and costs must be tracked.

- Because each project group is a separate OU, security between groups is easy to maintain.

Project-based design also has a couple of disadvantages:

- Projects often have a finite lifetime, so many OUs will have to be deleted and the resources redistributed.

- If projects change frequently, this type of structure will require a lot of maintenance.

I've found that a project-based structure will work for smaller companies with a limited product line. As a company grows (along with the number of active projects), the workload of maintaining a project-based design gets out of hand.

Division or Business Unit Model

The OU structure can also reflect a "well known" business structure if such a structure exists. A typical well known structure would be the various departments within a law enforcement agency. You can see an example in Figure 8.17.

FIGURE 8.17

Division or business
unit model

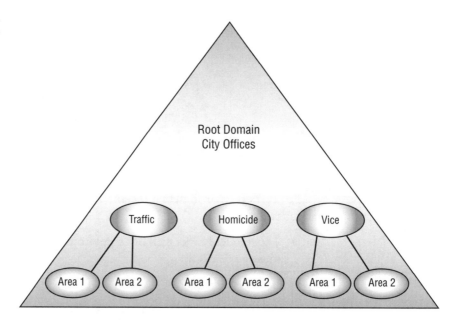

Here are some advantages of the division or business unit model:

- This structure is very user friendly, because it is based upon a structure with which users are already familiar.

- For the same reason, it is easy to locate resources.

And here is a disadvantage: Although the structure is based on a "well known" environment, there is always the chance that the business divisions will change. Any such change would force a redesign of the OU structure.

This model works very well in environments that are defined in a very rigid fashion, such as police departments and government offices.

Administration Model

One of the more frequently used models is a structure based upon common administrative groupings within a company, as shown in Figure 8.18. This model works well because it is based upon the actual business structure of the particular company.

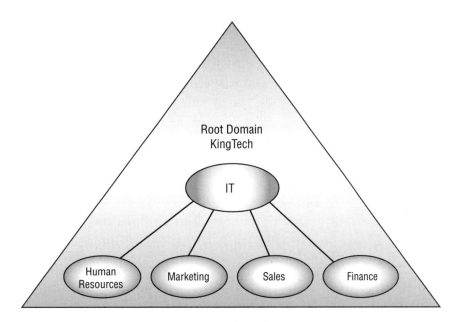

The administration model offers these advantages:

- This model is designed from the perspective of the network administrator and makes the administrator's job easier.

- Since most companies are departmental—from both a physical and a logical perspective—this model fits most enterprises.

It also has these disadvantages:

- Since this model is division oriented, all resources from a single division or department will be grouped under a single OU. This might be confusing for users.

- In companies where many resources are shared between departments, this model might not reflect the business model of the company.

This is one of the more commonly implemented OU models. It works reasonably well for most companies.

> Probably the biggest advantage of the administration model is that in most companies this design matches the organizational chart. In other words, the design has already been created—all the network administrator has to do is implement it!

The administration model also matches the way many NT 4 networks were created. First one department would install an NT server, creating its own domain and user accounts. Later, another department would see the benefits enjoyed by the first department and would in turn install its own NT server. In the process, this department would create its own domain and SAM (Security Accounts Manager) database. Next, the two departments would see the potential benefits of sharing resources and would create trusts. The end result is a network already modeled on the administrative groupings within the company.

During the upgrade to Windows 2000 Server, the administrator has the option of redesigning the structure, but since the users are already familiar with the "departmental" concept of multiple domains, it makes sense to keep the structure as it is. This results in less confusion for end-users, less retraining, and less productivity lost due to confusion.

Hybrid or Mixed Model

Most companies will settle on a hybrid structure that combines two or more of the "standard" models.

> Remember that a structure will be more stable and need fewer adjustments if it accurately reflects the business structure of your company. The standard models are often too rigid to do this.

A typical hybrid structure is shown in Figure 8.19.

F I G U R E 8.19

Hybrid model

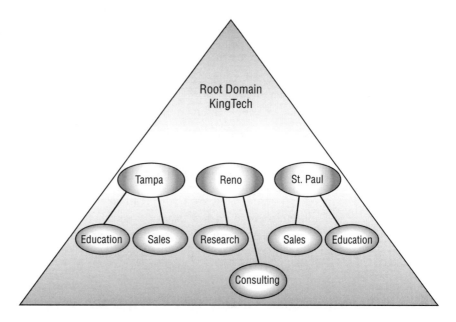

Advantages of a hybrid model follow:

- The structure can be customized to closely match the way in which business is conducted by the company.

- Employees are usually comfortable with the design, since it reflects the way they actually work.

This model does have one disadvantage: It requires a greater understanding than the other models do of the company for which it is intended. For this reason, many outside consultants will avoid hybrid models.

Because of its flexibility, the hybrid model is probably the best overall design. It does, however, require more planning before implementation than the other models. Administrators of a hybrid model ADS will have to create a set of rules governing when, why, and where new containers will be created. Here are some questions to ask yourself during this process:

- Which resources are departmental?

- Which resources are regional?

- Which resources are dedicated to a specific project?

Once you have answered these questions, you can start designing a structure that closely mirrors the way in which your business is structured.

The biggest problem with the hybrid model is that most businesses are dynamic. In other words, the way that they do business changes as the market changes. Such changes could result in a design that no longer meets the needs of the organization.

Other Aspects of Planning an OU Model

After you have chosen the overall structure that you will use for your OU model, there are a few other things to consider before you start implementation. Most of the following topics are administrative concerns. Proper planning of these details will make administering your network easier down the line.

Name Standards

The names you give to OUs are used internally within the domain and can be seen when searching for particular objects. It is important, therefore, that the names you choose are meaningful *both* to your users and to your administrators.

OU names are not part of the DNS namespace. Users do not use DNS services to "find" an OU. This makes sense, since OUs are not physical resources—they are logical structures used to organize the objects in your database.

OUs are identified by a distinguished name—also known as a *canonical name*—that describes their location in the hierarchical structure. Basically, this is the X.500 name for the object in the tree. An OU named Tampa that is located in the KingTech container would be known as Tampa.KingTech. These names are used most often for administrative tasks.

OU Ownership

Each OU in the structure has an object that acts as its owner. The owner of an OU can:

- Add, delete, and update objects within the container

- Decide whether permissions should be inherited from the parent container

- Control permissions to the container

- Decide whether permissions should be propagated to child containers

By default, the user who creates an OU is its owner.

Delegating Administration of OUs

For every OU in a domain there is a set of permissions that grant or deny Read and Write access to the OU. This allows for a delegation of administrative privileges down to the lowest level of your structure. Any permissions assigned at the OU level pertain to all objects within that OU. There are various levels of authority that you might want to delegate to other administrators:

Changing container properties   Administrators can change OU-wide properties, such as OU policies and other attributes.

Creating, deleting, and changing child objects   These objects can be users, groups, printers, and so on.

Updating attributes for a specific class of object   Perhaps your Help desk personnel should *only* be allowed to change users' passwords (but not any other attributes of a user account).

Creating new users or groups   You can limit the class of objects that an administrator has the permission to create.

Managing a small subgroup of objects within the tree   You might want an administrator to manage only objects in a particular office.

Trees and Forests

In our discussions so far, we have limited ourselves to environments with only one ADS tree. In a single-tree environment, each domain is added to the structure as a new partition of a single database to create the tree, as shown in Figure 8.20.

F I G U R E 8.20

Single-tree environment

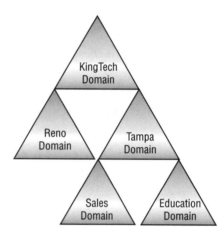

This configuration works well in most environments, but it has one big limitation: All objects within the structure *must* be a part of the same namespace.

Remember that a namespace can be defined as a system where all objects have a similar attribute to their name.

In the case of KingTech, the name of every object will end in .KingTech.com. Therein lies the problem: What if a company has a reason for some objects to belong to one namespace and other objects to a different namespace? Such a situation might occur when an environment requires a substantial amount of separation between domains that must still share resources. For instance, partnerships or joint ventures might require that two distinct businesses share resources. These two companies would each have a unique namespace, so both could not fall under a single root domain.

Two separate ADS trees can establish a relationship, thereby forming an ADS *forest*. A forest is just a collection of trees that share a common schema and Global Catalog server. The trees establish a trust relationship between their root domains, as shown in Figure 8.21.

FIGURE 8.21

An ADS forest

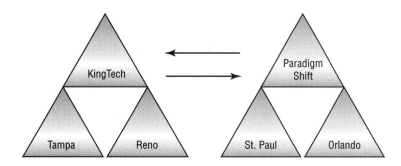

Once you've established this relationship, you have formed a forest. A forest allows you to do the following:

- Search across all domains through a common Global Catalog server.

- Maintain existing DNS names (during an acquisition, for instance).

- Control trust relationships with partnering systems. Rather than creating a two-way trust between the trees, you could opt for a one-way trust to limit access to one system.

A forest configuration can also come in handy if you need to establish a relationship with an outside company. As an example, let's say your company makes widgets. Your widgets come in many colors. You have the paint made to your custom specifications—your own version of candy apple red, perhaps. If the company that produces your paint is also working on a Windows 2000 network, you could create a trust between your two trees (thus creating a forest). This would allow your widget-color-scheme designers to be granted access to resources in your vendor's environment or to check on your orders to plan for paint production.

Special Types of ADS Servers

Over the last few chapters we've discussed various aspects of computers acting as Active Directory servers. We've discussed the Active Directory database, how it is partitioned into domains, and how these replicas stay in sync through a replication process. What we haven't talked about are some of the special function servers that exist in an Active Directory environment.

Global Catalog Servers

We briefly discussed the role of a Global Catalog server in the last chapter; now let's finish the topic. A Global Catalog server is an ADS server that holds a partial replica of the entire tree. This replica holds a limited amount of information about every object within the forest, usually those properties that are necessary for network functionality or those properties that are frequently asked for.

The list of properties will be different for each class of object. User objects, for instance, will need to store certain information for network functions—a great example is their "Group Membership" list. During the logon process, the user's object is checked to retrieve this list. ADS will then confirm the user's membership with each group using information stored in the Global Catalog. Once membership has been confirmed, the Security IDs for each group can be added to the user's security token. The Global Catalog might also contain various properties that might be frequently searched upon—telephone numbers, for example. On the other hand, the Global Catalog will probably store less information about Printer objects because fewer of their properties will be needed on a regular basis.

By default, the Global Catalog will be created on the first domain controller installed in the ADS forest. The service itself has two major functions. First, it is critical to the logon process. When a user logs onto the network, a security token is created for them. This token includes information about the groups of which they are a member. If a Global Catalog server is not available during the logon process, the user will not be able to log onto the network—instead they will be limited to logging onto the local computer.

Members of the Domain Admins group can log onto the network without accessing the Global Catalog. If this wasn't the case, a malfunctioning Global Catalog server could conceivably prevent an administrator from logging on to fix the problem.

The second function of the Global Catalog is to facilitate searches of the Active Directory database. If you perform a search for, let's say, the phone number property of a user in another domain, your request could be answered by the Global Catalog server rather than a domain controller from the target domain. To put it more simply, searches can take place on servers that are more local to the user—thereby reducing network traffic and decreasing the time it takes to receive results.

The second function of Global Catalog servers brings us to an important design issue. While by default only one Global Catalog server is created, the system can support an unlimited number of them. To reap the benefits of the Global Catalog, you must think about how many you would like, and place them appropriately. It is best to have a Global Catalog server at each physical location—otherwise, your search will cross your WAN links, thereby eliminating the benefits of the service. This design also prevents the situation where users are unable to log into the network because a WAN line has gone down.

On the flip side, though, too many Global Catalog servers can increase network traffic. Remember that the catalog contains an incomplete copy of every object in your forest. Let's say that user Joe changes his phone number; this change would have to be replicated to every Global Catalog server in your environment.

This explains why the Global Catalog does not contain every property of every object. The traffic generated to keep complete replicas up to date would probably exceed the bandwidth available on most networks.

Windows 2000 creates the first Global Catalog server for you and determines which properties of each object class it will store. In most cases, this default list of stored properties will be sufficient. There might be situations, though, where you want to add a property to the list that the Global Catalog stores. You can control the attributes of each object class stored in the partial partition of the Global Catalog by using the Active Directory Sites and Services tools. These tools will be discussed in more detail in Chapter 12, "Modifying the Active Directory Schema."

Single Master Functions

We've discussed the difference between single-master and multiple-master environments. In short, single-master environments use a single instance of a database to accept and then replicate changes. Multiple-master environments allow changes to any replica of the database. Each replica has the ability to update all other replicas with changed data. Most of the changes made to the Active Directory database are handled in a multiple-master manner. The change will occur at any local ADS server, and that server will synchronize those changes with the rest of the ADS servers in the domain (and the Global Catalog server, if necessary).

There are, however, certain operations that, by the nature of what they do, need to be handled in a single-master manner. For these operations, one server is designated as the *operation master*. All updates or changes occur at the operation master, and this server is responsible for synchronizing the changes to all other servers. Because these responsibilities can be moved from server to server (as best fits your network), Microsoft refers to them as "flexible single-master operations."

Do not let the word "flexible" confuse you—this is mostly a marketing phrase. These operations are truly "single-master." They are "flexible" only in the fact that you can determine which server will perform them.

Some of these single-master operations are forest-wide tasks. In other words, one server performs the task for your entire ADS forest. Other operations are performed by one server in each domain. In either case, only one server performs the operation, so it is important that you take these tasks into account when planning server functionality (and disaster recovery). By default, the first domain controller installed in your forest or in each domain, as appropriate, is assigned the role of operation master for each function.

Forest-wide Operations

There are two forest-wide operation master roles:

- Schema master
- Domain naming master

Once again, let me stress that only one server in the entire forest performs these tasks. You must ensure that this server is reliable and has enough horsepower to perform them. You should also place it in a physical location where any outside links are fairly reliable. If these servers or the links to them are unavailable, certain administrative functions will not be accessible.

The *schema master* controls the structure of the ADS database. Any updates or modifications made to the database structure must be made on this server first. It will then replicate these changes to the rest of the ADS servers in your forest. This ensures that all ADS servers are "speaking the same language." There should never be a case where one server knows about a new object class or property but another server does not.

The *domain naming master* is responsible for adding or removing domains from the forest. It ensures that each domain is given a unique name when added to the forest and that any reference to a removed domain is cleaned up.

Domain-wide Operations

There are three domain-wide operation master roles:

- Relative ID master

- Primary Domain Controller (PDC) emulator

- Infrastructure master

Once again, only one server in each domain performs each of these tasks. These servers will need to be both powerful enough to handle the extra workload and reliable enough to be available when necessary.

The *relative ID master* controls the creation of security IDs for new objects created in the domain. Each object has a security ID that is made up of a domain identifier (the same for every object in the domain), and a unique relative ID that differentiates the object from any other in the domain. To ensure that these IDs are unique, only one server in each domain generates them.

The *PDC emulator master* has the ability to act as a PDC for non–Windows 2000 clients and NT 4.0 (and earlier) BDCs. This allows for a mixed environment of Windows 2000 and earlier NT version servers on the same network. Even in a completely Windows 2000 ADS environment, though, the PDC emulator performs an important function. When a user changes their password, whichever domain controller accepts the change will first pass the change to the PDC emulator operation master. This server then uses a high-priority function to replicate this change to all of the other domain controllers in the domain.

Each domain controller in a domain knows which server is acting as the PDC emulator. If a user tries to log onto the network but provides an incorrect password, the domain controller will first query the PDC emulator to ensure that it has the latest password for the user before denying the request to log on. This prevents a denial of service in the event that a user attempts to use their new password before it has had a chance to be replicated to all of the domain controllers in the domain.

The *infrastructure master* is responsible for updating group-to-user references when group members are renamed or relocated. It updates the group object so that it knows the new name or location of its members.

In Short

Designing the structure of your Active Directory is an important task that should be completed *before* implementation. As you have seen, proper planning of domains and organizational units can make life easier for both users and administrators. Here are some suggestions for your design:

- Use as few domains as possible. Windows 2000 Server greatly increases the capacity of a single domain. You should use multiple domains only when there is a specific need for such a configuration.

- Limit the number of OU levels. As with the file system, the deeper things are hidden, the harder they are to find! Because of the way ADS searches for objects, deep structures are less efficient than shallower ones.

- Limit the number of child objects for any given OU. While a Windows 2000 Server domain can now support up to a million objects, no one wants to page through that many objects to find a specific user or printer.

- Remember that administrative privileges can be delegated at the OU level. You no longer have to create a new domain in order to limit administrative power.

In Chapter 9, we'll look at the actual implementation of ADS: creating domains, OUs, and other objects.

CHAPTER

9

Implementing
Your Design

Now that we have discussed some of the variables that go into planning your ADS tree, we can turn our attention to the mechanics involved. Once you have settled on a design, the next step is to install ADS, create your OUs, and populate the tree with objects. While most of these tasks are straightforward, it can take some time to master the tools used.

Installing ADS

In earlier, domain-based versions of Windows NT, the accounts database (known as the *SAM* for Security Accounts Manager) was stored on special servers known as *domain controllers*. There were two types of domain controllers:

- One primary domain controller (PDC) for each domain
- An unlimited number of backup domain controllers (BDCs)

As you will recall, the PDC was responsible for synchronizing changes to the database to all of the BDCs.

One of the biggest problems with this older system was the inability to reconfigure servers "on the fly." While you could promote a BDC to the position of PDC, it was impossible to demote a domain controller or promote a member server (any NT server that was not acting as a domain controller) without reinstalling Windows NT. In other words, once you chose a role for an NT server—domain controller or member server—you were stuck with that role. The only way to change a server's role was to pull out the NT CD-ROM and reinstall the operating system.

One of the biggest "incidental" advances that Microsoft has made to Windows 2000 Server is that ADS can be installed or removed without affecting the underlying operating system. If you decide that a certain server should act as an ADS server, only to learn later that the server just doesn't have the necessary horsepower to perform the task, you can remove ADS. If you install a Windows 2000 server without ADS and later decide you need to add the service, all you have to do is run an Administrative Wizard.

ADS has become "just another network component" of the Windows 2000 operating system. This flexibility allows network administrators the opportunity to make mistakes without fear of losing network functionality while *another* reinstallation takes place.

Before You Begin

Before you can begin the actual installation of the Active Directory service, you must complete certain preliminary tasks. Specifically, DNS *must* be configured and working properly before you begin the installation process. You should verify the following:

- You have decided on and configured DNS names for each of your Active Directory servers.

- DNS is installed and working.

- You have configured DNS for your environment. Specifically, ensure that

    - Lookups work properly.

    - All DNS servers are configured for forward lookups as needed.

    - Your reverse lookup zones are working properly.

- You have configured DNS to allow dynamic updates.

Testing DNS

Testing DNS is beyond the scope of this book, but here are a couple of suggestions:

- Use Ping to confirm communication between *all* Active Directory servers. If you Ping each server by its host name, you will also test DNS at the same time.

- Use NSLOOKUP to test functionality for forward lookup, reverse lookup, and root zones.

For more information on these tools I would suggest *Mastering Windows 2000 Server,* 2nd ed., by Mark Minasi, Christa Anderson, Brian M. Smith, and Doug Toombs (ISBN 0-7821-2774-6, Sybex, 2000) or *MCSE: TCP/IP for NT Server 4 Study Guide,* 4th ed., by Todd Lammle, Monica Lammle, and James Chellis (ISBN 0-7821-2725-8, Sybex, 2000).

Mixed Mode or Native Mode?

You must also decide on one other facet of your ADS environment: whether your ADS server should be configured to run in *mixed* or *native* mode.

A mixed-mode ADS server can interact with domain controllers running earlier versions of NT. Basically, the ADS server becomes the primary domain controller (PDC) for the existing domain, and it will update the older servers in a manner similar to that of an NT 4 server. (For this reason, ADS servers are sometimes referred to as *domain controllers.*) This allows you to update your servers one at a time without having to be concerned about backward compatibility issues. While this process is certainly not as efficient as moving everything to ADS, it does allow you a gradual upgrade of your environment.

Unfortunately, terminology in the Microsoft world is often a little confusing. A Windows 2000 Server acting as an ADS server has the ability to emulate the functions of a domain controller from earlier versions of Windows NT. Since it is performing the same functions as an NT domain controller, many documents will refer to it as a domain controller. You should be aware that there is a subtle difference between old and new— and an ADS server just acts like a PDC.

A native-mode ADS server does not have the ability to act as part of an older environment. As soon as all of your older servers have been upgraded to Windows 2000 and ADS, you should switch your servers to native mode. "Mixed mode" basically refers to a process running on your Windows 2000 server, using processor power and memory.

It is not necessary to use mixed mode if all of your servers are running Windows 2000.

The ADS Installation Wizard

ADS is installed by using the Active Directory Installation Wizard (the actual file is named `DCPromo.exe` and is located in the `<windows_root>`\`system32` directory). The Wizard leads you through the entire installation process, asking you for information on the first domain controller, domain, site, and other configuration information. ADS must be installed on a volume that has been formatted with NTFS 5 or higher.

The Wizard itself is fairly straightforward. It starts with the obligatory Microsoft Welcome screen to identify what you are about to do (just in case you ran the wrong program). On the second screen, you will be asked to select your server type, as shown in Figure 9.1.

F I G U R E   9.1

Domain controller type

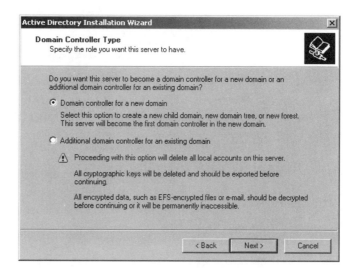

There are two choices on this screen:

Domain controller for a new domain This server will be the first domain controller. Make this choice if this is the first ADS server for a domain.

Additional domain controller for an existing domain Use this option if there is already an ADS server within this NT domain. This server will receive a replica of the local domain's partition.

The next screen also has two choices, as shown in Figure 9.2. Here you will have to decide if you would like to create a new domain tree or add this domain to an existing tree.

FIGURE 9.2

Create tree or child
domain

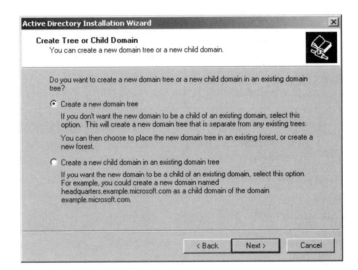

We discussed the tree and forest issue in the last chapter. Here you will make decisions that will affect the number of domains in your environment and how their namespaces will interact.

Finishing Your Installation

If you choose to create a new child domain, you will be asked for an administrative account and password for an existing domain in the tree, as shown in Figure 9.3.

FIGURE 9.3

Network credentials

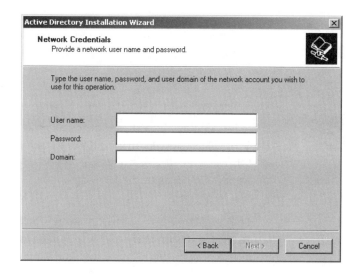

FIGURE 9.3

Network credentials

If you choose to create a new tree, the next screen will ask you for the full DNS name for the new domain, as shown in Figure 9.4. Remember that this name *must* be resolvable through DNS.

FIGURE 9.4

New domain name

Active Directory Installation Wizard	
New Domain Name	
Specify a name for the new domain.	

Type the full DNS name for the new domain.

If your organization already has a DNS domain name registered with an Internet naming authority, you can use that name.

Full DNS name for new domain:

Royal-Tech.com

Remember that the prerequisite for installing ADS is a working DNS system!

If the Installation Wizard cannot resolve the name of the server through DNS, it will ask you if you would like to have DNS installed and configured on this machine. If you say yes, it will do so automatically, adding the appropriate records to the DNS database.

That's all there is to the installation of ADS. So far, so good! Actually, creating a good design is the hardest part of moving to a directory-based environment—the mechanics are just knowing where to click.

What Does the Wizard Create?

The following items are created during the ADS installation process:

Database   This is the directory database for the new domain. The default location for the database and its associated log files is `<systemroot>`\Winnt\Ntds.

Shared system volume   All Windows 2000 domain controllers have a share point used to store scripts that are part of the group policy objects for both the local domain and the enterprise. The default location for these files is `<systemroot>`\Sysvol\sysvol.

Domain controller   The first domain controller for the domain is created during the first installation of ADS.

First site name   A *site* is a logical grouping of servers. By default, the first site contains the first domain controller.

Global Catalog server   The first domain controller in a site becomes the Global Catalog server. The Global Catalog server holds a partial replica of every domain in the forest. This replica holds a subset of the attributes for each object—those attributes most commonly used for searches. The Global Catalog server facilitates forest-wide searches for objects.

Root domain   If you create a new tree (rather than join an existing one), this domain will become the root domain for the new tree.

The installation also creates a series of organizational units:

Built-in   This contains default security groups, such as Account Operators, Administrators, and so on.

Foreign Security Principals   When a trust is made with a domain outside of the tree, this container is used to hold references to objects from the outside environment that have been granted local permissions.

Users   This is the default location for user accounts.

Computers   Likewise, this is the default location for computer accounts.

Domain controllers   I bet I don't even have to tell you. (Just in case, though, this container is the default location for domain controller accounts.)

After your installation is complete, all components are ready to go. The process even creates an OU structure for you. This structure is more than sufficient for many companies. The installation process also creates a log file that lists the results of each step in the process. This log file is located in the \winnt\debug folder.

Verifying Your Installation

Once you have completed the installation of ADS, it is a good idea to confirm that everything went as planned. The only real problem with Wizards is that you click, they do, and you are never sure if they have done what you wanted them to do! The most important process that must be completed during the installation is the addition of the service records, or *SRV records,* to the DNS database.

Since ADS uses DNS to find domain controllers, it is imperative that each server have a record in the database.

To confirm that DNS has been updated correctly, you need to do two things.

First, check the local DNS file to ensure that the proper entries have been made. This file is located in the \<*systemroot*>\System32\Config folder and is named Netlogon.dns. The first record you should see is the server's LDAP service record. The LDAP SRV record should look something like this:

```
_Ldap._tcp.<Active_directory_domain_name> IN SRV 0 0 389
<domain_controller_name>
```

Here's an example:

```
_Ldap._tcp.KingTech.com IN SRV 0 0 389 ADS1.KingTech.com
```

Second, to ensure that the SRV records in the DNS database are working correctly, use the NSLOOKUP tool. The following steps will confirm their functionality:

1. At the command prompt, type **NSLOOKUP** and hit the Enter key.

2. Type **SET TYPE = SRV** and press Enter.

3. Type **ldap.tcp.<*Active_directory_domain_name*>**, where <*Active_directory_domain_name*> is the name of your company's Active Directory domain. Press Enter.

If this process returns the server name and IP address, the SRV records are performing correctly.

Creating Organizational Units

To review: organizational units are used to organize the objects within your tree and to act as administrative boundaries. Many different types of structures can be created using OUs as the building blocks.

The only real limitation is that no OUs can be created within the default OUs created during the installation of ADS.

A user must have the appropriate permissions to create OUs within the tree. By default, members of the Administrators group have the permissions necessary to create OUs anywhere.

To create an OU, use the Active Directory Users and Computers tool, located in the Administrative Tools group. Expand your domain, and you will see the default containers shown in Figure 9.5.

FIGURE 9.5

Active Directory Users
and Computers tool

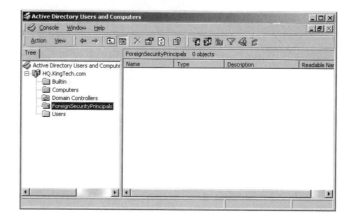

Right-click the container where you want to create a new OU and choose New, then Organizational Unit, as demonstrated in Figure 9.6.

FIGURE 9.6

New organizational
unit

You will see the window shown in Figure 9.7.

F I G U R E 9.7

Creating a new
organizational unit

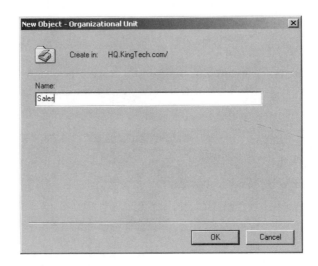

Provide a name for your new organizational unit and click the OK button. As you can see, creating new organizational units is about as easy as creating new directories in a DOS file system. Just as in DOS, there will be those people who create too many and those who create too few. In either case, we have a name for them: future consulting customers. Take the time to plan your structure (and play with a few test systems) before implementation!

Delegating Administration

One reason to create multiple OUs is to delegate administrative tasks. While the mechanics of delegation are straightforward, you will need to be aware of how permissions work in the ADS structure.

Permissions granted to an ADS container flow down the structure in the same way they do in the NTFS file system, as you can see in Figure 9.8.

If Susan is granted Full Control to the KingTech container, by default that set of permissions will flow down the ADS structure so that she has Full Control in every container below KingTech. As you will see when we walk through the process, you can limit the flow if you desire.

Delegating Control of a Container

To delegate control of a container, right-click the container in the Active Directory Users and Computers tool and choose the Delegate Control

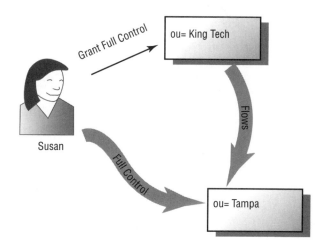

FIGURE 9.8

Permissions
inheritance

option. This will start the Delegation of Control Administrative Wizard. As
with all Wizards, the first screen is a Welcome screen. Clicking Next will
bring you to the window shown in Figure 9.9. Here, you are asked to choose
which users or groups should be given permissions.

FIGURE 9.9

Users or groups

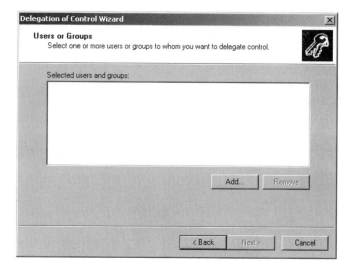

Clicking Add will bring you to a list of available users and groups, as shown in Figure 9.10.

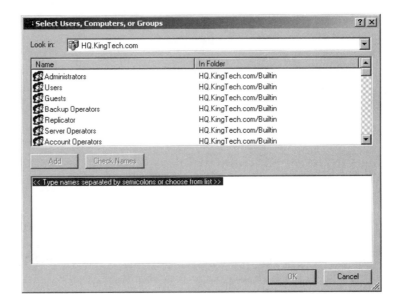

The next screen, shown in Figure 9.11, allows you to choose from a list of commonly delegated tasks or create a custom delegation.

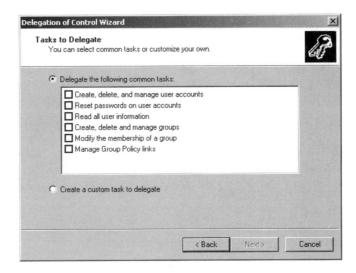

If you choose to create a custom delegation task, you will be presented with the window shown in Figure 9.12. Here you can either allow management of all objects in the container or limit the delegation to certain object classes.

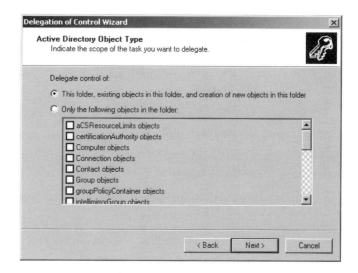

In the next window, shown in Figure 9.13, you determine exactly what administrative powers you wish to grant. Notice that there are three check boxes.

The first "General" check box gives a basic set of permissions as options. These permission are:

Full Control   Grants all other permissions (and the ability to take ownership) to all objects in the container

Read   Allows the recipient to read the access control list (ACL) of all objects

Write   Allows the recipient to write to the ACL of all objects within the container

Create All Child Objects   Allows the creation of any class of object within the container

Delete All Child Objects   Allows the deletion of any class of object within the container

Read All Properties   Allows the recipient to read the properties of objects within the container

Write All Properties   Grants the ability to change all properties for objects within the container

In reality, the list of permissions above should be sufficient in most cases. Actually, most companies will not even be as specific as this first list allows—most companies will give administrators Full Control and leave it at that. You have, however, the ability to micromanage the delegation of administrative permissions. If you check the "Property-specific" option (shown back in Figure 9.13), the list will expand to include a list of all of the various properties available. As an example, the list will include "Read Street" and "Write Street," allowing you to determine if the recipient can see or change the "Street" property of objects within the container. This level of granularity allows you to easily grant a person in Human Resources the ability to change user information such as addresses and phone numbers *without* having to give that person rights to any other properties.

Lastly, if you check "Creation/deletion of specific child objects," the list will expand to include the various classes of objects that can be created. Now you can control exactly what types of objects an assistant administrator can create. Perhaps you've got a person who is in charge of all printers in the company. You can easily give this person the ability to create printing-related objects *without* giving them the permission to create anything else.

The last screen of the Administrative Wizard confirms the changes that you are about to make. Clicking Finish will implement these changes.

Creating Users

Once you have created your ADS structure, the next step is to populate it with objects representing the resources on your network. While there are many different classes of objects available, there are a few that *every* network will require. To tell the truth, most objects within the directory are created in a similar manner. In the Active Directory Users and Computers tool, right-click the container in which you wish to create the object and choose "New"; you will be presented with a list of valid object classes, as shown in Figure 9.14. Choose the object class that you wish to create and enter the required information.

F I G U R E   9.14

Creating new objects

Without a doubt, the most important class of object is that of *user*. User accounts are the backbone upon which all network functionality is built—without them, no one accesses resources.

You are probably pretty comfortable with the concept of a user account. User accounts of one sort or another have been used since the dawn of networks to allow users to identify themselves to the network. Networks also use user accounts to authenticate access to resources. When a user—let's call him Tom—attempts to access the network, he will be asked for his logon name (Tom's user account). The network operating system will then check to see whether the account he provides exists and, if so, whether there are any restrictions that would mandate denying his request (such as time or station restrictions). If Tom successfully logs on to the network, his account information will be used to authenticate his requests for resource access. Every action that Tom takes on the network will be allowed or denied based on information in a user account (although not necessarily his own—many processes are accessed through system accounts, such as many Web-based resources).

Creating a New User Account

To create a user account, access the Active Directory Users and Computers program located in the Administrative Tools group. Right-click the container in which you wish to place the user account, then choose New ➢ User. You will be presented with the screen shown in Figure 9.15. Here you will enter the user's first, last, and logon names.

F I G U R E   9.15

Creating a user account

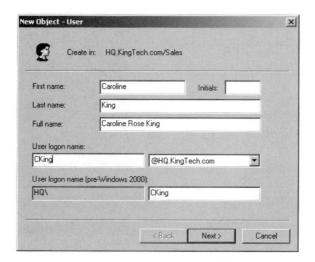

Click Next to move to the next window in the process, shown in Figure 9.16. Here you can assign the user her first password and make a

couple of choices regarding this account. Your choices are explained in the following list:

User must change password at next logon   The next time the user logs in to the network she will be forced to change her password. This forces the user to change her password from the one provided by the administrator, so that the user is the only person who knows her password.

User cannot change password   Some companies use a centrally controlled list of passwords, set by the administrator. If this is the case, this option will prevent a user from changing her password.

Password never expires   Most companies force users to change their passwords periodically. This option overrules that policy.

Account is disabled   This option can be used to disable an account.

Usually, the "Account is disabled" option is used when an employee has been terminated or goes on an extended leave. In a seasonal business, however, you might want to create user accounts for seasonal employees before your busy season, disable them, and then just re-enable them as the employees come on line.

FIGURE 9.16

User account setup

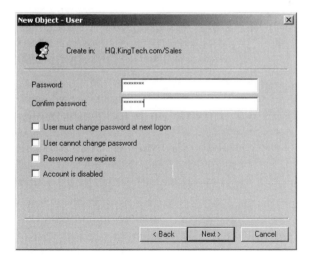

The process ends with a screen that confirms the choices you have made, as shown in Figure 9.17. Clicking Finish will create the account.

Adding Information about Users

Once you have created a user account, there is still a lot of information that you can add. I've been promising you that you can search for a user based on such criteria as location, department, or manager. To perform these searches, you will have to enter that information into the user's attributes. To do so, double-click the user account in the Active Directory Users and Computers tool. You will be presented with the User Properties window shown in Figure 9.18.

I'm going to include figures for each of the tabs on this object. Most of the attributes are self-explanatory; the e-mail attribute, for instance, is the user's e-mail address. Other attributes will need some explanation; for example, phone number and home page are both multivalue attributes. Clicking the Other button allows you to add multiple values for these attributes.

Figure 9.19 shows the Address tab of the User Properties dialog box. This tab contains parameters that pertain to the user's mailing address.

FIGURE 9.18

General tab of the User Properties window

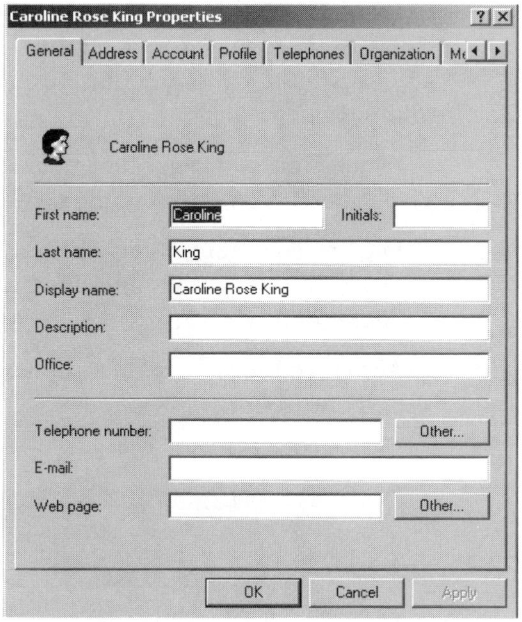

FIGURE 9.19

Address tab of the User Properties window

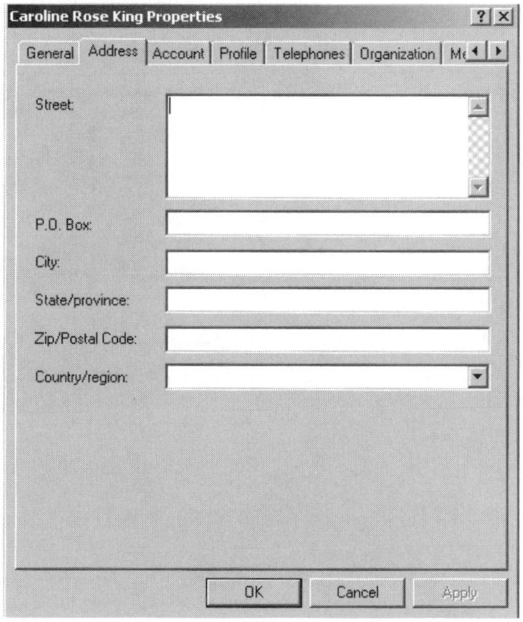

Figure 9.20 shows the Account tab. Notice that you can use this tab to set an expiration date for a user account. This option is handy if you hire a lot of temporary or seasonal personnel and do not want their accounts to be valid indefinitely. You can also provide values for the following:

Logon Hours   One of the initial access securities is the ability to limit when users can log on to the network.

Log On To   Controlling which computers a user logs on to can help to control those "social butterflies" who flit from desk to desk, logging on but never logging off!

Account options   This area allows you to set parameters for controlling password security.

FIGURE 9.20

Account tab of the User Properties window

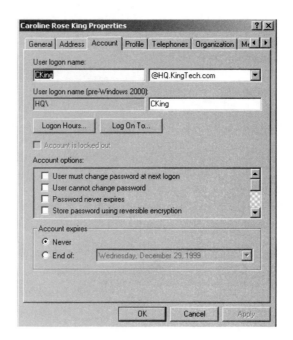

Figure 9.21 shows the Profile tab. This tab contains attributes pertaining to the placement of network files. There are three distinct areas of configuration:

User profile   Here you can set the location of a user's profile and login script.

Home folder   This lets you control the placement (local or network) of a user's home directory.

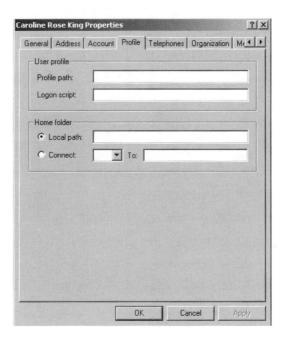

FIGURE 9.21

Profile tab of the User Properties window

Figure 9.22 shows the Telephones tab, which contains contact information for the user.

The attributes on the Telephones tab are all multivalue fields—clicking the Other button allows you to enter multiple values.

FIGURE 9.22

Telephones tab of the
User Properties
window

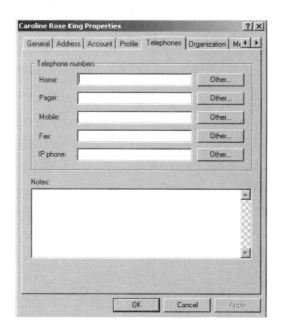

Figure 9.23 shows the Organization tab. This tab contains attributes that allow you to document the organizational hierarchy of your company. You can set the following values:

Title

Department

Company

Manager   This refers to the employee's manager (as opposed to the next attribute, Direct reports).

Direct reports   This refers to the people who are managed by this user.

At this time, ADS does not use the information stored on the Organization tab except for LDAP searches. Later, we can expect other applications to take advantage of this information. For example, imagine an e-mail system—Exchange Server, perhaps—that lets you send messages to "All users whose department attribute is Sales."

FIGURE 9.23

Organization tab of the
User Properties
window

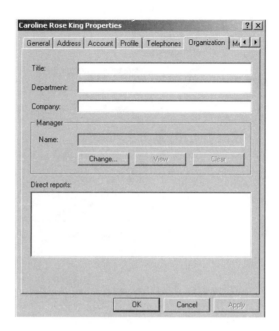

FIGURE 9.23

Organization tab of the
User Properties
window

The Member Of tab is shown in Figure 9.24. On this page you can add or remove users from Windows NT security groups.

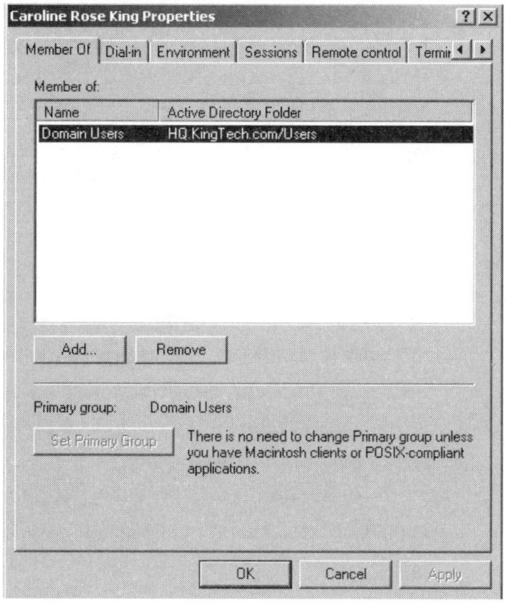

FIGURE 9.24

Member Of tab of the
User Properties
window

The Dial-in tab, shown in Figure 9.25, is used to configure a user's dial-in privileges. This tab is only valid if RAS has been configured.

F I G U R E 9.25

Dial-in tab of the User Properties window

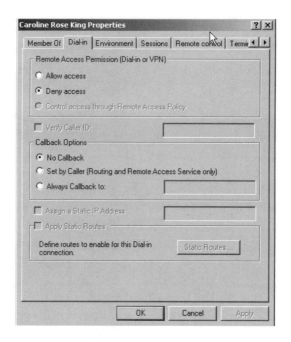

The Environment tab (Figure 9.26) allows you to configure the user's initial network environment as they log in. This is useful for users who move from computer to computer. Settings here will take effect no matter where the user is sitting.

The Sessions tab, shown in Figure 9.27, allows you to configure connections for clients utilizing the Terminal Server capabilities of Windows 2000.

Terminal Server is really beyond the scope of an ADS book. In short, it allows you to use less powerful PCs or dumb terminals to connect to a Windows 2000 server. All applications actually run on the server, with only screen updates being sent to the client machine. We use this quite effectively in the training industry—it allows us to move out-of-date equipment from technical classrooms into application training rooms. Here, they can run Windows 9x or NT applications without having to have the horsepower necessary to run those operating systems.

FIGURE 9.26

Environment tab of the
User Properties
window

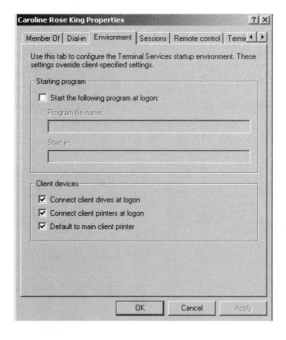

FIGURE 9.27

Sessions tab of the
User Properties
window

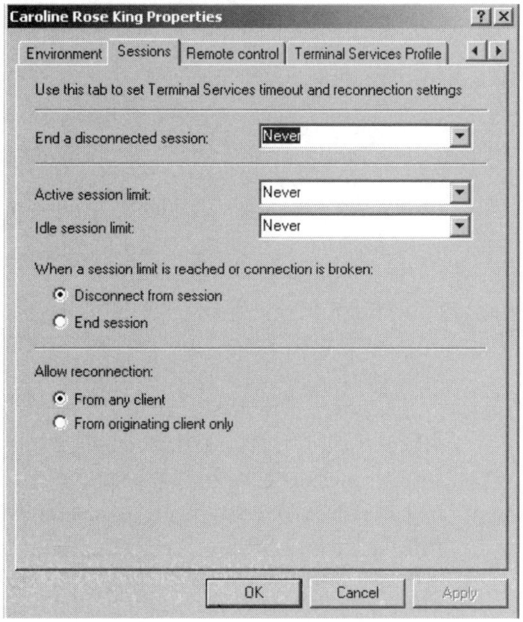

The Remote Control tab also pertains to Terminal Services. As shown in Figure 9.28, you can configure aspects of observing or controlling a user's session from a remote location.

NOTE This can really save time for Help desk personnel. They can call a user on the phone and walk him through the process he is having trouble with—without ever leaving their own desks!

F I G U R E 9.28

Remote Control tab of the User Properties window

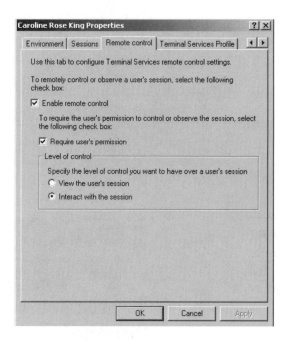

Lastly, the Terminal Services Profile tab, shown in Figure 9.29, allows you to configure the location where terminal services clients should find their session profile and assign the folder they should use as their home directory.

I know that this seems like a lot of information about a user—especially when compared to earlier network operating systems. Remember the big difference here is that in ADS we are not just creating a user account for network access, we are trying to create a database of user information. This information, once entered, can be utilized in many ways.

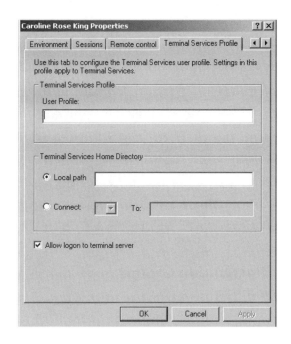

FIGURE 9.29

Terminal Services
Profile tab of the User
Properties window

Creating Groups

Groups are a means to organize individual user or computer accounts. They are used for security and distribution purposes. Most of your management should be done through groups, rather than to individual users or computers. The *scope,* or area of influence, for a group can be limited to a single domain, to multiple domains (through trusts), or to the entire network. Group objects are named in the same way as any other object in the directory.

Take special care to give each group a name that describes its purpose. If a group is used to grant access to accounting information, for instance, its name should imply that, such as AcctInfo.

Types of Groups

New to Windows 2000 Server are two types of group objects:

- Security groups
- Distribution groups

Each type of group is used for a specific function.

Security Groups

Security groups are used to grant permissions to resources. Computers, users, and other groups can be members of a security group. If you wanted to grant users permissions on a share point, for instance, you could create a group, grant that group the appropriate permissions, and then add users (or other groups) as members of that group.

Distribution Groups

Distribution groups are used for non-security functions, such as e-mail. Distribution groups cannot be assigned permissions or rights.

Access Tokens

When an object is created in the directory database, it is given a unique identifier known as a SID (System Identification). Rather than the user-friendly X.500 names, the operating system uses SIDs to identify objects. SIDs are used to control access to all resources on the network.

When a user logs in to the network, the system requires that she provide a valid login name (and password if one exists for her account). NT then puts the SID for the user, and the SIDs of any groups that she is a member of, into an object known as the *access token* and sends the access token back to the user.

As the user attempts to access resources, she will send her access token to the resources for authentication. The SIDs in the token are compared against a list of SIDs for objects that have permissions to the resource. This list, known as the access control list (ACL), controls who may access the resource. If the user's access token contains the SID of an object that has been granted the necessary permissions to use the resource, the user's request is granted.

Scopes of Groups

Windows 2000 Server provides the ability to limit the area of influence for a group. A group can be

- A domain local group
- A global group
- A universal group

These terms are defined in the sections that follow.

Domain Local Groups

Domain local groups are limited to a single domain. They can be used to grant permissions to resources only within that domain.

These groups should be used when the permissions are to be granted specifically within a domain: Domain local groups are not visible outside of their own domain.

Global Groups

Global groups are used to grant permissions to objects in multiple domains and are visible to all trusted domains. Global groups, though, can have as members only users and groups from within their own domain. If your ADS database is configured for native-mode operation, global groups can be *nested;* in other words, a global group can contain other global groups.

Universal Groups

Universal groups are similar to global groups in that they can be used to grant permissions across multiple domains. The big difference is that universal groups can contain any combination of user and global group accounts from *any* trusted domain in the forest. Microsoft suggests the following procedure for granting permissions across multiple domains:

1. Create a global group in each domain, and add the appropriate users as members.

2. Create a universal group and grant it the appropriate permissions.

3. Add the global groups as members of the universal group.

Adding groups to other groups is known as *nesting*. Each group "deep" into a nest is called a *layer*, as shown in Figure 9.30. Group 1 is a member of Group 2; this is one layer. Group 2 is a member of Group 3; this is another layer.

While there is no limit to the number of layers that can be applied, tracing permissions becomes much more complex as the depth increases.

FIGURE 9.30

Nesting groups

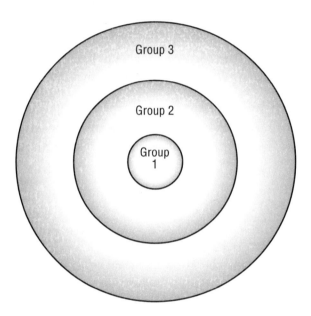

The Mechanics of Creating Groups

Groups are created using the Active Directory Users and Computers tool located in the Administrative Tools group. Right-click the container in which you wish to create a group, choose New, then choose Group. This will bring up the Create New Object—Group screen depicted in Figure 9.31. Here you will name your group, choose a type (security or distribution), and choose a scope (domain local, global, or universal). The universal option will be available only in a multidomain environment (in other words, in ADS structures where trusts exist).

FIGURE 9.31

Creating a group

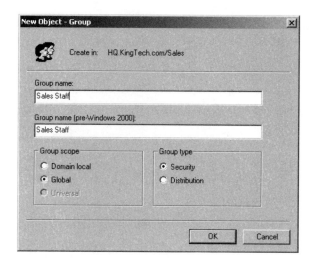

Once you have created the group, you can manage the object's properties by double-clicking the group object in the Active Directory management tool. You will be presented with the Properties page for the group. As you can see in Figure 9.32, the Properties page for a group object has four tabs:

- General

- Members

- Member Of

- Managed By

On the General tab, you can change a group's type, scope, and name, and even provide an e-mail address for addressing mail to the group.

The properties on the other three tabs are fairly straightforward.

The Members tab, shown in Figure 9.33, lists those users and groups that are members of this group.

F I G U R E 9.32

General tab of the
Group Properties
window

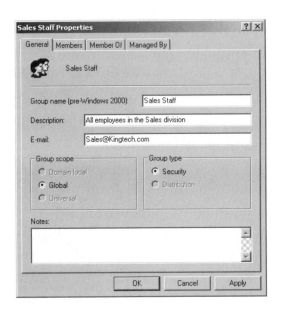

F I G U R E 9.33

Members tab of the
Group Properties
window

The Member Of tab, which you can see in Figure 9.34, lists the groups that this group is a member of.

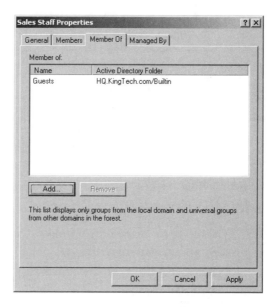

Figure 9.35 shows the Managed By tab, which allows you to document who is responsible for management of this group.

Creating Printers

There are two types of printers that you might create in your Windows 2000 Server environment:

- Those that are attached to Windows 2000 computers

- Those that are not

Since Windows 2000 Server is fully ADS enabled, publishing a printer in the ADS database is as simple as creating a new printer. For printers attached to non–Windows 2000 computers, use the Active Directory management tool to create a printer object.

Printers in Windows 2000 Server

Printers are created on a Windows 2000 computer in the same manner that they are created in earlier versions of NT. Access the Printers folder and double-click the Add Printer icon. This will run the Add Printer Administrative Wizard. The Wizard opens with a Welcome screen. Clicking Next will bring you to the first configuration window, in which you determine whether you are adding a local printer or attaching to a printer across the network. If you are adding a local printer, the next window, shown in Figure 9.36, will ask you which port the printer is attached to.

FIGURE 9.36

Port selection

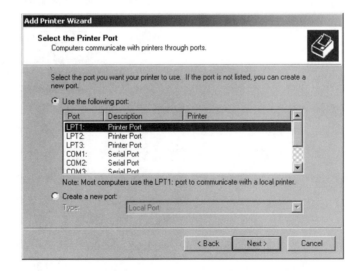

The next screen, which you can see in Figure 9.37, will ask you to identify the make and model of your printer. This ensures that the appropriate printer drivers are installed.

FIGURE 9.37

Printer model

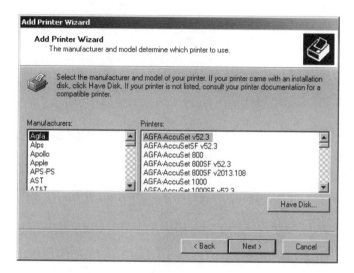

The next screen asks you to name the printer. After you have done that, you are asked if you want to share the printer, and if so, what the shared printer should be named.

A new option for Windows 2000 Server appears in the next screen, shown in Figure 9.38. Here you can add a few comments about the printer. These comments will be available to users through an ADS query.

The rest of the Wizard is standard. It asks whether you want to print a test page and shows you a review of the choices you have made. Clicking Finish on the last page will complete the process.

Once the printer has been created, you can right-click it and access its properties. On the Sharing tab, shown in Figure 9.39, you will see that the "List in the Directory" option is selected by default. In other words, this printer will automatically be listed in the ADS database.

F I G U R E 9.38

Location and
Comment

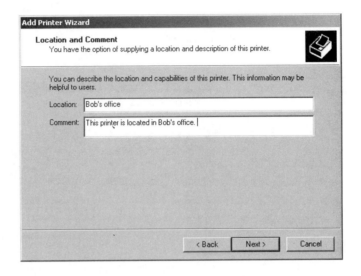

F I G U R E 9.39

Printer Properties

Non–Windows 2000 Printers

To add to your directory any printers that are attached to computers not running Windows 2000, you must use the Active Directory management tool. Before you begin, ensure that the printer is properly configured on the host computer. Document the make, model, and name of the printer for use in this process.

In the Active Directory management tool, right-click the container in which you want the printer created. Choose New and then Printer. You will be presented with the Create New Object—Printer dialog box, as shown in Figure 9.40. Provide the UNC path to the printer, and you are done!

FIGURE 9.40

Creating a printer in
ADS Manager

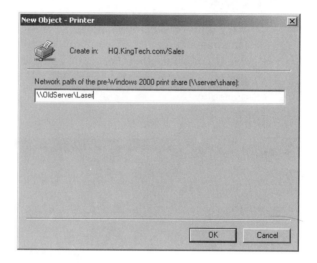

Creating Other Objects

While OUs, users, groups, and printers will be the mainstay of most directories, ADS defines numerous other types of objects: computers, contacts, shares, and more. Some of these object types are for special use and beyond the scope of this book, but others will become an integral part of your environment as you get more and more comfortable with Windows 2000 Server. As an introduction to some of the other types of objects available, we'll take a look at the following classes:

- Computer
- Contact
- Shared folder

Creating each of these objects starts in the same way: In the Active Directory Users and Computers tool, right-click the appropriate container, choose Properties ➢ New, then choose the class of object you wish to create.

Computer Objects

A *computer object* is used to represent computers that have joined the domain. Creating a computer object requires one screen, shown in Figure 9.41. Here you provide the computer name and the DNS name of the host, and identify the type of computer (Windows 2000 workstation, member server, or domain controller).

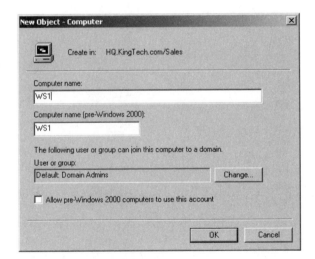

Once you have created a computer object, you can configure the properties of the object by double-clicking it. Figure 9.42 shows the tabs that are available for configuration.

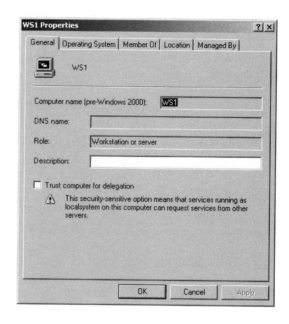

Each tab represents a different type of information:

General   This tab shows the information given during the creation of the device, names, and roles.

Operating System   This tab documents the name and version of the operating system running on the machine, as well as any service packs that have been applied to the operating system.

Member Of   This tab shows the ADS security groups of which this computer is a member.

Location   This tab allows you to document the physical location of the computer—Tampa Building 1, for instance.

Managed By   This tab shows properties that describe who is responsible for this computer.

Contact Objects

A *contact* is an object designed to hold information about a person who is not a part of the local forest. Users can then access this information using an

LDAP-enabled tool. The creation process involves providing first, last, and full names for the contact.

Once created, the contact has numerous properties. The Properties page of a contact object is shown in Figure 9.43.

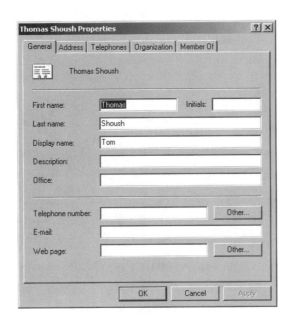

Each tab represents a different type of information:

General   This tab contains generic contact information such as names, phone numbers, and e-mail addresses.

Address   This tab shows the mailing address of the contact.

Telephones/Notes   This tab lets you record more contact information.

Organization   This tab shows title, department, and company information.

Member Of   This tab shows the ADS security group of which this contact is a member.

Share Objects

Share points can also be published through the ADS database. Once the share has been created at the host computer, you create a share object in

ADS. Configuring a share is just a matter of providing the UNC path to the actual share point, as shown in Figure 9.44.

FIGURE 9.44

Creating a share object

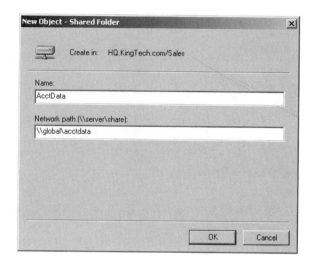

Share objects do not have a lot of properties, as you can see in Figure 9.45.

FIGURE 9.45

Configuring a share
object

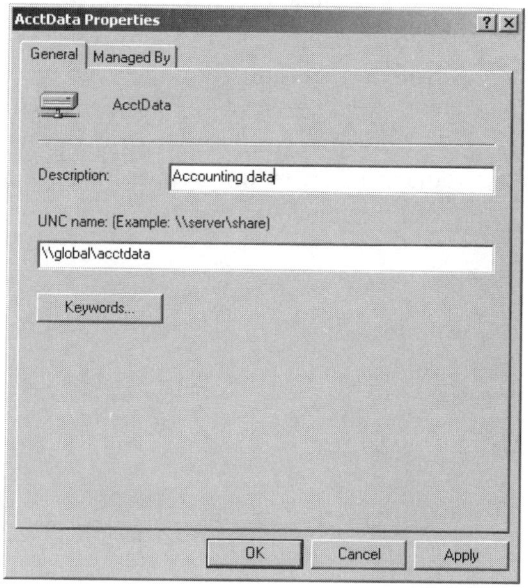

The most interesting property of a share object is the ability to create a list of keywords that can later be used to find this share with an LDAP query, as shown in Figure 9.46.

FIGURE 9.46

Creating a keyword list
for a shared folder

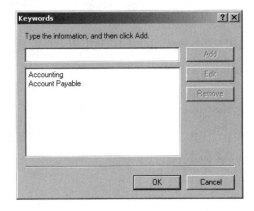

In Short

Installing and populating an Active Directory database is really just a matter of knowing where to click. More important than the mechanics is a firm understanding of the design principles discussed in Chapter 8 and the function of each object class, as discussed in this chapter.

Now that you have created your ADS structure, the next step is to ensure that it is secure. In Chapter 10, we will discuss the theory and techniques of securing an ADS directory database.

CHAPTER
10

Securing the Active
Directory Database

Most of the information stored within the ADS directory database is specifically designed to be for public consumption: things like telephone numbers, departments, and company names. There are, however, certain attributes of objects that you might *not* want to be published to the world at large. A user object, for instance, has certain properties that could be considered confidential (depending upon the types of data you store). For example, in some companies the human resources department uses "job titles" to describe employees' salary ranges. In such a case, federal, state, or local legislation might mandate that salary information be kept confidential.

One way to avoid this problem would be to ignore the title attribute of all user accounts—after all, if the information is not there it most certainly is not at risk of disclosure. Another way to approach this issue would be to secure the title attribute so that only members of the appropriate groups could see this information.

Another issue, one that we touched upon earlier, is that of delegating administrative privileges. The ability to limit administrative capabilities is one of the most important security features of Active Directory. We'll revisit this topic in this chapter, not so much for new information as to drive home the concepts presented earlier.

Although this is not one of those "test preparation" manuals, if you are considering chasing your Microsoft Certified System Engineer (MCSE) certificate you should understand the concept of administrative delegation inside and out! Microsoft is pushing this feature very hard—and they are known for testing on the features that they are most proud of.

We'll begin this chapter, though, with a discussion of the basics of security. While most of the Windows 2000 Server security features work the same as they did in NT 4, there are a few subtle differences, as well as a few new features pertaining to Active Directory.

> For many of you, this chapter will be a great review of NT security. For those of you who are new to NT, this chapter might not be in-depth enough. If you need more information about NT security, I would suggest *Mastering Network Security* by Chris Brenton (ISBN 0-7821-2343-0, Sybex, 1998).

Security Basics

NT security follows a security model that was created in the '60s for mainframe environments. Because this model is a mature technology, we can rest assured that NT security is stable and well supported in the industry. This does not mean, however, that it is intuitive or simplistic. NT security can be extremely complex, but that is the price we usually pay for sophisticated and powerful systems.

You must understand two main concepts to fully appreciate the strengths (and weaknesses) of NT security:

- System identifiers (SIDs)

- Access control lists (ACLs)

SIDs and ACLs work together to provide security for the resources on your network. We'll look at each in turn.

System Identifiers (SIDs)

As each object is created in the directory database, it is assigned a unique value known as its *SID*. The SID is used by internal operations to identify that object when it attempts to access some resource.

For our purposes, we will limit our discussion to the use of SIDs for user and group objects, but you should be aware that every object in the tree has a unique SID assigned to it.

Any discussion of how best to use SIDs starts with the logon process. As an NT computer boots, a series of processes starts. One of these processes is the *NETLOGON* process. Among its tasks, the NETLOGON process is responsible for the act of "logging on" (hence the name) to the network.

The NETLOGON process, working in conjunction with a few other components, opens a secure communication channel to a domain controller. The user provides a username and password, and is either granted or denied access to the network. If the user is granted access, the domain controller will gather together the user's SID and the SIDs of all groups that the user is a member of. These SIDs are placed in an *access token* and sent back to the user, as shown in Figure 10.1.

FIGURE 10.1

Acquiring the access token

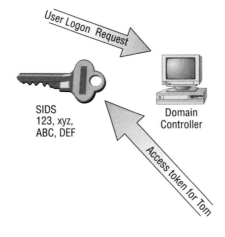

User Logon Request

SIDS
123, xyz,
ABC, DEF

Domain
Controller

Access token for Tom

Active Directory Database

Tom-SID : 123
Member of: Acct
            Managers
            Montana

Acct SID = xyz

Managers SID = ABC

Montana SID = DEF

Many people picture the access token as a set of keys. Each key opens a different aspect of some network resource. If you attempt to read a file and you have the "read key" for that file, for example, you will be granted access.

The system identifier is only half the story. For it to have any value, there must be a mechanism for connecting SIDs to resources. That mechanism is the *access control list*.

Access Control List (ACL)

The record for each object in the directory database has a header known as the *security descriptor*. The security descriptor defines the access permissions that have been granted to the object. To be more specific, the security descriptor contains

- The SID of the owner of the object

- A group SID (used only by the POSIX subsystem and Services for Macintosh)

- Two access control lists

You can see the contents of a security descriptor in Figure 10.2. The object being granted rights is known as the *security principal*. Security principals receive rights or permissions.

F I G U R E   10.2

Security descriptors

Security Descriptor
for a Container Object

	Access Control Entries
Owner SID	Grant Owner Full Control
Group SID	Grant World List
Discretionary ACL	Grant Joe Create Child
System ACL	

The *discretionary access control list* (DACL) contains the SIDs of objects that have been granted permissions to the object and the specific permissions granted. The objects within the DACL are referred to as *access control entries* (ACEs). All permissions and rights are assigned through ACEs. The *system access control list* (SACL) contains systemwide policies, such as the settings for auditing. As such, it is not really relevant to our discussion.

Access Control Entries

Access control entries are part of the DACL and are designed to protect the object. There are many levels of ACEs available:

Object class   You might set an ACE for every instance of a class of object in the tree. You might, for example, want to create an ACE that allows your Help desk personnel to change user passwords.

Object   You can create ACEs that apply only to a specific object in the tree. You might, for instance, want to protect a particular application object from being tampered with.

Object properties   You can also protect specific attributes of an object. For example, you might want to limit the anonymous user account's ability to view the configuration parameters of your e-mail server.

This combination of abilities lets administrators get as granular as they want in their management practices. You can make assignments that are sweeping in nature (affecting large numbers of objects, such as all user objects), more controlled (such as the ability to read and write to all properties for a specific printer), or very specific (such as the ability to read all properties of user Joe *except* his title property).

Applying ACEs to a Request for Access

ACEs are applied to requests in the same manner in which ACEs are applied to requests in the NTFS file system (both the newest version that ships with Windows 2000 Server and earlier versions). We'll look at a standard request first and then at the exception that makes the rule.

In a standard request, a user—Tom, for instance—wants to change the value of the telephone number property of user Susan. Tom's computer will send his request, along with his access token, to the Active Directory server, as shown in Figure 10.3.

The ADS server finds Susan's object and compares the SIDs in Tom's access token with the SIDs in Susan's DACL. You can see this in Figure 10.4.

ADS will search for a matching SID that allows Tom to change the attribute in question. If a match is found, Tom can make the change. If not, Tom's request will be denied.

FIGURE 10.3

Request for
information

FIGURE 10.3

Request for
information

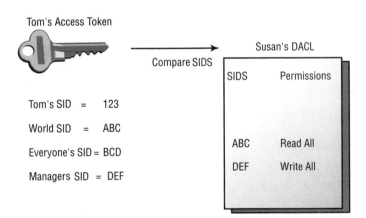

FIGURE 10.4

Authenticating a
request

There is one exception to the statement "ADS will search for a matching SID." If the access token contains a SID for an object that has been granted the Deny Access permission, the object would be denied access. Notice the blank space at the beginning of Susan's DACL in Figure 10.4. All Deny Access permissions are placed at the beginning of the DACL. Let's change the scenario a bit and see what happens. Tom will still be a member of the Managers group, but we'll also make him a member of the "Security Problems" group. (Either Tom is a manager who knows just enough to be dangerous or his position is such that he shouldn't be granted excessive permissions.) In Figure 10.5, the graphic has been updated to reflect this small change.

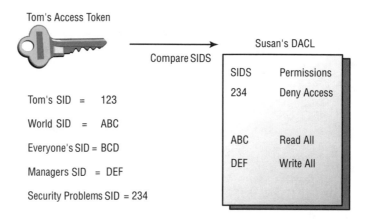

FIGURE 10.5

Deny Access permission

Figure 10.5 shows the Deny Access permission at the top of the DACL. When the comparison is made, ADS will see that Tom is a member of a group that has been denied access. Even though Tom is a member of another group with the appropriate permissions, his request will be denied. ADS will search no further once it finds a Deny Access permission.

Ownership

Every object in the ADS database has an *owner*. The person who creates an object becomes the owner of that object. The owner has complete control over an object. The owner has the ability to control how permissions are set for an object and to whom permissions are granted. In short, ownership of an object delegates administrative responsibility of that object to the listed owner.

If a member of the Domain Administrators group creates an object, the group (rather than the individual) is listed as its owner. Members of the Domain Administrators group also have the ability to take ownership of any object within their domain.

Taking ownership of an object is as simple as right-clicking the object in the Active Directory Users and Computers, choosing Properties, choosing the Security tab, then clicking Take Ownership.

Delegating Control

We've taken a look at delegating control of an OU before, but this topic is extremely important, so I think it warrants revisiting here. To delegate complete control of an OU, run the Active Directory Users and Computers tool located in your Administrative Tools group. Right-click the appropriate OU and choose Delegate Control. This will start the Delegation of Control Wizard. You will be asked to provide the names of any users or groups that you want to delegate control to, as shown in Figure 10.6.

FIGURE 10.6

Users and groups

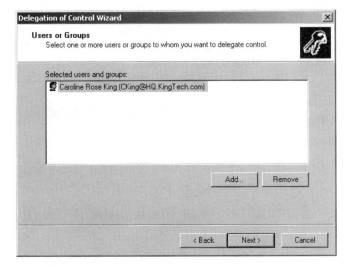

In the dialog box depicted in Figure 10.7, you will be asked to determine which administrative rights you wish to grant. You can choose from the list of common tasks or decide to create a custom delegation. If you choose from the list of common tasks, this is the last decision you have to make. The next screen will be a summary of the changes you are about to make—click the Finish button and you are done.

FIGURE 10.7

Tasks to delegate

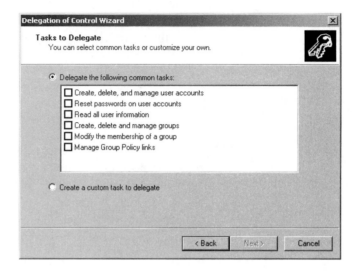

If you choose to create a custom delegation, the next window (shown in Figure 10.8) allows you to decide if the user or group should be allowed to manage all classes of object or if you would like to limit their ability to a set of object classes.

FIGURE 10.8

Scope of delegation

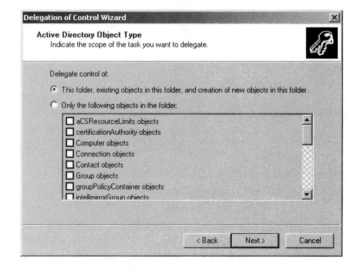

Next, you will be asked to list the actual permission you wish to grant. There are three levels of control—general, property-specific, and creation/ deletion of specific child objects. The general tasks contain the "tree management" abilities that an administrator might need, such as read or write permissions to access control lists and read or write permissions to all properties. The property-specific list allows control over the ability to read and write to each individual property of the objects in this container. Finally, the creation/deletion of specific child objects lets you control which object classes this security principal will be able to manage. Just make the appropriate selection on the dialog box shown in Figure 10.9, and choose the permissions from the list.

FIGURE 10.9

Permissions list

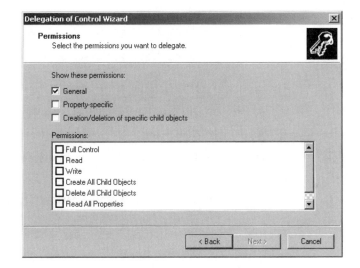

Authentication Security

The initial security that any user encounters is the security involved in the logon, or authentication, process. Windows 2000 Server supports multiple protocols for network security and authentication. In a perfect world, one—and only one—security protocol would be used to access the network. Unfortunately, in the heterogeneous networks of today's business market, most networks must use multiple security protocols. Rather than force administrators to make a choice, and in an effort to provide an open architecture, Microsoft has designed a security architecture that is both modular and extensible. Windows 2000 Server will support the following network security protocols:

Windows NT LAN Manager (NTLM)   NTLM is the security protocol used by earlier versions of Windows NT. NTLM will continue to be supported to provide backward compatibility with these operating systems.

Kerberos version 5   The Kerberos protocol replaces NTLM as the primary security protocol for access to resources within or across NT domains. Kerberos provides

- Mutual authentication of both client and server (in other words, authentication becomes a two-way street)

- Less overhead on the server during authentication

- Support of delegation of authority from clients to servers through the use of proxy mechanisms

We'll take a closer look at Kerberos in the next section of this chapter.

Distributed Password Authentication (DPA)   DPA is the shared secret authentication protocol used by some of the largest Internet membership organizations, such as CompuServe and MSN. It was specifically designed to allow members to use the same username and password to access multiple Internet resources that are part of the membership organization. In other words, a user can access different resources without having to enter (and remember) multiple usernames and passwords.

Public-key-based protocols   Secure Sockets Layer (SSL) is the *de facto* standard for secure connections between Internet browsers and Internet servers. These protocols use public-key certificates to authenticate clients.

We'll discuss certificates in more detail later in this chapter.

The ability to mix and match security mechanisms as needed is critical in any large organization. Microsoft has implemented a modular security architecture known as the *Security Support Provider Interface* (SSPI) to provide this functionality. This SSPI architecture is shown in Figure 10.10.

FIGURE 10.10

Security Support Provider Interface architecture

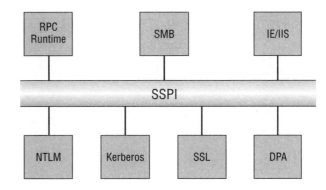

SSPI is a Win32 system API that acts as an interpreter between application protocols (such as those used by Internet Explorer) and security protocols (such as Kerberos).

Kerberos Basics

Kerberos version 5 has been implemented in numerous systems and can be used to provide a single point of authentication to mixed resources. Kerberos provides a common protocol that allows a single account database to authenticate users across a heterogeneous environment. As such, utilizing Kerberos security can greatly reduce the administrative overhead involved in supporting a mixed network.

Kerberos security uses a computer designated as the Key Distribution Center (KDC). Kerberos is known as a *shared secret authentication protocol* because both the client and the KDC know the user's password. The KDC acts as the middleman between clients and resources during the authentication process. You can see this process in Figure 10.11.

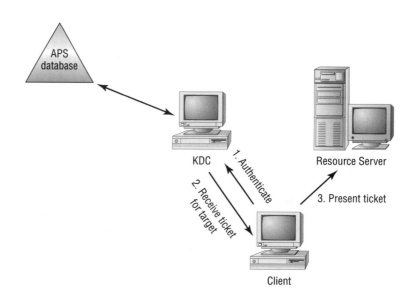

Here's what happens:

1. The client authenticates to the Key Distribution Center computer, using a valid username and password. In Windows 2000 Server, this account information is held in the Active Directory database. In other words, Kerberos is fully integrated into the ADS environment.

2. The client requests a *session ticket* for the target server. The Kerberos session ticket identifies the user. In a Windows 2000 Server environment, the session ticket contains the user's SID as well as the SIDs of any groups the user is a member of. The session ticket also contains an encrypted key that the target server can use to ensure that the ticket was generated by the KDC.

3. The client then presents the session ticket to the target server. The target server checks whether the ticket is valid and grants or denies access as appropriate.

The session ticket is stored on the client computer for a random amount of time (between five minutes and eight hours) so that it can be used to request access to that resource in the future. If the ticket expires, it is flushed from memory and the process is repeated at the next access attempt.

Kerberos is a great technology—secure, dependable, and mature. It is not something that most administrators will, under normal circumstances, have to concern themselves with. The Kerberos authentication process happens in the background as users attach to network resources, much as the NTLM authentication process did in earlier releases of NT.

Public-Key Security

Windows 2000 Server also supports the use of public-key schemes, the most common being X.509, for granting resource access to users who do not have Kerberos credentials. Most commonly, this scenario will involve granting access to someone outside of the organization. You might, for instance, wish to allow clients the ability to access an inventory database, rather than forcing them to call a salesperson for information. Another potential X.509 certificate user would be a company that uses contractors to perform internal functions. Rather than create an internal account for the contractors, an administrator could use certificates to authenticate contractors to the resources they need. Whatever the purpose, using public-key security, or certificates, for authentication is common practice in today's world.

Public Key Basics

Public-key security is based on the science of *cryptography*. Cryptography uses mathematical algorithms that combine input (plain text) and an encryption key to generate encrypted data, known as *ciphertext*. With a good algorithm, it is mathematically infeasible (notice I did not say "impossible") to reverse the encryption process with only the ciphertext; some additional data is needed to perform this task, namely an *encryption key*.

In traditional cryptography, the same key is used to encrypt and decrypt messages. You have probably seen such encryption in some spy novel you have read. The spy steals the master code for all communication from the enemy, and the hero is one step ahead of the enemy from that point on. Usually, the master key is stolen during its transfer from one party to another. This is the biggest weakness of traditional cryptography: Both parties must have the key, so some secure method of transferring that key is crucial.

In public-key cryptography, the encryption and decryption keys are related, but different. An encryption key is used to encrypt data, but it has no place in the decryption process. A different key (mathematically related but not identical), known as the *decryption key*, is used for decryption. In a public-key environment, every user has a pair of keys: a public key (to encrypt) and a private key (to decrypt). By making the public key available, you can enable others to send you data that is encrypted in such as way that only your private key can decrypt it. Public-key encryption schemes avoid the biggest weakness of older systems: The key used to decrypt data does *not* have to be transferred and thus can be kept in a secure location.

This separation of public and private keys has allowed the creation of a number of new technologies that are becoming a part of today's networks:

- Digital signatures

- Distributed authentication

- Bulk data encryption without prior shared secrets

The following sections give an overview of these technologies.

Digital Signatures

A *digital signature* is used to validate the authenticity of a message by the receiver. Using the private key, the client creates a small piece of data that can be decrypted only with the use of the corresponding public key. This electronic signature provides the following benefits:

- It ensures that the data is from someone who possesses the matching private key (either the originator of the message or a trusted certificate server).

- Anyone with access to the public key can verify the signature.

- Any change to the data (as small as modifying a single bit) invalidates the signature—letting the recipient know that the message has been tampered with or corrupted in transit.

Using digital signatures can provide a high level of confidence in the integrity of transferred data. Not only is this a good security mechanism, it can also be used to ensure that network problems have not corrupted data in transit.

Distributed Authentication

Public-key security can also be used as a form of authentication security. The public/private key combination can be used to guarantee the identity of the sender of data, much like using the digital signatures described in the previous section. This allows an NT system to grant access to users outside of its environment. As long as both parties (the NT system and the user) trust a third-party key provider or certificate server, users can use their public/private key mechanism to identify themselves to an NT server.

Bulk Data Encryption without Prior Shared Secrets

Current public-key technologies are processor intensive compared to more traditional cryptographic methods. They are secure, though, because the decryption key does not need to be passed from sender to recipient. Bulk encryption takes advantage of the security of public-key mechanisms without incurring the greater processor overhead. If two computers need to transfer data, the sender will use the recipient's public key to encrypt a *master key* and send it to the recipient. Since only the recipient has the private key to decrypt this message, we can trust that the master key has arrived securely. Now that both parties have the master key, traditional encryption can be used during the actual transfer of data.

Certificates

A service known as the Certificate Authority (CA) issues *certificates* that guarantee the binding between a public key and the originator of data. In other words, both the sender and the recipient trust that the CA will correctly authenticate the certificate that the sender transfers to the recipient. If it does so, the recipient can trust that the certificate is from whom it is supposed to be from, and the rest of the public/private key security mechanism can proceed.

Another way to look at this is to think about the process of sending a signed message. The sender creates a message and attaches the digital signature. The recipient performs the algorithm against the signature to determine whether the message has been tampered with. What the recipient cannot guarantee is that the message came from the appropriate sender. In other words, the recipient can use the public key to verify the message, but what does she use to verify that the public key belongs to the appropriate sender? In other words, *anyone* can request a public/private key pair from a KDC using any name at all. How does the recipient know that some other user hasn't generated a key pair under a false name?

This is where CA services enter the picture. CA services guarantee the binding between the originator and the public key. As long as the recipient trusts the CA to do its job correctly, the recipient can rest assured that the sender is indeed who he claims to be.

In a large environment, the recipient might need to verify the CA server by using another CA server. This second CA server might also need to be verified using a third server. Ultimately, the recipient will build a chain of "trusts" back to a CA server that the user implicitly trusts, known as a *trusted root certificate server*.

Microsoft Windows 2000 Server ships with the software to build a Microsoft Certificate Server. This software is compliant with the industry's leading certificate standard—X.509. Once in place, an Active Directory server can trust X.509 certificates and thus allow outside accounts access to internal resources.

In Short

This has been a fairly short chapter, but a big topic in terms of the administrative capabilities of Windows 2000 Server and Active Directory. The ability to selectively delegate administrative privileges is a *very* big selling point of Windows 2000 Server! Also important is the ability to incorporate external security methods into your NT network. Understanding the implications of these new features can be the turning point in the learning curve for ADS.

In the next chapter, we will expand upon our discussion of security with the addition of group policies. This tool gives you the power to completely control who accesses your network and what their environment will look like.

CHAPTER
11

Implementing
Group Policies

In NT 4, you could create system policies (using the System Policy Editor) to configure user and computer settings stored in the Windows NT Registry. System policies could be used to control the user environment and user actions, as well as to enforce system configuration settings for computers running Windows NT Workstation, Windows NT Server, and Windows 95. Basically, though, system policies in earlier versions of NT are really just Registry settings that define the behavior of operating system components.

Windows 2000 Server introduces a whole new level of central control over user environments. The Group Policy Editor, a new utility for Windows 2000 Server, extends the functionality of the System Policy Editor and enhances administrators' abilities to configure user and computer settings by fully leveraging the Active Directory database.

What Are Group Policies?

Many articles have appeared in the trade magazines lately about the Total Cost of Ownership (TCO) of personal computers. TCO represents not only the original cost of the hardware and software used on the desktop, but also the ongoing support costs associated with personal computers. Lost productivity due to configuration errors is cited as one of the largest costs involved in long-term support. This brings us to our discussion of *group policies*.

Group policies are used to define user or computer settings for an entire group of users or computers at one time. The settings that you configure are stored in a *group policy object (GPO)*, which is then associated with Active Directory objects such as sites, domains, or organizational units.

Many different aspects of the network, desktop, and software configuration environments can be managed through group policies. The following list describes, in general terms, the different types of policies that can be created (and enforced) using Windows 2000 Server's Group Policy Editor:

Application deployment policies   These policies affect the applications that users access on the network. These policies are used to automate the installation of software in one of two ways:

- Application assignment: The group policy installs or upgrades applications automatically or provides users with a shortcut that they cannot delete.

- Application publication: The group policy advertises applications in the directory. The applications then appear in the Add/Remove Programs list found in Control Panel. This gives users the ability to install and remove programs using a process with which they are already familiar.

File deployment policies   These policies allow the administrator to place files in special folders on the user's computer, such as the Desktop or My Documents areas. For example, an employee telephone directory could be placed in the My Documents folder each time a user logs on to the network.

Script policies   These policies allow an administrator to specify scripts that should run at specific times, such as logon/logoff or system start-up/shutdown.

Software policies   These policies work much like system policies did in earlier versions of NT. Administrators can use them to globally configure most of the settings in user profiles, such as Desktop settings, Start menu options, and applications.

Security policies   These policies are some of the more important ones that you will configure. Using security policies, an administrator can restrict user access to files and folders, configure how many failed login attempts will lock an account, and control user rights (such as which users are able to log on locally at domain servers).

As you can see from this list, you can make policies do more than in earlier versions of Windows NT. Most of this additional functionality comes from the integration of policies with Active Directory Services.

Microsoft Management Console

Before we begin our discussion of policy-based administration, this is as good a time as any to introduce a new tool—the Microsoft Management Console (MMC). In earlier chapters, we discussed specific tools to do specific jobs—for instance, using Active Directory Users and Computers to create organizational units and the objects that populate them. While this is a valid method (using a separate tool for each management function), Microsoft has provided us with a single tool that is capable of performing almost every administrative task required in a Windows 2000 environment—the MMC.

I think of the MMC as a big software pincushion. On its own it does very little, but if you plug in additional software, known as *snap-ins*, its functionality knows no bounds.

To run the MMC, type **MMC** in the Run window. Before any snap-ins have been added, the interface will look like the window shown in Figure 11.1.

FIGURE 11.1

The Microsoft
Management Console

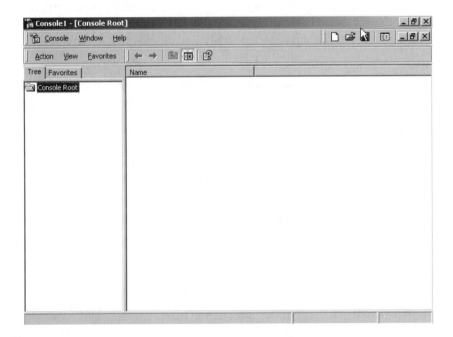

From here you'll need to install a few snap-ins. On the Console menu, choose Add/Remove Snap-in. You'll be presented with the list shown in Figure 11.2. As you can see, I've already added the Active Directory Users and Computers snap-in.

FIGURE 11.2

Add/Remove Snap-in dialog box

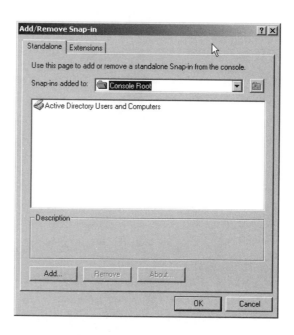

Click the Add button to be presented with a list of available snap-ins. For our purposes here I'll add the Group Policy snap-in by highlighting it and choosing Add, as shown in Figure 11.3.

The next screen allows you to choose where the group policies will be stored, whether on the local machine or in a container in your ADS structure. I've decided to place a group policy object named "KingTech Education Policy" in the Education OU in my tree, as shown in Figure 11.4. We'll discuss the significance of this placement a little later in this chapter. For now, be aware that policies can be created that affect sites, domains, or organizational units.

FIGURE 11.3

Adding the Group
Policy snap-in

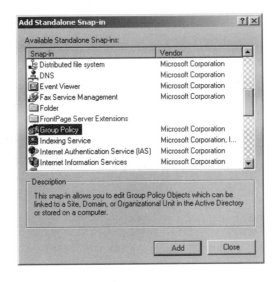

FIGURE 11.4

Creating the policy
object

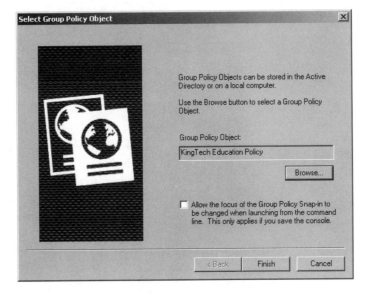

Now that I have created the Policy in my tree, the MMC reflects its existence, as shown in Figure 11.5. From now on, I can manage the policy using the MMC, rather than some external tool.

FIGURE 11.5

KingTech Education
Policy

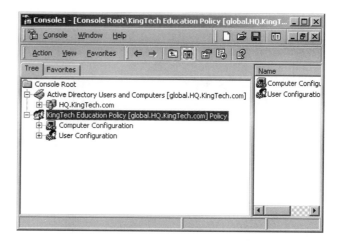

FIGURE 11.5

KingTech Education
Policy

Policy Objects in ADS

As you've seen, group policies are stored in group policy objects (GPOs), which are associated with sites, domains, or organizational unit objects within the directory. We'll discuss the procedures for creating and modifying group policies later in this chapter. We will begin, though, by looking at the structure of group policies. GPOs are a special object within the ADS structure.

In effect, the group policy objects for each container define their own folder structure, which works like namespaces. These structures are tied to one of the three places at which a GPO can exist in the Active Directory tree: site, domain, or organizational unit. Their placement will determine which users or computers will be affected by the settings in the GPO. The first rule to remember with policies in Windows 2000 is that they can be applied only to users or computers—they will have no effect upon other classes of objects in the ADS tree.

At the root of the GPO structure are two subfolders, `Computer Configuration` and `User Configuration`, as shown in Figure 11.6.

As the names imply, each of these subfolders contains parameters that can be configured based upon either the computer that is attaching to the network (Computer Configuration) or the user who is logging into the network (User Configuration).

FIGURE 11.6

The root of the GPO
structure

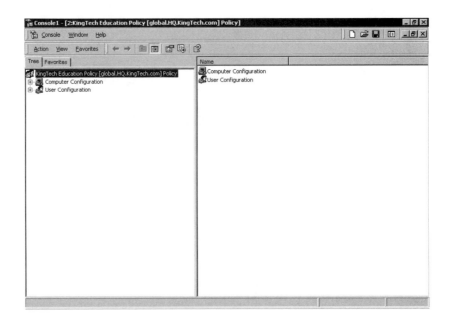

Computer Configuration

Among the options available within the Computer Configuration area are
the abilities to:

- Create policies that specify operating system behavior and the appearance of the Desktop

- Assign applications

- Assign settings

- Set file deployment options

- Specify security settings

- Specify computer start-up and shutdown scripts

Computer-related policies are applied when the operating system
initializes.

User Configuration

Among the options available within the User Configuration area are parameters that can be used to

- Create policies that determine operating system behavior, Desktop settings, application settings, and assigned and published applications

- Set file deployment options

- Set security options

- Assign user logon and logoff scripts

 User Configuration policy options are applied when a user logs on to the computer.

Using Computer and User Configuration

The bottom-line difference between the Computer Configuration and User Configuration settings is when they are applied. For Computer Configuration options, the policy is applied as the operating system boots. This means that the configuration options set in the Computer Configuration area will affect *any* user who logs on at the specified computer. User Configuration policies, on the other hand, are applied *after* the operating system has initialized and *only* to specified users or groups based upon a fairly complex series of rules that we'll discuss later.

For example, if you were trying to lock down user Bob, you would use a policy created within the User Configuration area. If, however, you were trying to lock down a particular computer, you would create a policy within the Computer Configuration area.

 At first glance, the ability to apply a policy to a particular computer might not appear too useful. If your company has a computer located in a public area, however, these options can be very beneficial. Imagine a computer in a public library. It could have a policy set up so that all temp files are deleted at shutdown—or better yet, at logoff. This would delete any private e-mail or Internet browser temporary files that had been copied to the local machine. Using Computer Configuration settings would clean up the computer's environment and secure files against undesired access at the same time!

Each of these folders—Computer Configuration and User Configuration—acts as the root of a GPO structure. Within each you will find a series of folders and subfolders. Each of these folders, also known as *GPO nodes*, contains configurable options for a specific area of your environment.

While group policies are managed through ADS-based tools, the actual policies are still specific files, just like in NT 4. These files are located in a structure called the *group policy template* in the System Volume folder of the domain controllers in the Policies subfolder. As an object in the directory, each policy you create has a unique SID. Within the Policies subfolder you will find a series of subfolders, as shown in Figure 11.7. Each subfolder is named with the SID of the GPO that it contains. As you can see in the right-hand side of the figure, within each GPO folder are two folders, MACHINE and USER, and a file, GPT. The GPT file contains a version number that is used to determine if the policy has been changed since the last time it was applied to a user or computer. The version number is used to prevent processing a policy when it is not necessary.

FIGURE 11.7

Policies folders

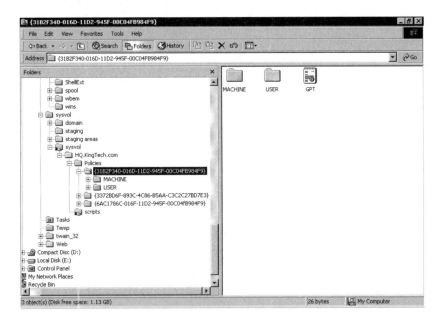

The following sections highlight the various nodes of the group policy object and some of the specific configuration parameters that can be controlled. The reality is that there are so many options available in group policies that there is no way anyone could adequately describe them unless they were writing a book about group policies. We'll limit our discussion to an overview of the types of parameters that can be controlled—and concentrate on the impact of group policies on managing Active Directory Services.

Software Settings Node

The Software Settings node of the GPO is the same for both the user and computer policies. This node allows you to manage the installation and maintenance of software for a user or computer. Applications can be managed in one of two different modes: assigned or published.

Assigned Mode

Assigned mode is used when you want everyone using the policy to have an application on his or her computer. Suppose, for instance, that you want everyone in the education department at KingTech to have Microsoft Power Point on their computers. Your first step would be to create a *package*. A software package contains all of the files necessary to install an application along with a description of all system changes needed (Registry changes, file locations, etc.). Many applications now include a pre-made package when you purchase them (or have a package available for download on their Web site). If the application does not have a package, one must be created. There are many third-party products on the market that can accomplish this task. Place the application package in some shared folder available to the network.

Once you have your package, adding it to a policy is a straightforward procedure. First, decide if you wish to assign the application based upon user identity (we'll talk about that later in this chapter) or if you wish this application to be available on all computers within a site, container, or organizational unit. The answer to this question will determine whether you should work in the Computer Configuration node or the User Configuration node of the policy. In either event, open the appropriate node (Computer or User), expand the Software Settings subnode in the MMC as shown in Figure 11.8, right-click Software Installation, and choose Package on the New menu.

FIGURE 11.8

Software installation

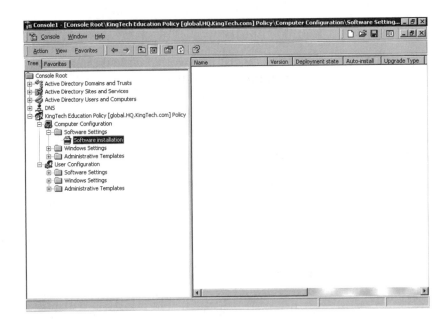

You will be presented with the dialog box shown in Figure 11.9. Choose the package file for the application that you wish to associate with this policy.

FIGURE 11.9

Choosing the package

You will then have to choose how this application should be distributed, as shown in Figure 11.10. Your choices are to *assign* or to *publish* the application.

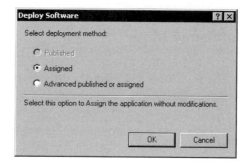

When an application is assigned, the policy will advertise it to the user the next time they log in (or to a computer the next time it initializes). When an application is advertised, it is not actually installed on the computer. Only enough information is installed to make its shortcut appear on the Start menu and to create the appropriate file associations. In our example, for instance, the Microsoft Power Point icon would appear in the Start menu and the appropriate file types (.PPT, .PPS, and a few others) would be associated with the application.

The first time a user tries to run MS Power Point (by either using the icon on their Start menu or attempting to open an associated file type), the application would be installed on their computer. The user can delete an assigned application, but since it is advertised, the icon and associations will be recreated the next time they log on.

Using the software installation mechanism of group policies can greatly ease administration of the applications in use by your users. In my education center in Grand Rapids, Michigan, we use Windows 2000 and group policies to control the computers in our classrooms. I've created packages for each of the applications that we teach. I then assign them to whichever user accounts our students will use to access our network. Each night we can put a new clean image down on our classroom computers (avoiding the hassle of cleaning up student work manually and greatly reducing our risk for virus infection), and when a student logs in the next day, all of the applications they need are available. The best part for us is that we don't have to worry about setting up specific machines for specific classes. We use the same clean image on all of the computers; who logs in at a computer will determine which applications are made available.

If your users move from computer to computer, you can reap the same benefits. Administrators no longer have to worry about installing applications on computers—that task will happen automatically when a user tries to use the tools they need.

Published Mode

Another option available is to publish the application package. When an application is published, nothing is installed automatically on the client computer. Instead, the application is added to the list of available programs in the Add/Remove Programs applet in Control Panel. This allows users to install the application on their own if they so desire. They do so by using a familiar interface—the Add/Remove Programs applet. They also do not have to have the disks (floppies or CD-ROM) at their computer—all of the files needed to install the application are part of the package.

Computer Configuration Node

The settings in the Computer Configuration node are applied to the local machine's Registry as the computer initializes. As the network components of the operating system load, the computer will obtain a list of group policies that should be applied. The next few sections outline the various subnodes of Computer Configuration.

As you can see in Figure 11.11, the Computer Configuration node has quite a few subnodes. This area is the closest to the options available in the policies of earlier versions of Windows NT.

FIGURE 11.11

Windows Settings

Computer Configuration\Windows Settings

In Figure 11.12 you can see the subnodes in the Computer Configuration: \ Windows Settings area of the Group Policy structure.

> As with most of the administrative actions that you can take within the Windows 2000 operating system, there are numerous ways to accomplish many of these tasks. I've gotten used to adding the appropriate snap-in to the MMC (if necessary) and using it for most of my administration. The figures in this chapter were all made using the MMC—but be aware that there is also a separate tool called the Group Policy Editor that can perform these tasks.

FIGURE 11.12

Computer Configuration: Windows Settings

Windows Settings\Scripts

In this subnode you can designate scripts (basically batch files) that will run at either system start-up or shutdown. Some of the actions you might include in these scripts are

- Deleting temporary files
- Running anti-virus software
- Performing system diagnostics

The list is limited only by your imagination!

Windows Settings\Security Settings

This section of the Computer Configuration policy settings is most like those options available in the policies of earlier versions of Windows NT.

Windows Settings\Security Settings\Account Policies

As you can see in Figure 11.13, there are three subnodes in this section.

- Password Policy includes options to control the use of passwords such as minimum length, maximum age, and whether a password history should be maintained. One of the new options here is the ability to define rules that govern the password a user is allowed to choose. You can define a template, for instance, that mandates the use of at least one alpha and one numeric character.

- Account Lockout Policy includes how long an account is locked out and how many bad login attempts will trigger lockout.

- Kerberos Policy includes the ability to configure various attributes of the Kerberos security environment.

Windows Settings\Security Settings\Local Policies

As shown in Figure 11.14, the Local Policies node also contains three subnodes.

- Audit Policy allows you to control which events should be audited on this computer.

- User Rights Assignment includes the ability to control who can use specific system rights (such as the right to change the system time or shut down the system) on this computer.

- Security Options include parameters to control numerous aspects of the computer's environment—everything from who can eject removable media to who can rename the administrator account.

The next few nodes are shown in Figure 11.15.

FIGURE 11.15

Additional Security
Settings nodes

- Event Log
- Restricted Groups
- System Services
- Registry
- File System
- Public Key Policies
  - Encrypted Data Recovery Agents
  - Automatic Certificate Request Settings
  - Trusted Root Certification Authorities
  - Enterprise Trust
- IP Security Policies on Active Directory

Windows Settings\Security Settings\Event Log

This node includes only one subnode, Settings for Event Logs. Here you can configure options such as the maximum size of the log files and what should happen when the log files are full.

Windows Settings\Security Settings\Restricted Groups

This is a new feature in Windows 2000. You can define which user accounts can be a member of any group by making it a *restricted group*. In the policy, the computer will honor only those users who are listed in the allowed member list. This prevents someone from managing to add him- or herself to an administrative group and then using those privileges.

Windows Settings\Security Settings\System Services

In this node, you will find settings that allow you to control the various services that load on the computer. The options for each service are the following:

- Load automatically at system startup
- Set for manual load
- Disable

It took me awhile to think of a use for this one, but once I did, it opened up a lot of options. I now configure a policy for all of my servers, limiting which services they can run. This prevents a remote administrator from loading a service that I wish to control, such as putting up his own DHCP server.

Windows Settings\Security Settings\Registry

In this area, you can add new keys to the local Registry of the computer.

This is an option that should only be used by experienced Windows 2000 administrators!

Windows Settings\Security Settings\File System

In this node you can set permissions to files or folders, thus enforcing security through the group policy.

Windows Settings\Security Settings\Public Key Policies

Here you can manage various aspects of certificate-based security.

Windows Settings\Security Settings\IP Security Policies on Active Directory

Here you can manage various aspects of the secure IP environment.

Computer Configuration\Administrative Templates

This node has four subnodes as shown in Figure 11.16.

FIGURE 11.16

Administrative
Templates

```
⊟ ⬜ Administrative Templates
   ⊞ ⬜ Windows Components
   ⊞ ⬜ System
   ⊞ ⬜ Network
      ⬜ Printers
```

- Windows Components

- System

- Network

- Printers

Administrative Templates\Windows Components

This node has the subnodes shown in Figure 11.17. The basic functionality of this area is to configure aspects of some of the fundamental pieces of the Windows 2000 environment.

FIGURE 11.17

Windows Components

- NetMeeting

- Internet Explorer

- Task Scheduler

- Windows Installer

Administrative Templates\System

This node contains the five subnodes shown in Figure 11.18. This is one of the more useful areas of the group policy object—there are many options here that will be useful in even the smallest of environments.

FIGURE 11.18

System

- Logon
- Disk Quotas
- DNS Clients

- Group Policy
- Windows File Protection

System\Logon

Here you can control various aspects of the logon process, such as whether start-up scripts should be visible when they run or whether cached copies of roaming profiles should be deleted.

System\Disk Quotas

One of the new features of Windows 2000 is the ability to set usage limits on disk space. This section allows you to turn this feature on and then configure various options, such as the space limit and what should happen when the limit is reached.

System\DNS Client

Here you can mandate the suffix used to identify the computer in DNS.

System\Group Policy

In this node, you can configure how group policies are processed on the computer. You can determine which nodes should be processed, whether they should refresh in the background, and how slow links should be dealt with.

System\Windows File Protection

Windows 2000 scans system files on a regular basis to determine if changes have occurred. This protects against a corrupted driver causing problems in the operating system itself. Here you can configure various options of this process.

The next two subnodes of Administrative Templates are shown in Figure 11.19.

FIGURE 11.19

Network and Printers nodes

- Network node
- Printers node

In the Network node, you will find options to control the Offline Files service and the Network and Dial-up Connections services. The Printers node controls options involved with the printing environment, such as whether printers can be published to the directory.

User Configuration

In the User Configuration node, shown in Figure 11.20, you will find three subnodes:

- Software Settings, which we discussed earlier

- Windows Settings, which include options to control aspects of the Windows 2000 environment

- Administrative Templates, which expand upon the capabilities available in the Computer Configuration node

FIGURE 11.20

User Configuration

```
User Configuration
  Software Settings
  Windows Settings
  Administrative Templates
```

User Configuration\Windows Settings

The Windows Settings node contains the subnodes shown in Figure 11.21.

FIGURE 11.21

Windows Settings

```
Windows Settings
  Internet Explorer Maintenance
  Scripts (Logon/Logoff)
  Security Settings
  Remote Installation Services
  Folder Redirection
```

- Internet Explorer Maintenance allows you to configure various options for users' use of Internet Explorer. Some of the more interesting options include the ability to define entries for the users'

Favorites List, set the Home Page parameter, and configure Channels (including turning them off).

- Scripts allows you to write scripts to run as the user logs on to or off of the network.

- Security Settings allows you to configure various aspects of the Public Key encryption security environment.

- Remote Installation Services allows you to configure parameters of a remote installation of the Windows 2000 operating system, if you are set up for that installation.

- Folder Redirection allows you to redirect a user's application data, Documents folder, Desktop preferences, or Start menu through a policy. Enabling this useful policy option means that a user can log on at *any* computer and always access their own environment (assuming you have redirected it to a place accessible from the network).

User Configuration\Administrative Templates

For users, this is the area that contains options most like those that were offered in earlier versions of Windows NT policies. As shown in Figure 11.22, there are six subnodes to the Administrative Templates node.

FIGURE 11.22

Administrative
Templates

```
└─ Administrative Templates
   ├─ Windows Components
   ├─ Start Menu & Taskbar
   ├─ Desktop
   ├─ Control Panel
   ├─ Network
   └─ System
```

- Windows Components allows you (as in the Computer Configuration node) to configure various aspects of Windows 2000, such as Net-Meeting, Internet Explorer, and Windows Explorer.

- Start Menu & Taskbar allows you to configure the various options that will appear in the Start menu and how they will look to the user. You can, for instance, disable or remove the links to the Windows Update, remove common program groups, remove the Help menu, or disable logoff.

- **Desktop** allows you to configure the appearance of the user's Desktop. Options include the ability to hide specific icons (My Network or Internet Explorer), prohibit the user from changing the My Documents path, or (my personal favorite) Don't save settings at exit.

- **Control Panel** allows you to configure which applets appear in the Control Panel.

- **Network** gives you the same options as the **Network** node of the Computer Configuration area.

- **System** allows you to configure various options of the operating system, such as disabling access to the command prompt, disabling Autoplay, or disabling Registry-editing tools.

Whew—quite a list isn't it? The amount of control available through the use of group policies in Windows 2000 is staggering (and maybe even overwhelming). Now that we've looked at the types of things you can control, let's look at the procedures involved in using group policies.

Configuring Group Policy Settings

Since the options available within the group policy realm are so diverse, there are differences in the ways that many of them are configured. Fortunately, there will be certain similarities among "types" of parameters. In this section, we will look at a few of the different configuration procedures that you will use to set policy parameters.

The Three-Way Toggle

Many of the options will be a basic on/off switch with a twist. The twist is inherent in the way that policies work. Remember that a policy writes to the local Registry of the client computer. *Enabling* the policy turns something on, *disabling* a policy turns something off—so far so good, right? There is one last option, the *Not Configured* option. You can see these three options in the sample shown in Figure 11.23.

FIGURE 11.23

Three configuration
options

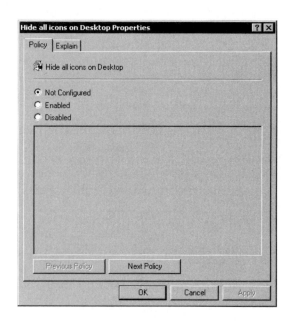

There are two issues to be aware of when making these choices. First, read the description of the parameter carefully. Often descriptions are written in the negative, such as Don't turn on XYZ. If you enable this type of policy option, XYZ will be turned *off* instead of on. Watch for double negatives!

The second issue to be aware of is the action taken when you choose Not Configured. You might assume that this would reverse an option that was configured earlier—not so! Whatever is already in the Registry will remain there! To reverse a decision, you must pick the opposite of what your original choice was.

Setting Amounts

Some options will allow you to configure a limit of some sort. You might, for instance, want to place a default limit on the amount of disk space that users can use. This option is shown in Figure 11.24.

Here you will type your value in the dialog boxes provided.

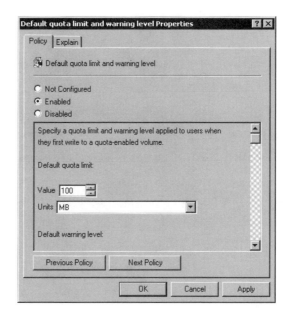

FIGURE 11.24

Setting Volume quotas

Creating Lists

Some options might be made up of a list, such as the option to limit the applets available in Control Panel. Here you would add the name of the applet to the list by clicking the Show button, as shown in Figure 11.25.

As you can see, configuring most of the options will be a matter of common sense (and figuring out where they are in the list of available options).

Determining Which Policy Will Be Applied

Having looked at the options available and how to configure them, the next step is to determine how and why policies are applied to users, groups, and computers. We'll look at how policies are applied by default and then we'll look at how those defaults can be changed.

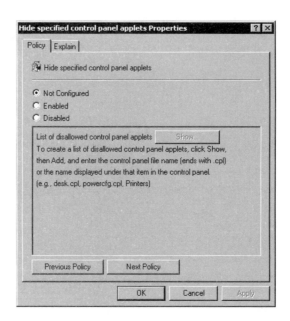

First, let me stress one last time:

- User policies are obtained when a *user* logs on to the network.

- Computer policies are obtained when a computer boots.

No other classes of objects receive policies—just users and computers.

The Order in Which Policies Are Applied

As we discussed earlier, policies can be associated with various objects in the Active Directory structure—domains, sites, and organizational units. There is also a local policy that is stored on and managed at the local client computer. Since we have the option to place policies at various points in our hierarchy, the first question that should come to mind is "Which policy or policies will apply to which users and computers?" In a perfect world, the answer to this question would be short and sweet. Unfortunately, a simple answer would probably also imply a simple solution, and a simple solution would not meet the needs of today's complex networks. The truth of the matter is that most of the rest of this chapter will revolve around answering that "simple" question.

Default Order of Application

The default order in which group policies are applied is:

1. The local policy, if one exists.

2. Policies assigned to the ADS site object, in an order specified by the administrator.

3. Policies assigned to the domain, in an order specified by the administrator.

4. Policies assigned to organizational units, starting at the top of the ADS tree and working from parent to child OU until the context of the object (user or computer) has been reached. Once again, if an OU has more than one policy, they will be applied in an order set by the administrator.

This order can be influenced in numerous ways, but the default behavior is that the policies are applied in the order listed above. Each policy that is processed will override those settings made in policies applied earlier in the process. In other words, if a parameter is set to "true" in the local policy, the site policy could change it to "false," the domain policy could change it back to "true," and then various OU policies could change it back and forth so many times that it could be hard to determine what the settings will be once the process is done! The point here is that the implementation of group policies takes some prior planning to avoid these kinds of issues.

The general philosophy is that the policies should be designed so that the least restrictive are applied first. You should plan your policy strategy so that the policies are more restrictive as they work through the order. This means that:

- Local policies should be the least restrictive. In most companies, local policies won't be used at all so that all policy management can occur within the Active Directory database.

- Site policies should be extremely generic. Perhaps you have decided that no computer should display the last logged-in username in the "Log onto Windows" dialog box. This type of overall configuration is best done in the policy that will affect the most users, such as the policy assigned to the site.

We'll talk about sites in Chapter 13, "Understanding and Controlling ADS Sites and Replications."

- Domain policies should contain configurations that are specific to the needs of the users and computers defined within the domain. This sounds obvious, but as you'll see in Chapter 13, it is possible for a single site to contain resources from multiple domains. This option allows you to be a little more specific as to who or what will be affected by a policy. Here you might want to configure the DNS suffix that all computers within the domain will use when dynamically updating DNS.

- Organizational unit policies should contain configuration parameters that apply to a branch of your ADS tree. Perhaps no users in the Sales OU (and those OUs under it in the tree) should be allowed to run programs other than those that are company approved. Here you could configure the policy with the list of approved programs.

You can use this cascading effect to reduce the number of places in which you have to manage certain parameters—sweeping parameters only have to be configured once (in the site or domain policy), rather than in each OU policy.

Creating Policy Objects

Look at the ADS organizational unit structure shown in Figure 11.26. In our example, we have an education OU that contains a Michigan OU, and contains OUs for each of the levels of schools that we support. This seems like a workable design—resources from each type of school can be placed within a container that represents their type (K-6, Middle, or High schools). (Under these three containers, we could also have containers for each individual school—but we'll leave out that level of container to avoid confusing the issue.)

Within this type of structure, certain aspects of our users' environment will be similar. All of our students, for instance, should be able to use Internet Explorer. Other items of control, though, will differ based upon age group—first-graders should probably have a different Home Page setting

F I G U R E   11.26

The education
department

than high-school students. This is where the cascading nature of group policies comes in handy.

Our first step will be to determine which type of policy files we wish to use—local, site, domain, or organizational. Because we won't discuss ADS sites until Chapter 13, we'll avoid them here. The process of assigning a policy to a site is the same as for assigning one to a domain or OU. In real life we would sit down with the teachers and administrators and ask for input: What types of controls do they desire, and how sweeping should those decisions be? After our research we might come up with a list that looks something like this:

All students:

- Advertise basic programs to all computers—word processing, spreadsheet, and database.

- Run a script that checks for viruses each time a user logs on.

- Do not allow printers to be published to ADS.

- Limit access to the Display Options in Control Panel.

Based upon grade:

- Add appropriate URLs to the Favorites List in Internet Explorer.

- Assign specific applications.

- Redirect all data, desktop settings, and other personal information to network locations.

In a real-world scenario, the list would probably cover pages, but for our purposes this should be sufficient. As you can see, there are certain policies that should apply to all students, and others that should only be applied to specific groups of students.

The second step in our process will be to determine which policies should be applied to computers and which to users. Some of the parameters will only be available to one or the other, but some can be configured in either manner.

The next step is to determine the type of policy to use—local, site, domain, or organizational unit. Since our environment is a single domain and a single site, we could use either a site or a domain policy as our most generic. Given our single-branch scenario, we could even use a higher-level OU as our least restrictive policy—but since this would be rare in a true business, we'll follow a more conventional strategy.

Creating a Policy for a Site, Domain, or Organizational Unit

To create a policy, start the MMC. On the Console menu, choose Add/ Remove Snap-in, as shown in Figure 11.27.

F I G U R E 11.27

Add/Remove Snap-in

The Add/Remove Snap-in dialog box, shown in Figure 11.28, will appear. This dialog box shows the snap-in modules that you have already added to your console. (Remember that the point of the MMC tool is to allow you to manage almost everything using a single application. Notice that I've added quite a few snap-ins to my interface.)

Click the Add button and you will be presented with a list of the available snap-ins. Double-click the Group Policy option and the Group Policy Object wizard will begin, as shown in Figure 11.29.

Your first decision is whether to work with the group policy of the local machine or to work with/create an ADS group policy object. To accomplish the latter option, click the Browse button. As you can see in Figure 11.30, you will then be able to determine what type (site, domain, or organizational unit) policy you wish to work with.

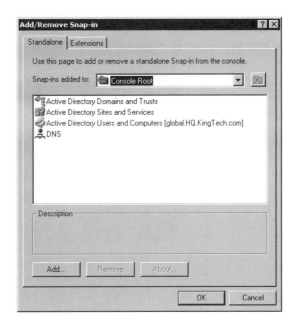

F I G U R E   11.28

Add/Remove Snap-in
dialog box

F I G U R E   11.29

The Group Policy
Object wizard

FIGURE 11.30

Browse for a Group
Policy Object

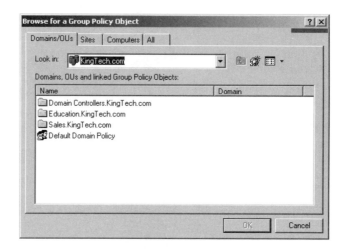

If you wish to add an existing policy to your MMC console, browse this
screen and select it. To create a new GPO, browse to the domain, site, or container you wish to associate your new GPO with, right-click empty space in
the list, and choose New, as shown in Figure 11.31.

FIGURE 11.31

Creating a new GPO

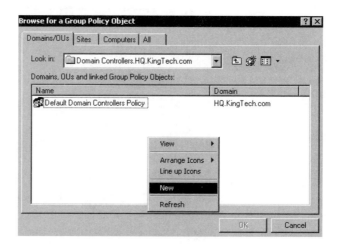

Click OK and Finish, and your new GPO will appear in the MMC console. We follow the same steps to assign policies to each of the organizational

units in which we want to create a group policy object. For our example, I'm also going to create one in the K-6 container. Our final MMC console will contain both GPOs, as shown in Figure 11.32.

FIGURE 11.32

KingTech Domain Policies

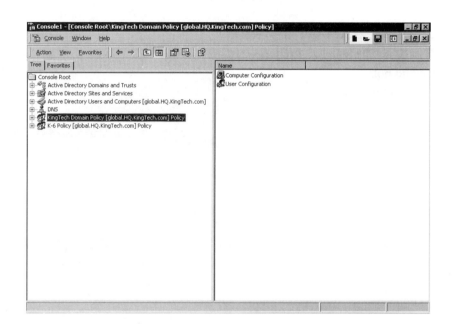

 Notice that the names that I've given my group policy object readily identify where they exist in my ADS structure. Look at Figure 11.32 again—without proper naming standards, it wouldn't be clear where they would be applied.

Linking Policies to Containers

While basic inheritance will see to it that a policy created in one organizational unit will flow down the ADS structure to lower OUs, there might be instances where you would like to apply the same GPO to containers that are not related in a parent/child relationship—in other words, one policy that applied to two different branches of your structure. To do this, link your policy to whichever container you want it to apply to. Linking is accomplished by accessing the properties of the container itself. In MMC, highlight the container, right-click, and choose Properties. On the Group Policy tab, shown in Figure 11.33, you will find a list of policies that have been linked to this container.

FIGURE 11.33

Linking policies to containers

If more than one policy is linked to a container, this same list will determine the order in which they are processed. Those higher in the list have higher priority, which means they are processed last. (That can take a little thought—just remember that since policies can overwrite each others' settings, the last one to process will make the final changes.)

Taking Control

If planned carefully, the default order of cascading group policies can work fairly well. The problem is that it is often necessary to have a policy apply to one group of users but not another, even if those users exist in the same organizational unit. At other times, you might want to allow one container within your ADS structure to set its own policy without having to worry about it being overwritten by a policy in a lower container. The opposite is also true—there might be a time where you want a lower level policy to be the *only* policy applied to the users in an organizational unit.

Based upon what we've discussed so far, these cases would require very careful planning of both the placement of policies *and* the very ADS organizational units themselves. Luckily, Microsoft has provided us with three methods for taking control of which policies will be applied in any given situation. Those three methods are:

- Filtering policies by security group membership

- Blocking policy inheritance

- Preventing a policy from being overwritten by policies above it in the ADS tree

By understanding the default mechanisms involved in policy inheritance and the various methods available to override those defaults, an administrator can use group policies to take complete control over their network.

Filtering Policies through Group Membership

Each GPO created has its own set of properties as an object in the ADS structure. These properties refer to the *object*—not to the parameters that the GPO passes to the user or computer applying the policy itself. To see these properties, right-click the GPO in the MMC and choose Properties, as shown in Figure 11.34.

FIGURE 11.34

Accessing the properties of a GPO

You will be presented with the Properties dialog box of the group policy object, an example of which is shown in Figure 11.35.

The Properties dialog box of a GPO can be used to gather information about the policy, manage the policy, determine where the policy will be applied, and manage who will use the policy.

F I G U R E 11.35

Properties of a GPO

Figure 11.35 shows the General tab of the GPO Properties dialog box. As you can see, this opening screen provides some useful information, such as when the GPO was created, the last time it was modified, and its SID. You can also disable the computer or user portion of the policy to improve performance: If you create a policy but only use one portion or the other (user or computer), you can disable the other, thus preventing the unused portion from being downloaded to the client computer for processing.

The Links tab of the GPO Properties dialog box is shown in Figure 11.36. Here you can have the system perform a search to determine which sites, domains, and organizational units will use this policy. The results of this search can be useful when troubleshooting a policy problem. Because of the complex set of inheritance rules for GPO application, it is sometimes difficult to determine which policies are in effect in each container.

The Security tab of the GPO Properties dialog box is shown in Figure 11.37. Like any other object in the ADS database, GPOs have access control lists (ACLs). The ACL lists those objects that have been granted permissions to the object itself. GPOs have a unique permission—look at the bottom of the permissions list in Figure 11.37 and you will see the "Apply Group Policy" permission.

FIGURE 11.36

Links tab of the GPO
Properties dialog box

FIGURE 11.37

Security tab of
the GPO Properties
dialog box

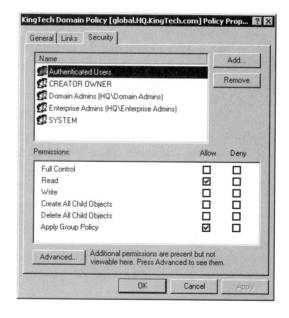

The permissions shown in Figure 11.37 are the default permissions granted when a group policy object is created. Table 11.1 lists these default permissions.

TABLE 11.1 Default Permissions to a GPO	User or Group	Permissions
	Authenticated Users	Read, Apply Group Policy
	Creator Owner	None
	Domain Admins	Read, Write, Create All Child Objects, Delete All Child Objects
	Enterprise Admins	Read, Write, Create All Child Objects, Delete All Child Objects
	System	Read, Write, Create All Child Objects, Delete All Child Objects

The important assignment for our discussion here is that assignment made to all authenticated users. Basically, this assignment is what creates the default rules. Any user who logs into the network and whose user object exists in this domain (since this is a domain policy) will have the policy applied to them.

As an example, let's return to the KingTech education department. The policies we've discussed so far have all revolved around the needs of the students—limiting their ability to change configurations, or adding tools that they will need to their Desktops and applications. The problem with the default GPO assignments is that this policy will also be applied to the teachers and administrative staff at KingTech (since they too will be authenticated users in this domain). To correct this, we could create a security group—perhaps named "Students"—and change the default permissions to this GPO. Remove the Authenticated Users from the list and add the Students security group, as shown in Figure 11.38.

FIGURE 11.38

Using security groups
to limit GPOs

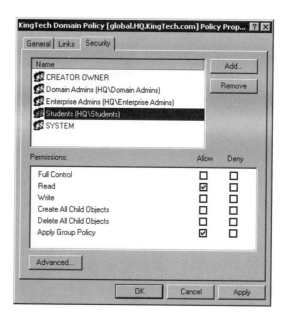

Make sure to give the Students group both the Read permission and the Apply Group Policy permission. Without the Read permission, they would be unable to read the various parameters set in the policy itself.

Blocking Policy Inheritance

At any site, domain, or organizational unit, group policy inheritance can be set to block the inheritance of group policies. Because this setting is made directly to the site, domain, or OU, instead of to a particular GPO, it will block *all* policies from reaching the designated area. In effect, you are creating an autonomous branch of your structure that will not inherit policies from above itself in the tree.

To block the inheritance of group policies, access the properties of the site, domain, or OU where you wish the block to begin. To do this, highlight it in the MMC, right-click, and choose Properties. You will be presented with the Properties dialog box of the object. On the Group Policy tab, shown in Figure 11.39, you will find an option to Block Policy inheritance. Select this option, and inheritance will be blocked.

FIGURE 11.39

Blocking inheritance

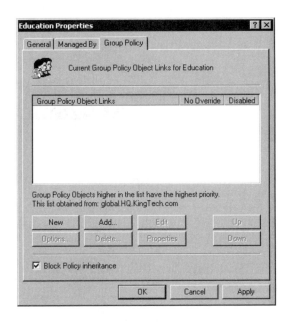

FIGURE 11.39

Blocking inheritance

Mandating a Policy

While there will be times when you want to block inheritance as we just discussed, there will be other times when you want to ensure that a higher level policy setting is not overwritten by a policy later in the policy list. To prevent a policy from being overwritten, access the properties of the container in which you wish to protect the policy. On the Group Policy tab, click the Options button. You will be presented with the dialog box shown in Figure 11.40.

FIGURE 11.40

Policy Options dialog box

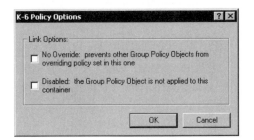

Here you can either select the No Override option or disable the policy in this container.

In Short

Group policies give a network administrator complete control over the user's environment. Given that many Help desk calls revolve around user configuration errors—"I was just trying to change my color scheme" or "I didn't know I couldn't pick my own IP address"—properly configured group policies should reduce the administration necessary to support end-users.

In the next chapter, we will look at the process for extending the ADS schema to include objects that are specific to your environment—perhaps some software package needs a new object class defined or perhaps you would like to store employee identification numbers as an attribute of each user's network account. Whatever the reason, you will probably need to extend the ADS schema at some point.

CHAPTER
12

Modifying the Active
Directory Schema

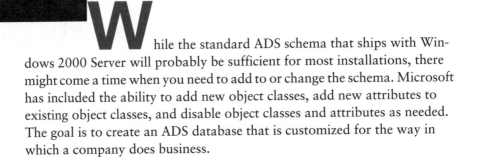

While the standard ADS schema that ships with Windows 2000 Server will probably be sufficient for most installations, there might come a time when you need to add to or change the schema. Microsoft has included the ability to add new object classes, add new attributes to existing object classes, and disable object classes and attributes as needed. The goal is to create an ADS database that is customized for the way in which a company does business.

Schema Basics

To review, the *schema* of the Active Directory database defines the objects that can be stored there. It is the formal definition of the object classes and attributes that exist in the database. The ADS database is no different from any other database that you have worked with in the past. Before you can place information within it, you must lay out a structure to define how to store that data.

What's in a Schema?

Imagine you were going to build a database to hold the telephone numbers and addresses of your business contacts. You wouldn't just start entering names and addresses, would you? The first step would be to decide exactly what information you would like to store. Your list might include:

- Company
- First name

- Last name
- Nickname
- Address
- City
- State
- Zip code
- Country
- Telephone number
- Pager/cellular phone number
- Fax number
- E-mail address

The next step would be to lay out the fields for each record, as shown in Table 12.1. You will need to decide the type of data each field will hold and the maximum size of each field, as well as add any special formatting requirements that are necessary for consistency.

T A B L E 12.1:   Contact Database Structure

Field	Type	Size (Characters)	Formatting
Company	Text	50	
First name	Text	20	
Last name	Text	20	
Nickname	Text	20	
Address	Text	50	
City	Text	25	
State	Text	2	Should provide a pick list for consistent abbreviations

T A B L E 12.1: Contact Database Structure *(continued)*

Field	Type	Size (Characters)	Formatting
Zip code	Text	9	#####-####
Country	Text	2	Should provide a pick list for consistent abbreviations; use the two-letter abbreviations provided by the X.500 committee
Telephone number	Text	11	#-###-###-####
Fax number	Text	11	#-###-###-####
Pager/cellular phone number	Text	11	#-###-###-####
E-mail address	Text	25	

Once you have decided the structure of each record, you are ready to build your database—unless you decide to add a bit more functionality. (To programmers this is known as *feature creep.*) You might also want to store records of each time you have been in touch with each of your contacts. You could do this by expanding the list in Table 12.1 to include a unique identifier, then using that unique field to relate to another database file. In the second file, you would then repeat the process of defining the fields that it would contain, as shown in Table 12.2.

T A B L E 12.2: Related Files

Field	Type	Size	Formatting	Related to
Unique ID	Numeric	3		Unique ID in contact list
Date	Date		US standard	
Length of contact	Numeric	10	Number of minutes	
Notes	Text	Variable length		

NOTE The total description of your contacts database, including the description of each field, the relationships between files, any pre-made drop-down lists, and any other information about how the database is structured is known as its schema. Every database has a schema, some more complex than others.

The Active Directory Schema

The schema of the Active Directory database is much more complex than that of our contact list database. Within the ADS database, each different type of record defined is known as an *object class*. The fields, known as *attributes*, for each class might be different from those for other defined classes. The ADS schema, for instance, must include definitions for the following database attributes:

Multiple record types in a single database   Traditional databases had one record type defined for each file in the related system of files. In the ADS database, we must define a record type for each class of object that we wish to use in our environment.

Multivalue attributes   Certain characteristics of an object class need to store more than one value. A user's telephone number attribute, for instance, might need to store multiple telephone numbers for a single user.

How the various pieces of the database fit together   This is necessary due to the distributed nature of the ADS database. Remember that this database is divided into partitions (domains), which are spread across multiple servers. Something in the schema must define how these partitions find each other, communicate, and share information as needed.

Attributes holding pointers to all other replicas of the same partition   There might be multiple copies of a single partition; without these attributes, the replication of database changes could not take place.

A mechanism to track changes   The replication process requires this of each object and each attribute of each object. This mechanism includes both the up-to-date vector and a time stamp.

Variable, rather than static, attribute lengths   Some of the data that the database will hold might be textual and the database might grow quite large—over a million objects in a single partition. In other words, each record in the database should take up only as much disk space as necessary but should have the ability to grow as more information is added.

A hierarchy of object classes   To reduce redundant design, the schema is built upon this hierarchy, with subordinate classes inheriting attributes from higher-level object classes.

To make matters even more complex, the Active Directory database schema must be fully—and easily—extensible so that it can grow to meet the changing needs of a dynamic business environment. In other words, the schema must be readily accessible so that changes to the database structure can be made. Make changes to the Active Directory schema by using the Active Directory Schema Manager included with Windows 2000 Server.

You can also write scripts that make Active Directory Services interface calls to accomplish this task. We'll discuss the Active Directory Schema Manager later in this chapter.

At the top of any LDAP-compliant directory service (such as Microsoft Active Directory), there is a special container known as rootDSE. When referring to this container, the appropriate syntax is to refer to LDAP:// rootDSE. The rootDSE container contains a number of entries, including the definition of the namespace of the LDAP structure and the schema of the database. The schema itself is stored in the subcontainer that follows the naming context:

CN=schema, CN=configuration, DC=domain_name, DC=domain_root

For our purposes, we really don't even have to know where the actual schema is stored—the tools provided by Microsoft will find it. But it is interesting to note that Microsoft has used the industry standard location so that other LDAP-compliant directory services can communicate (and perhaps synchronize) with ADS.

Who Can Modify the Schema?

To make changes to the schema, a user must be a member of the Schema Admins group. By default, the Administrator user account is a member of this group. While you can add other user accounts to the Schema Admins group, due to the nature of the task—which is complex and has far-reaching consequences—most companies will probably stick with the default.

What Can Be Modified?

When modifying the directory schema, you may perform the following tasks:

- Create new classes
- Modify existing classes
- Create new attributes
- Modify existing attributes
- Deactivate classes
- Deactivate attributes

When you modify the schema, you are making a change that impacts the structure of the Active Directory database. This is not something that should be done lightly! Before you modify the schema, Microsoft suggests that you review the existing schema to determine if an existing object class or attribute can fulfill your needs.

Modifying Existing Classes or Attributes

Once you have determined that no existing class or attribute will fit your needs, consider modifying the schema. If at all possible, try to modify an existing object or attribute rather than creating a new one.

A user object, for example, has many attributes that might not be applicable to your environment. There are numerous tabs filled with attributes for a user object. You will probably not use all of these attributes in your environment.

Changing a display name for an existing attribute is one of the least intrusive ways to modify the schema to meet your needs.

Modify an existing object class if all you need are new attributes. User objects are probably the best example of this situation. Many companies will want to store specific information about users in the directory. Often the generic definition of a user will not contain the additional attributes necessary. If your users do a lot of traveling, for instance, you might want to add attributes that store travel preferences, such as airline frequent-flyer information or smoking/nonsmoking preferences.

Creating an Auxiliary Class

An *auxiliary class* is really just an extension of an existing object class. For example, you might have two types of users: permanent and temporary. While the normal user object might be perfect for your permanent employees, you might wish to create an auxiliary class for your temporary workers. The auxiliary class Temp Workers would be based upon the User class, inheriting all of the attributes of the User class, but could be modified to fit your needs. Basically, an auxiliary class acts as a shortcut—rather than starting from scratch creating a new class, you can start with an existing set of attributes and work from there.

Adding New Classes and Attributes

Add new attributes when no existing attribute meets your needs or can be modified to meet your needs. This can be an extensive change to the directory database, and you should think carefully before you do it.

The most intrusive and potentially dangerous change is to add a new object class. You should take this action only when no other option will fit the needs of your environment.

Can Classes and Attributes Be Deleted?

There is no way to delete an object class or attribute that is in the schema. You can, however, *deactivate* either a class or an attribute. We'll discuss deactivation in the next section.

As you can see, there are numerous types of modifications that can be made to the Active Directory database. While the process is straightforward (albeit not exactly easy), modifying the schema is not something that you should do without prior planning. Any time you change the structure of a database you risk damaging it—not something you want to happen to your network's directory!

Deactivating Classes and Attributes

Classes and attributes are never removed from the schema. Instead, they are deactivated and marked as unused. This prevents irreversible mistakes and improves performance by not forcing a time-consuming cleanup of removed items.

Deactivating an item is functionally the same as deleting it, but deactivation leaves you the option of reversing your action at a later date.

Here is what happens when you deactivate an object class or attribute:

- That object class or attribute is no longer replicated throughout the network or to the global catalog server.

- You may no longer create objects that are part of the deactivated class or enter data into the attribute. Attempts to do so will return the same error as if the class or attribute had never existed.

- When an attribute is deactivated, you may no longer use it in definitions of new object classes or add it to an existing class.

- Objects created prior to the deactivation remain in the ADS database and will appear in the various tools. You may not, however, change attributes of them; your only real management option is to delete them.

- Deactivated object classes and attributes still appear in searches, for two reasons:

  - You can search for the deactivated information in order to clean up your directory.

  - You might not have deleted those objects that were created before the deactivation (which means you might need to search for them at some point).

- You cannot create new objects or attributes with the same name, LDAP display name, or object identifier. This rule is only common sense, since the deactivated object class or attribute is still defined in the schema.

We'll discuss object identifiers later in this chapter.

What Cannot Be Modified?

The bulleted list at the end of the "What Can Be Modified?" section seems to imply that you can make just about any type of change to the directory that you desire. For the most part, this assumption is true. There are, however, a few notable exceptions.

There are certain attributes and object classes that cannot be disabled or changed. Any attribute whose name begins with the word system cannot be changed. This allows Active Directory to protect those attributes that are critical to its functioning.

This rule also applies to object classes that you create. If at the time of creation you list any attribute as system, that attribute cannot be changed later.

Modifying the Schema

Earlier, you read about the concepts of multiple-master and single-master environments. Both *multiple master* and *single master* refer to the process used to replicate changes throughout a distributed replicated database. In a multiple-master environment, all copies of the database can accept changes and can replicate those changes to all other copies. In a single-master environment, such as the PDC/BDC relationship used in earlier versions of NT, only one copy of the database can accept changes, and the server that holds the copy (the primary domain controller) is responsible for replicating them to all other domain controllers.

While Windows 2000 Server is a multiple-master environment when it comes to replicating changes to the information stored within the directory database, it is a single-master environment when it comes to replicating changes to the schema. In other words, there is only one domain controller, known as the *schema master*, on which schema modifications can be made at any given time. In Active Directory, these single-master operations are known as *Floating Single Master Operations* (FSMO). The domain controller that is acting as the schema master is also known as the *schema FSMO*.

What Happens When the Schema Is Modified?

When the schema is modified, there is a delay before the changes take effect. This delay is incurred because there are actually two copies of the schema:

- One in memory
- One in the Active Directory

When a modification is made, the change is written to the Active Directory database. Active Directory waits for five minutes after the schema update before it commits the changes to the copy in memory. The copy in memory, known as the *cache schema*, is the schema that is current.

> In other words, the copy of the schema used by various system processes and threads is the one stored in memory. This means that approximately five minutes will pass between the time you stop making changes to the schema and the time those changes become apparent.

The reason that the time is approximate is that there might be processes running at the time of the change. Rather than replace the old schema with the new one (in memory), the old and new schemas coexist until all current processes have ended. All new processes are pointed to the new schema, but any running processes continue to use the old. This prevents the introduction of a new schema from corrupting an active process.

During this five-minute interval, you cannot add objects that use a new or modified class or attribute. In other words, you must wait until the update has completed before making use of your changes.

Preparing for Schema Modifications

There are four preliminary steps you must complete before you can proceed with the task of modifying the Active Directory schema:

1. Obtain an OID (Object Identifier) for each new class or attribute you intend to create.

2. Verify your membership in the Schema Admins group.

3. Install Active Directory Schema Manager.

4. Set Registry settings that allow schema modifications.

So far, we've discussed the process of making modifications to the directory as if it were a common administrative practice. As you'll see, this is far from the case!

Obtaining OIDs

OIDs are globally unique object identifiers. By global, I mean that these identifiers are used to define objects and attributes as they are applied to *any* directory service, from Microsoft Active Directory to Novell Directory Services. OIDs are registered with the International Standards Organization (ISO) issuing agency. By having a central group control how object classes and attributes are implemented, the industry can avoid incompatible network directories.

OIDs uniquely define data elements, syntaxes, and various other parts of distributed applications. ISO-issued OIDs are used in many standard technologies, including Open System Interconnection (OSI) applications, X.500 directories, Simple Network Management Protocol (SNMP), and many other applications where a unique identifier is important. Each object class and attribute must have a unique OID if it is to exist in the ADS schema. OIDs are organized in a hierarchical structure managed by the ISO.

While you probably won't need to understand the entire OID naming process, it is important to know that the OID represents a tree-like structure much like the container/subcontainer structure of ADS.

LDAP is an important protocol used for accessing information in network directories, such as Microsoft Active Directory. LDAP applications use the ISO-issued OIDs to identify the objects and attributes that are available in *any* directory to which they connect. In other words, to be LDAP accessible, every object and attribute within a directory must have an OID. (The OID itself becomes an attribute of each object defined.)

As stated earlier, the International Standards Organization acts as the issuing agent for new OIDs. To create a new object class or attribute within the ADS schema, the first step is to apply to the ISO for an OID. The OID will be expressed as a string of numbers delimited by decimals, such as 1.2.840.xxxxxx.w.y.z. Table 12.3 describes the purpose of each piece of our sample OID.

T A B L E 12.3	**Number**	**Represents**
Decoding OID 1.2.840.xxxxxx.w.y.z	1	This value acts as the root of the ISO hierarchy.
	2	American National Standards Institute (ANSI).
	840	United States.
	xxxxxx	The organization applying for the OID is given a unique identifier.
	w	A location within the organization.
	y	A division within the location.
	z	A group within the division.

Verifying Membership in the Schema Admins Group

Before anyone attempts to make any schema modifications, verify that the person who will perform the procedure is a member of the Schema Admins group. By default, the only member of this group is the Administrator account. (The Administrator account is automatically made a member of the Administrators, Domain Admins, Domain Users, Enterprise Admins, and Schema Admins groups.) Verify membership using the Active Directory Users and Computers tool found in the Administrative Tools group or in the MMC (after adding the appropriate snap-in). The process requires the following steps:

1. Start the Active Directory Users and Computers utility.

2. Click the domain, then double-click the Users OU. Groups and users will appear in the Details pane, as shown in Figure 12.1.

3. Find the Schema Admins group and double-click it. You will see the Schema Admins Properties dialog box, which is shown in Figure 12.2.

4. Click the Members tab, and ensure that the appropriate user is listed as a member. You can see this tab in Figure 12.3.

FIGURE 12.1

Active Directory Users and Groups

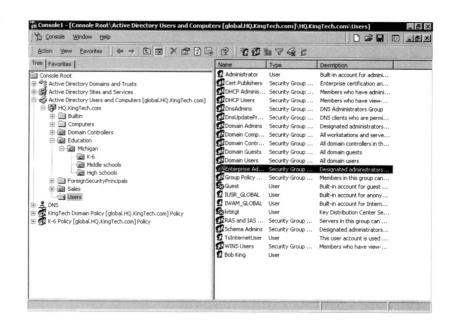

FIGURE 12.2

Schema Admins Properties dialog box

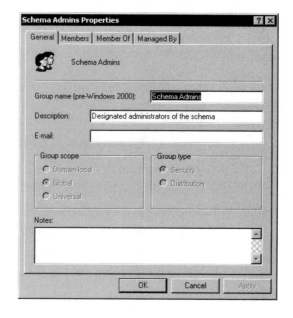

FIGURE 12.3

Members tab of the
Schema Admins
Properties window

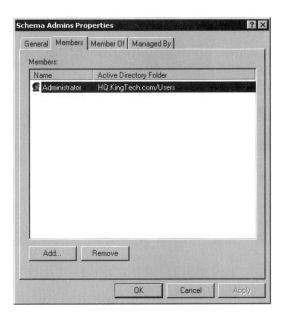

The default membership list, consisting only of the Administrator account, will be sufficient for most organizations.

WARNING Modifying the directory schema is not something that many people should be doing, and there should never be multiple people performing modifications simultaneously!

Installing Active Directory Schema Manager

Administrators do not modify the schema as a matter of course, so Microsoft has not installed the Active Directory Schema Manager utility as part of the standard Windows 2000 installation. Follow these steps to add this tool:

1. On the Run command, type **MMC** (for Microsoft Management Console). The MMC will appear, as shown in Figure 12.4.

2. From the Console menu, choose Add/Remove Snap-in. The Add/Remove Snap-in dialog box will appear, which you can see in Figure 12.5.

FIGURE 12.4

Microsoft
Management Console

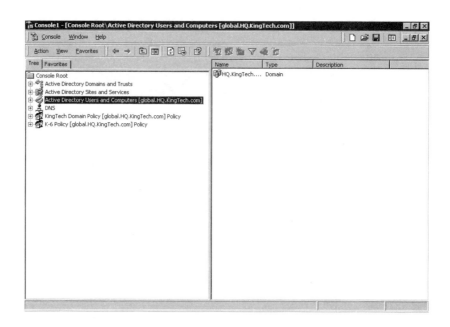

FIGURE 12.5

Add/Remove Snap-in
dialog box

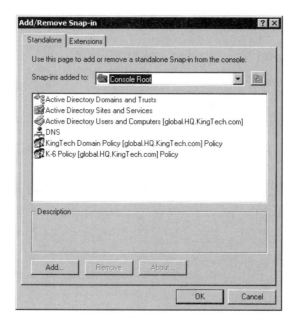

3. Click the Add button to access the Add Standalone Snap-in dialog box, as shown in Figure 12.6.

4. Highlight the Active Directory Schema Manager option and click Add.

If you do not see an entry for Active Directory Schema in the Add/Remove Snap-in dialog box, you need to install the Schema Manager. The Schema Manager is part of the Windows 2000 Administration Tools Package in Add/Remove Programs in the Control Panel. The option pack is located on the Windows 2000 Server Installation as `adminpak.msi`.

5. Click Close, and the Active Directory Schema option will be added to your MMC.

The Active Directory Schema Manager utility must be connected to the current FSMO before modifications can take place. To ensure that the utility is pointing to the correct server, highlight the Active Directory Schema Manager option in the MMC, right-click, and choose Advanced. The Advanced Schema Manager Properties dialog box will appear. You can see this dialog box in Figure 12.7.

FIGURE 12.7

Advanced Schema
Manager Properties
dialog box

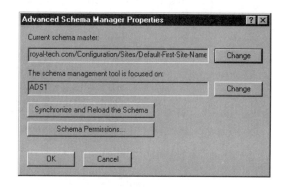

From here you can change the server that the Active Directory Schema Manager utility points to when making schema modifications. You can also set permissions to control which users and groups can perform certain functions in the ADS database, as shown in Figure 12.8.

FIGURE 12.8

Permissions for
Schema dialog box

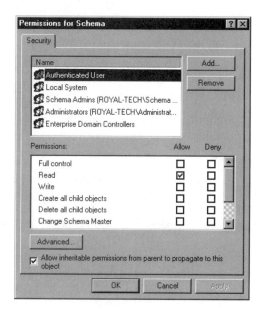

Here are the permissions available for the schema:

- Full control
- Read
- Write
- Create all child objects
- Delete all child objects
- Change Schema Master
- Replicate directory changes
- Manage replication topology
- Synchronize replication
- Update Schema Cache

The default permissions assignments are described in Table 12.4.

T A B L E 12.4 Default Schema Permissions	**User or Group**	**Permissions**
	Authenticated User	Read
	Local System	All permissions
	Schema Admins	All permissions except Full control and Delete all child objects
	Administrators	Replicate directory changes, Manage replication topology, Synchronize replication
	Enterprise Domain Controllers	Replicate directory changes, Manage replication topology, Synchronize replication

Setting the Registry to Allow Schema Modifications

By default, all domain controllers have Read-only access to the schema. To allow modifications, you must set a Registry setting on the domain controller that will act as the FSMO. The Registry parameter must be added to the Registry under the following key:

```
HKEY_Local_Machine\System\Current Control Set\
Services\NTDS\Parameters
```

Add the parameter **Schema Update Allowed** with a data type of REG_DWORD. Set this value to anything other than 0 to enable modifications.

Since only one domain controller can act as the FSMO, setting this parameter in the Registry automatically promotes the current domain controller to the FSMO (and demotes the old one).

Since the Registry is a critical component of the Windows 2000 environment, be sure that you back it up before making any changes. One wrong move and you'll end up having to reinstall NT because of a corrupted Registry!

The Five Types of Schema Modifications

As you read earlier, there are five types of modifications that you can make to the schema:

- Creating a new class
- Modifying an existing class
- Creating a new attribute
- Modifying an existing attribute
- Deactivating a class or an attribute

The next few sections discuss the procedures for accomplishing each of these tasks. All of them are accomplished through the Active Directory Schema Manager (ADSM) snap-in to the MMC that you read about earlier.

Creating a New Class

To create a new class, you create a *class-definition object*. In effect, this class-definition object becomes a container for the attributes that describe the object class. Within the ADSM utility, right-click the Class container and choose New ➤ Class. You will be presented with the Create New Class dialog box, which you can see in Figure 12.9.

FIGURE 12.9

Create New Class
dialog box

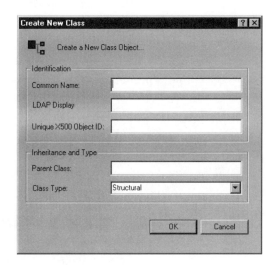

You will have to provide the following information:

Common Name This is mandatory and is used as the Common Name attribute for the object class. This is an indexed field and is used for searches of the database.

LDAP Display This is another mandatory field. This is what LDAP tools will display to users when they access the directory.

Unique X.500 Object ID This is the OID you received from the ISO.

You will also have to determine whether this class should be a child to another class. Children inherit the attributes of their parents. This section can be used to create a subtype of object without having to apply for redundant OIDs or set up redundant attributes. An example would be my company's ADS tree. While we have "normal employees," we also have a subset known as "instructors." The instructors subclass inherits all of the properties of the user object class, but it also has attributes that are specific to that type of user (vendor certifications, a list of courses taught, and so on).

There are three types of classes:

Structural Structural object classes are those from which ADS objects can be created.

Abstract   Abstract object classes are templates used to build structural objects. An example of an abstract object class is the Top class. It contains all of the attributes that are mandatory for *every* other object class.

Auxiliary   Auxiliary objects are just a list of attributes that can be added to other object classes.

Modifying an Existing Class

To modify a class, expand the Class container within the ADSM. Right-click the appropriate class and choose Properties. You will see the class Properties dialog box illustrated in Figure 12.10.

FIGURE 12.10

Class Properties
dialog box

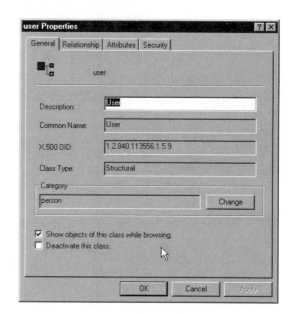

There are four tabs available:

- General
- Relationship
- Attributes
- Security

Each of these tabs controls a different aspect of the object class.

Look back to Figure 12.10 to see the General tab. Here you can change items pertaining to how the class fits into the schema.

Figure 12.11 shows the Relationship tab. Here you can assign auxiliary object classes to this structural class.

FIGURE 12.11

Relationship tab of class Properties

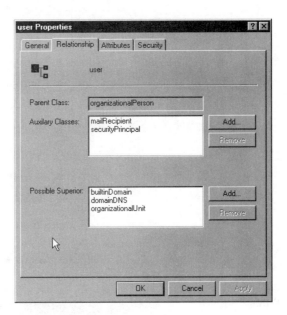

The Attributes tab is shown in Figure 12.12. Here you can add either mandatory or optional attributes to the object class.

Finally, Figure 12.13 shows the Security tab. Here you can assign default permissions to this class of object. This can be useful if you need to apply special security to a class of objects but do not want to have to repeat the assignments each time you create an object. You might, for instance, want a certain type of object to be visible only to members of the Administrators group. By applying the permissions here, these permissions would become the default for this class of object.

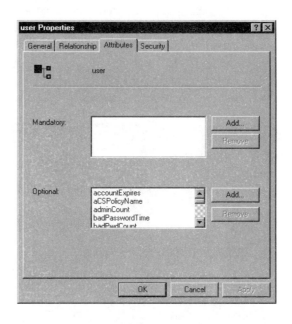

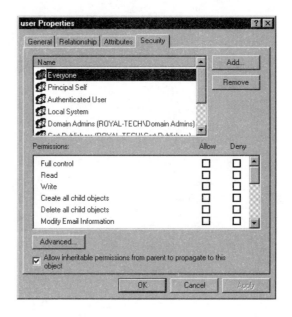

Creating a New Attribute

To create a new attribute, you create an *attribute-definition object*. The process is much like that of creating a new object class. Within the ADSM, right-click the Attributes container, then choose New ≻ Attribute. You will see the Create New Attribute dialog box, shown in Figure 12.14.

Here you enter the following information:

Common Name   This field becomes the Common Name attribute of the attribute.

Yes, attributes themselves have attributes—it can become confusing.

LDAP Display   This is the string that the LDAP utility will display to users when they access the directory.

Unique X.500 Object ID   This is the OID you received from the ISO.

You must also configure the type of data that the attribute will hold. In the Syntax box, you will decide whether the property will hold a string of data, numeric data, a case-sensitive set of information, and so on. You may also set valid ranges for the data entered to avoid incorrect information. Finally, check the Multi-Valued box if the attribute will contain more than one value (such as the telephone number attribute).

Modifying an Existing Attribute

To modify an existing attribute, follow exactly the process for modifying an existing object class, which was described earlier. Right-click the attribute and choose Properties. The same four tabs are available:

- General
- Relationship
- Attributes
- Security

These tabs offer the same set of configuration options as for modifying an object class.

See the earlier section "Modifying an Existing Class" for information about these tabs.

Deactivating a Class or an Attribute

In the ADSM, expand either the Class or the Attribute container, depending on what you want to deactivate. Within the container, find the item you wish to deactivate, right-click it, and choose Properties. On the General tab you will find a check box titled Deactivate this <Class or Attribute>. Select this check box.

If you choose to deactivate an item that another object is dependent upon, ADS will return an error describing the problem. This prevents you from making a deactivation that would interfere with the functionality of another class or attribute.

In Short

While you can make changes to the structure of the Active Directory database, this is not something you would do as part of the day-to-day administration of an ADS environment. The modification process involves acquiring a valid OID for any new classes or attributes and, since it changes the schema, could have a negative effect on your network—such as corrupting your ADS database.

Microsoft offers the following suggestions for schema modifications:

- Modify the schema only when absolutely necessary.

- Use existing attributes when creating new object classes. This allows you to avoid the process of applying for numerous attribute OIDs.

- Avoid multivalued attributes as much as possible. Large attributes are costly to store (in terms of disk space) and to retrieve (in terms of network bandwidth), and therefore should be avoided.

- Use meaningful names for any new classes or attributes to avoid ambiguity.

In the next chapter we will change gears, moving from the logical structure of the database to its impact on the physical aspects of the network. Through proper design and implementation of ADS sites, an administrator can avoid much of the overhead involved in maintaining a large, distributed, replicated database like the Active Directory database.

CHAPTER
13

Understanding and Controlling ADS Sites and Replication

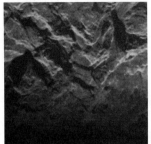

So far in our discussion of Active Directory Services, we have concentrated on ADS as a logical representation of your network—a way to present a complex physical environment in a logical manner. Our entire focus has been on creating an environment that matches the logical manner in which a company does business. In other words, we have looked at ADS as a way to present our network without considering the two main physical concerns of every business:

- Bandwidth

- Cost

Every network consists of some medium, be it copper, fiber, or even some wireless technology. On that medium we move packets of information from one point to another. This is the essence of networking: moving information from one point to another. This means that no matter how logical we make the structure or how graphical we make the interface, when all is said and done, everything comes back to the plumbing—the "pipes" we use to move data. It's just not feasible to design any portion of your network without taking into consideration available bandwidth and communication costs. This includes the design of your Active Directory database.

Previously, we looked at the logical organization of ADS to meet business needs. In this chapter, we will change our perspective, focusing on the organization of the ADS environment to meet the realities of your physical network.

Understanding Active Directory Sites

Within the Active Directory hierarchy, the directory tree structure does not need to match the physical organization of resources on the network. By "physical organization" I mean the physical location of computers and the connections between them. Take, for example, the ADS tree presented in Figure 13.1.

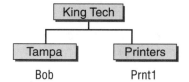

If user Bob needed to print to the printer named Prnt1, it would appear as a "local" resource. In other words, as Bob used his graphical interface to the network, Prnt1 would appear in a container named Printers. Based on the structure of the ADS tree and the naming conventions used, we have no idea where printer Prnt1 is physically located. In Figure 13.2, we see that Bob works in the Tampa office, but the printer named Prnt1 is located in the Reno office.

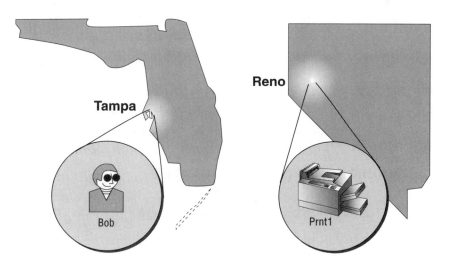

Figures 13.1 and 13.2 drive home the fact that ADS is *logical* in nature. Bob didn't have to know anything about the physical layout of the network; he just accessed a printer and used it. From the user's perspective, this simplicity is exactly what ADS is all about.

Network administrators, on the other hand, need to consider the physical path between resources when designing their networks. In Active Directory, the physical nature of the LAN is registered by defining *sites*. A site is a grouping of one or more Transmission Control Protocol/Internet Protocol (TCP/IP) subnets. Sites are defined to control two types of traffic generated on the network:

Logon traffic   Every time a user logs on to the network, NT will attempt to find a domain controller in the same site as the workstation.

Replication traffic   The act of updating domain controllers with changes to the database is known as *replication*. Sites can be used to control how and when this traffic will be generated on the network. (We'll discuss replication in detail later in this chapter.)

The subnets defined within a single site should be connected by high-speed, reliable links. The bottom line is that LAN lines (as opposed to WAN links) should connect all resources within a site. Any resources that connect through a router, dial-up connection, or other slow or unreliable link should be defined as separate sites.

Sites are not associated with the Active Directory namespace in any way, so a site can contain servers from multiple domains, and the servers from a single domain can be spread out among multiple sites.

Determining Site Boundaries

The first step in designing the boundaries of your ADS sites is to determine the placement of domain controllers throughout your network.

To review, sites are used to control two types of traffic: logon traffic and directory replication traffic. All of this traffic is specific to domain controllers. Users generate logon traffic as they attach and authenticate to the network through a domain controller. Replication is the process of updating changes to the directory database between the copies stored on multiple domain controllers. In other words, sites exist to control the traffic to and from domain controllers. Therefore, you should first decide on the placement of your domain controllers before considering the design of your site boundaries.

For each of your business locations, you will need to determine whether a domain controller is necessary. There are numerous factors that will determine your final decision. Table 13.1 lists the tradeoffs involved in having no domain controller at a location.

T A B L E 13.1 No Domain Controller at a Location	**Advantages**	**Disadvantages**
	No ADS database replication traffic to and from the location.	Since there is no local domain controller, all logon traffic will have to cross whatever links exist to a location with a domain controller.
	No need to define a site for the location.	Slower logins and authentication to network resources.
	No remote domain controllers to manage.	If all domain controllers are in a single location, you have a single point of physical failure (a natural disaster or even a telephone outage could cut all users off from network resources).

Table 13.2 outlines some of the tradeoffs of having a domain controller at a location.

T A B L E 13.2	**Advantages**	**Disadvantages**
Placing a Domain Controller at a Location	Logon traffic will not cross the WAN link.	Replication traffic will cross the WAN link.
	User logons will be faster.	Multiple locations will be needed, which might require on-site management.

When you are deciding on domain controller placement, the two most important factors to consider are the following:

- User convenience

- Available bandwidth

In most cases, users will see the best performance if they are authenticating through a local domain controller. A lack of available bandwidth, however, could result in periods where replication traffic floods the WAN link, slowing down access to resources across the network.

When it's all said and done, domain controller placement starts out as a judgment call. I usually err on the side of user convenience.

Placing a server at a site provides two big benefits:

- The logon process is much faster, since users are not crossing the WAN link for authentication.

- Placing a domain controller at a site gives me another server to play with. If the link has limited bandwidth, this might provide an opportunity to move resources or services to the new server (and thus local to the users), reducing the traffic on the line.

Bandwidth Considerations

Available bandwidth will often be the determining factor in domain controller placement, so we should take the time to properly define the phrase. *Available bandwidth* refers to the amount of throughput that is left after normal traffic has been taken into account. Many administrators assume that the fastest line will always have the most available bandwidth. This is not always the case. The "fastest" line is often also the most used line.

NOTE Think of it this way: Most companies will not purchase more bandwidth than necessary. If a company leases a fast T1 line, it is usually because they plan on using the link for large amounts of traffic. While the line might have a faster overall rating, it is also more likely to be near saturation (without the addition of logon or replication traffic). A smaller pipe, such as a 256Kbps leased line, might actually have more bandwidth available.

The only way to accurately determine the amount of available bandwidth on a link is to analyze traffic with a protocol analyzer, such as Microsoft Network Manager. You will need to analyze the traffic on each segment over a period of time. This period should include peak-usage and non-business hours so that you have a fairly good idea of how the link is utilized at different times of the day. Later in this chapter, we will discuss the ability to schedule replication traffic. If you know when a line usually has available bandwidth, you can easily determine the replication schedule that will be most efficient for your environment.

Along with the amount of available bandwidth, you will have to consider the cost of transmission on each link. Some telecommunications companies charge for the amount of data transmitted. If this is the case, even though a link might have plenty of bandwidth available, you might not want to add traffic to the line.

Analyzing traffic patterns and balancing use versus cost is one of the most challenging tasks facing network administrators. The cost structure for many WAN lines is confusing at best (and downright misleading at worst). Spending some time considering these factors can prevent unnecessary costs in the future—or worse, a complete redesign of your structure to control those costs.

Domain Controller Placement Strategies

There are three main strategies you can use when planning for the placement of domain controllers:

- Placement to control logon traffic
- Placement to control replication traffic
- Placement to provide a balance between replication and logon traffic

Each type of design has its advantages and disadvantages. You should analyze each network in order to choose the correct placement strategies for its unique properties.

Placement to Control Logon Traffic

One reason to create sites is to control logon traffic on the network. When a user logs on to the network, a workstation will attempt to find a domain controller in its local site. To determine this, the workstation compares its own TCP/IP address and subnet mask against those that define sites within the Active Directory database. If an organization is only concerned that a workstation log on to servers that can be connected to over fast and reliable lines, the site boundaries will usually match the physical boundaries of each location, as shown in Figure 13.3.

We'll discuss the mechanics and objects pertaining to sites a little later in this chapter.

FIGURE 13.3
Location-based
boundaries

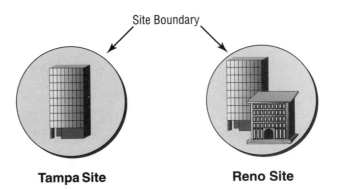

Site Boundary

Tampa Site   **Reno Site**

If, however, a company would like more control over which domain controllers are used by each user to log on, multiple sites can be created in a single physical location, as you can see in Figure 13.4. You should place each workstation in a site that contains the domain controllers the workstation should use during the logon process.

F I G U R E 13.4

Controlling domain
controller overhead

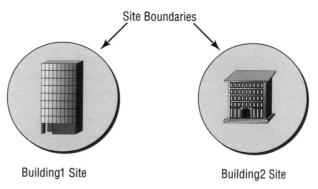

Site Boundaries

Building1 Site

Building2 Site

Reno Location

There is one potential problem with having multiple sites defined for a
single location. In the event that a domain controller from the same site is not
available, the workstation will query ADS for a domain controller from
another site. ADS does not consider physical proximity during this search, so
it is conceivable that a user would be sent to a domain controller that is
across a WAN link (even though there might be a local server available).

This is not as big a deal as it sounds. While the login and authentication
process will be slower than normal, the user will still be able to access the
network resources that they need. Since most users will access resources
that are local to them, most functions will not be affected. In other words,
it'll take a little longer to be authenticated, but everything else should function normally.

While this could degrade performance during the logon process, the
workstation will correct the problem as soon as possible. Every so often,
the workstation will check to see if a domain controller from its own site
has become available. If so, all future authentication requests will be
routed to that local server.

Placement to Control Replication Traffic

The other reason to create an ADS site is to control replication traffic. You
do not have as much control over replication within a site, also known as

intrasite replication, as you have over the replication traffic between two sites, also known as *intersite replication.* Intersite replication offers the following advantages:

- Control over when replication will occur. Replication will occur on a schedule, with the only exception being a case where replication could not occur at the scheduled time.

- Control over the network transport that will be used.

- Compression of all traffic generated (the average compression ratio is 10–12 percent).

Windows 2000 Server does its best to reduce the amount of traffic generated by the replication process. Changes are replicated at the attribute level; in other words, if a user's telephone number is changed, only the *new* information will be replicated to other domain controllers (as opposed to the entire record for that user object). All data transferred is also compressed, decreasing the amount of traffic by approximately 10–12 percent. Ultimately, though, the amount of traffic that will be generated by the replication process depends on the number of changes made to the database. Companies that experience constant growth, numerous reorganizations, or just plain old changes will generate more traffic than companies that experience little change.

Placement to Provide a Balance between Replication and Logon Traffic

Neither a design based upon optimization for replication traffic nor a design that solely reflects controlling logon traffic will be the perfect solution for most environments. In most cases, you will need to design the site boundaries with both considerations in mind. For each location in your intranet, you will need to analyze the links to other locations and decide (on an individual basis) whether each link should support logon or replication traffic.

The Default Placement

When you install Active Directory Services for the first time within a Windows 2000 Server environment, a default site will be created. This first site will be named `Default-First-Site-Name`. You can rename this site later using the Active Directory Site and Services tool. Until additional sites are created, all domain controllers will be placed in the default site.

All new domain controllers will be placed in the site that applies to them at the time of installation. In other words, during the installation process, the ADS Installation Wizard will search the ADS database for a site that includes the subnet upon which the server is placed. The new domain controller will be placed within this site. Figure 13.5 demonstrates this principle. The new domain controller, FS1, is created in the Reno office. ADS contains a site definition that describes the Reno site as all TCP/IP subnets that exist in the Reno network. Since the server is installed with an IP address that is defined as part of the Reno site, the server will be placed within the Reno site.

F I G U R E   13.5

Placing a domain
controller

Later, if you were to move the FS1 server shown in Figure 13.5 to somewhere in the Tampa location, you would need to redefine the site property of the server. If you don't, the server will still think it is a part of the site defined in Reno and will replicate with the Reno servers (across that expensive and slow WAN link).

Moving a server from one site to another is easy, but be careful when you do it. Placing a server from one site within the defined boundaries of another site could result in unnecessary logon or replication traffic.

Implementing Active Directory Sites

Sites are not part of the namespace defined by an ADS database. The ADS namespace contains users and groups (and other classes of objects) divided into logical groupings through the creation of domains and containers. Sites contain only server objects and are used to configure intersite replication. To manage sites, use the Active Directory Sites and Services tool or add the snap-in of the same name to the Microsoft Management Console.

There are three objects involved in the creation and configuration of ADS sites:

- Sites

- Subnets

- Site links

Objects of these three classes work together to define your site boundaries and configure replication between them.

Creating Sites

To create a site, use the Active Directory Sites and Services tool, found in the Administrative Tools group of your Start menu. You can see this tool in Figure 13.6.

FIGURE 13.6

Active Directory Sites and Services tool

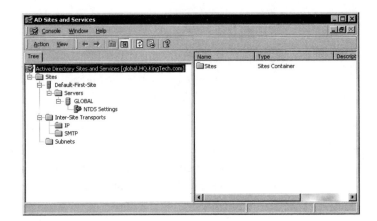

Highlight the Sites folder, right-click, and choose New Site. The New Object—Site dialog box will appear, as shown in Figure 13.7.

In the Name box, enter a name that describes this site. The name should adequately describe the purpose of the site, such as the name of the physical location or the department whose servers will be a member.

FIGURE 13.7

New Object—Site

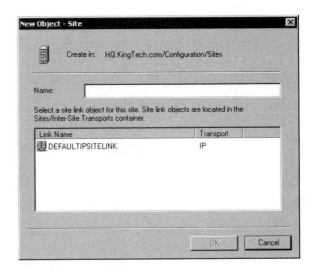

Once you have created a site, you can move servers into it by right-clicking the server and choosing Move. Just select the appropriate site from the list in the Move Server dialog box, as shown in Figure 13.8.

FIGURE 13.8

Moving a server to a new site

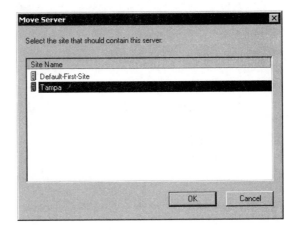

Creating Subnets

The next step in configuring a site environment is to define subnets. An ADS subnet is a collection of TCP/IP subnets. ADS subnets are created using the Active Directory Sites and Services tool. To create a subnet, right-click the subnet's container and choose New ➤ Subnet. The New Object—Subnet dialog box will appear, as shown in Figure 13.9.

FIGURE 13.9

New Object—Subnet

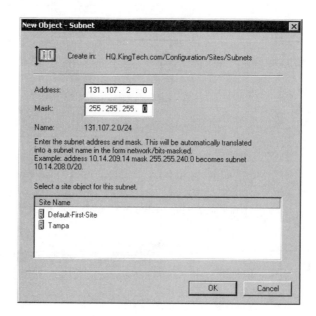

The name is made up of the IP address subnet and subnet mask for the physical network that the ADS subnet will represent. If, for instance, your IP subnet were 131.107.2.0 with a subnet mask of 255.255.255.0, the name of the ADS subnet would be 131.107.2.0/24. The 24 represents the number of bits being masked by the subnet mask.

Subnet masking is a complex concept that is well beyond the scope of this book. For more information, read *MCSE: TCP/IP for NT Server 4 Study Guide,* 4th ed., by Todd Lammle, Monica Lammle, and James Chellis (ISBN 0-7821-2725-8, Sybex, 2000).

A computer with multiple network interface cards (also known as a *multihomed* computer) and multiple IP addresses can belong to only one site. It is recommended that all subnets attached to a multihomed computer be in the same ADS site.

Associating Subnets with Sites

The next step is to associate your subnets with sites. Associating a subnet with a site tells ADS which physical networks are represented by the site. To associate a site with a subnet, access the properties of the subnet to be associated. You will be presented with the dialog box shown in Figure 13.10.

F I G U R E 13.10

Properties of a subnet

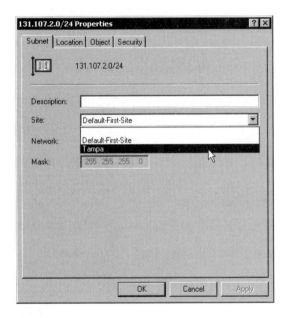

In the Description box, enter a description for the association, such as the physical location. In the Site box, enter the site with which you wish to associate this subnet. Click OK when finished.

Creating Site Links

So far we have created the sites and defined the scope of each site, listing which IP subnets make up our sites. The next step in the site configuration process is to configure the connections between our sites. The connections between sites are represented within the ADS database by site link objects. There are four components to each site link:

Transport The networking technology used to transfer the replication traffic

Sites The sites that the site link connects

Cost A value used to determine the site link that will be used for transfer in the event that redundant links are available

Schedule The times that replication will occur

Site links represent the path and method used to transfer replication traffic. As such, a well thought-out plan can greatly reduce congestion on wide-area connections. The first step is to plan your site boundaries to minimize network traffic; the next step is to create your site links to control that traffic.

You can connect a site to other sites using any number of site links. These site links can be established over many different networking technologies, such as T1 lines, network connections, dial-up links, or ATM. Some technologies provide a "cloud" in which a single hop connects any two physical locations. This concept is shown in Figure 13.11. In this type of environment, a single site link to the cloud provides replication connections to multiple locations.

FIGURE 13.11

Multiple sites connected through a single site link

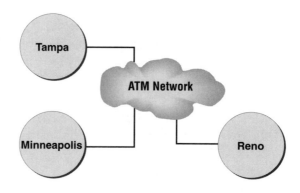

How Will Data Be Transferred?

When you create a site link, you will have to determine the method of data transfer. There are two options available:

TCP/IP   Uses normal TCP/IP connections to transfer data. All data is compressed to reduce overall traffic.

Simple Mail Transfer Protocol (SMTP)   All replication traffic is converted to e-mail messages to send between sites.

A site link should not be considered a single connection between two locations. Site links can be configured so that the same object links multiple ADS sites. This is depicted in Figure 13.12. If a company had three sites—X, Y, and Z—a single site link object could be configured to allow replication between all of them. Site links do not take into consideration the physical connections between sites; in other words, the site link represents "who talks to whom" rather than the path that traffic will take. Controlling the path is accomplished through setting costs on site links, as we will discuss in the next section.

FIGURE 13.12

Multiple connections with a single site link object

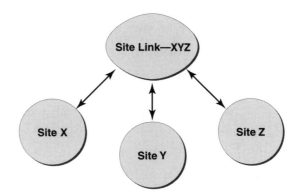

Site Link Costs

A site link's *cost* represents how expensive an organization considers the network connection between two sites that the site link is connecting. Consider the environment presented in Figure 13.12. We have three sites—X, Y, and Z—connected by a single site link object; let's name it XYZ. If that site link had been given a cost of 5, it would mean that the cost of sending traffic between any of the sites (X–Y, X–Z, Y–Z, Y–X, Z–X, Z–Y) would be 5. Higher costs represent more expensive connections. If there are two site links available between two sites, the lowest cost site link will be chosen.

The sites connected through a site link are specifically designated. Consider the environment depicted in Figure 13.13. Sites A and B are connected through a site link named AB with a cost of 5. Sites B and C are connected through a site link named BC with a cost of 3. This configuration in no way implies that traffic can be routed from Site A to Site C with a cost of 8 (or any cost). Another way to say this is that site link connections are *non-transitive* in nature.

FIGURE 13.13

Site link costs

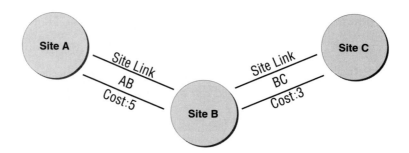

Site Link Schedules

The site link schedule specifies the times during which the site link is available. Two sites, for instance, connected by a dial-up connection, might be configured to use a site link with a schedule set so that it is only available during evenings and weekends. This configuration could reduce communication costs.

Setting Up a Site Link

Using the Active Directory Sites and Services tool, double-click the site's container, then double-click Inter-Site Transports. The available transports will appear within the Inter-Site Transports container, as shown in Figure 13.14.

Right-click the transport to be used, and then click New Site Link. You will be presented with the New Object—Site Link dialog box, as shown in Figure 13.15.

F I G U R E   13.14

Inter-Site transports

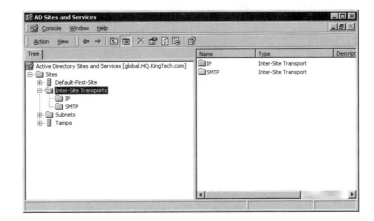

F I G U R E   13.15

New Object—Site Link

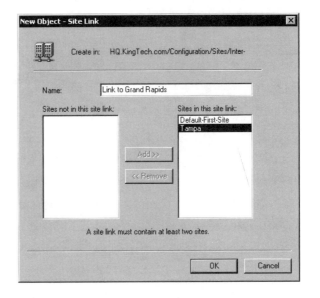

You must provide a name for the site link and a list of all sites that it should connect. The default settings for a site link object are a cost of 100 and a replication schedule set to replicate every three hours. To change either setting, right-click the site link object and click Properties.

Site Link Bridges

A *site link bridge* represents a set of site links, all of which can communicate using a common transport. A site link bridge is used to overcome the limitations of a non-transitive environment. Earlier we looked at an environment made up of three sites—A, B, and C—connected by two site links:

- AB (cost 5)
- BC (cost 3)

In a non-transitive environment, replication traffic will not be routed between Sites A and C unless some other configuration is available. The site link bridge is the tool used to create these types of connections. In this situation, we would create a site link bridge that included the site links AB and BC. Once the bridge is in place, replication will occur between Sites A and C with a cost of 8 (the cost of each site link involved in the transfer), as shown in Figure 13.16.

FIGURE 13.16

Site link bridge

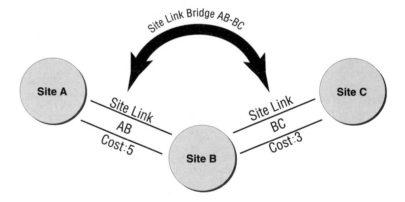

Site link bridges can reduce some of the management overhead involved in linking sites. We *could* have created another site link between Sites A and C, thus negating a need for a site link bridge. Bridges reduce the effort necessary when connecting sites in a large environment.

Creating a Site Link Bridge

In the Active Directory Sites and Services tool, click the Sites container to expand it. Double-click the Inter-Site Transports object. Right-click the transport to be used and choose New Site Link Bridge. The New Object—(Site Link Bridge) dialog box appears, as shown in Figure 13.17.

FIGURE 13.17

New Object—(Site
Link Bridge)

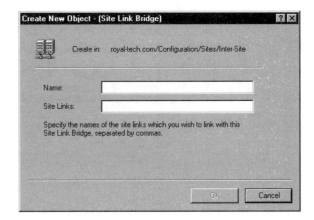

Give the bridge a descriptive name, and choose which sites are to be included in the bridge.

Connection Objects

There is one last object class associated with the replication process: the connection object. Connection objects represent a replication connection from one domain controller to another domain controller. In other words, connection objects define the two end points for replication traffic.

A process known as the *Knowledge Consistency Checker* (KCC) automatically creates connection objects. In most cases, the criteria used by the KCC to create connection objects will suffice. In other words, in most cases network administrators will not need to manually create or configure connection objects; this work will be done automatically by the KCC.

We'll expand our discussion of the KCC later in this chapter.

In the event that the KCC's default connectors are not sufficient, you can manually create and configure connection objects. Here are a couple of reasons for performing this task manually:

- To control the number of hops involved in the replication process. The KCC tries to limit the number of networks that traffic must cross during replication to three. In most cases, this will be sufficient. There might be times, however, when an administrator needs to limit traffic. You can manually add more connection objects to reduce the number of hops involved in replication.

- To increase the efficiency of a network by adding another path for traffic on the network.

Understanding Replication

Now that we have looked at the various configuration issues involved in controlling replication traffic, we should include a detailed discussion of that traffic. Each Windows 2000 domain has at least one server that acts as a domain controller. Unlike earlier versions of NT, each domain controller is involved in managing changes and updates to the database. Earlier versions of NT were configured in a *single-master environment*. The Primary Domain Controller (PDC) maintained and managed the master copy of the domain database and was in charge of replicating changes to the Backup Domain Controllers (BDCs) of its domain. In a single-master environment, the master (in our case, the PDC) is a single point of failure. If for some reason the PDC is unavailable, no changes can be made to the database.

In Windows 2000 Server, each domain controller holds a complete copy of the ADS directory for its own domain. In this respect, it is much like earlier versions. The difference, however, is that each Windows 2000 domain controller can accept and make changes to the database and then replicate those changes to other domain controllers. An environment like this, where multiple computers are responsible for managing changes, is known as a *multiple-master environment*. A multiple-master environment offers numerous advantages over the old single-master configuration. Here are some of those advantages:

- There is no single point of failure. Since every domain controller can accept changes to the database, there is no domain controller that is *critical* to the process.

- Domain controllers that can accept changes to the database can be distributed throughout the physical network. This allows administrators to make changes on a local computer and let a background process (replication) ensure that those changes are updated on all other domain controllers in a timely and efficient manner.

Replication vs. Synchronization

The first important concept to understand when looking at ADS updates is the difference between replication and synchronization. These two terms are often used interchangeably in the industry. Microsoft has a specific definition for each.

Replication

Directory *replication* is the process that takes place when one Windows 2000 domain controller updates another with changes to the ADS database. Replication relies on a homogeneous environment: All domain controllers involved must be Windows 2000 servers and have identical schemas, and there must be a high level of trust between the servers involved.

Synchronization

Directory *synchronization* occurs between dissimilar implementations of a directory service. For example, since both Active Directory Services and Novell Directory Services follow an industry standard method of access, it is possible for each environment to update the other with information from its own database. You might, for instance, want to create users in the Novell directory, but manage them from within the Active Directory environment.

In such a case, an agent, known as a *security principal*, would perform the synchronization, importing or exporting objects and changes from one directory to the other. Microsoft supplies security principals that can synchronize data between:

- Windows 2000 Server ADS and Novell Directory Services (NDS). This agent allows you to create and manage "Novell" accounts in Microsoft ADS. You can create an object in ADS and the agent will push that object to NDS.

- An agent that allows synchronization between the ADS database and a Microsoft Exchange Server directory.

Because Windows 2000 Server ADS is fully LDAP-compliant, it is conceivable that other environments will be added to this list in the future. For now, though, only these two are available.

Types of Replication

There are two basic types of replication in a Windows 2000 Server environment:

- *Intrasite* replication occurs between domain controllers within a site.

- *Intersite* replication occurs between domain controllers in different sites.

When planning your site structure and replication strategy, it is important to understand the methods used for each type of replication traffic.

Intrasite Replication

As you saw earlier, intrasite replication involves domain controllers from the same site. These computers use *Remote Procedure Calls* (*RPCs*) to perform the replication process.

Within a site, the Knowledge Consistency Checker (KCC), which you read about in the section on connection objects, generates a *ring topology* for replication among the domain controllers within the site, as shown in Figure 13.18. This ring topology defines the path through which changes will flow within the domain. Any changes will follow the ring until all domain controllers have received them.

Creating a ring topology ensures that there are two paths that changes can follow from one domain controller to another (either direction on the ring).

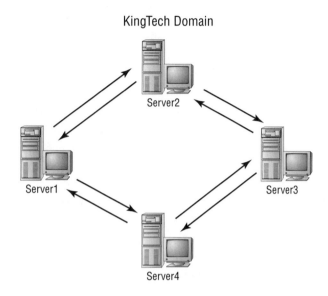

KingTech Domain

The KCC will also configure the ring so that there are no more than three
hops between any two domain controllers within the domain. On occasion,
this will call for the creation of multiple rings within a single domain, as you
can see in Figure 13.19.

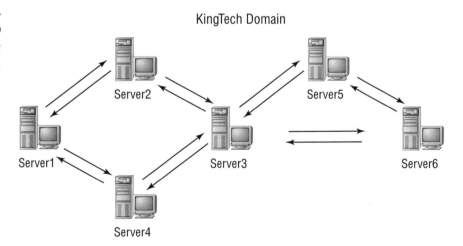

KingTech Domain

The KCC periodically analyzes the replication topology within a site to ensure efficiency. If a domain controller has been added or removed, the KCC will reconfigure the ring for optimum efficiency.

Intersite Replication

Intersite replication occurs between domain controllers in different sites. If an environment has only one site, all replication will be intrasite. The biggest drawback to intersite communication is that it is not automatic. It must be configured manually, as you saw earlier in this chapter.

Intersite replication is the best choice if the traffic must cross a slower Internet link.

Intersite replication can be configured to use either the TCP/IP transport or SMTP. All traffic sent is compressed to reduce the overhead on the network.

Behind the Scenes of Replication

We've discussed the objects, optimization techniques, and tools used for managing replication, but we have not yet looked at the actual process used by Windows 2000 Server and Active Directory Services to update multiple copies of the same database. There is a very good reason for this: There really isn't much that we, as administrators, can do to influence the process, other than having a properly designed site structure.

With that said, though, most of us will have an academic interest in the replication process. Knowing how it works can also help you to design an efficient and stable site structure.

Update Sequence Numbers

When a change is made to the database stored on a domain controller, either through a user action or through replication from another domain controller, the domain controller assigns the change an *Update Sequence Number (USN)*. Each domain controller keeps its own USNs and increments the value for each change that occurs.

NOTE

With respect to a single domain controller, you can think of the USN as a change counter. Each domain controller will have different values for changes that occur on its copy of the directory database. These values are not synchronized between domain controllers within a domain.

When the domain controller writes the change to the database, it also writes the USN of the change to that property. This is seen as a single transaction and will succeed or fail as a whole. In other words, ADS will protect against a change being applied to the database without a corresponding USN also being recorded. This is an important feature, since USNs are used to determine which changes need to be replicated to other domain controllers. This process is depicted in Figure 13.20.

F I G U R E 13.20

Applying a change to the database

Object—Bob

Property	USN	Value
Telephone number	6	555-1000

If the value of the telephone number property for user Bob needs to be changed, the domain controller will check its current value for the database USN. Let's say the last USN applied to a change was 3. When the system writes Bob's new telephone number to the database, it will increment the USN and write *both* the changed data and the USN to Bob's object. The system USN will also be incremented to reflect this new value (so that the next change to the database will receive a higher USN).

Multiple USNs

There are a couple of new concepts to keep in mind here. First, notice that the domain controller is keeping track of the highest USN value that it has assigned to a change. (Microsoft doesn't really have a name for this value, but I'm going to call it the DCUSN for *Domain Controller USN*.) This allows the domain controller to increment the value for each change, ensuring that no duplicate USNs exist and that each USN is larger than the one before it. Second, each property of every object really stores two values: the actual data (like Bob's telephone number) and the USN assigned to the value the last time the attribute was changed.

NOTE

Reread that last paragraph! Its two main concepts—a domain controller USN value that represents the highest USN assigned and the fact that every property stores the USN assigned at the time of change—are crucial to understanding how replication works.

The Process of Replication

Now we can discuss the process of replicating Bob's new telephone number to all domain controllers within the domain. Each domain controller stores the DCUSN from all other domain controllers at the last time of replication, as shown in Figure 13.21.

FIGURE 13.21

DCUSN tables

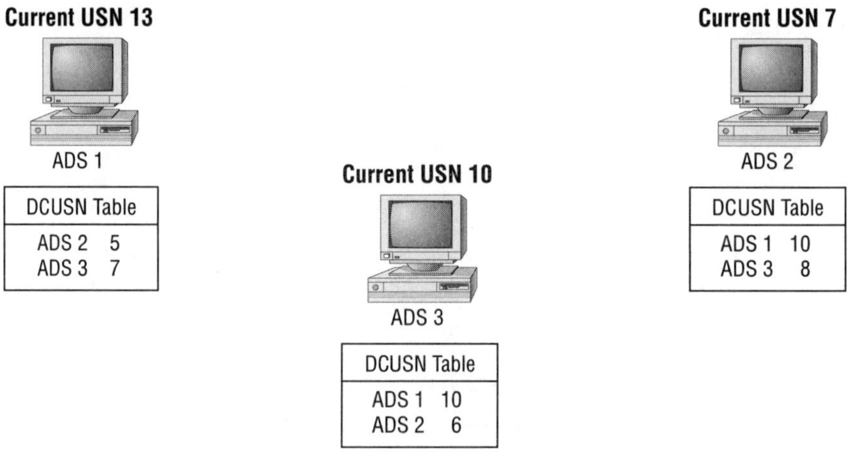

Current USN 13

ADS 1

DCUSN Table	
ADS 2	5
ADS 3	7

Current USN 10

ADS 3

DCUSN Table	
ADS 1	10
ADS 2	6

Current USN 7

ADS 2

DCUSN Table	
ADS 1	10
ADS 3	8

During the replication process, each domain controller sends its current DCUSN value to all of the other domain controllers in the domain. These servers compare this current value to the value that they have stored in their DCUSN table. If the current value is higher than the stored value, changes need to be replicated.

Look back at Figure 13.21. During replication, domain controller ADS 2 will send its current DCUSN, which is 7, to both domain controllers ADS 1 and ADS 3. The last time that replication occurred with ADS 1, the USN for ADS 2 was 5. Since the current value is 7, ADS 1 will request changes 6 and 7 from ADS 2. ADS 2 will search its database for the properties with these USN values and replicate them to ADS 1, as shown in Figure 13.22.

F I G U R E   13.22

Replication of specific changes

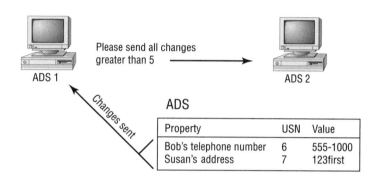

Property	USN	Value
Bob's telephone number	6	555-1000
Susan's address	7	123first

Benefits of Using USNs

Using USN values to determine which changes to replicate eliminates the need for precise time stamps for changes (and for time to be synchronized among the domain controllers). Time stamps are also assigned to each change, however, for tie-breaking purposes. These time stamps decide which change should be implemented if a specific attribute was changed on two or more domain controllers during the replication interval. In that event, the change with the latest time stamp is placed in the database; any other changes are discarded.

Using USNs also simplifies the recovery process after a failure. When a domain controller comes back online after a recovery, it just needs to ask all of the other domain controllers for all changes with higher USN values than the last value stored in its DCUSN table. This is true even if the replication process is temporarily interrupted (a wide-area link goes down, for instance). When communication is reestablished, the domain controller will request all changes with USNs greater than the last change applied to the database.

Propagation Dampening

As you saw earlier in this chapter, the KCC creates the replication topology for intrasite replication. The KCC creates a loop topology so that domain controllers have multiple paths for sending and receiving updates, as shown in Figure 13.23.

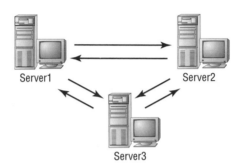

While a loop topology increases fault tolerance and can increase performance, it can also result in a domain controller receiving the same update from two different domain controllers. To prevent this, Active Directory uses a *propagation dampening* scheme. Propagation dampening is the process of preventing unnecessary replication of directory changes.

Up-to-Date Vectors

While USNs can be used to determine which changes have been replicated from another domain controller, they do nothing to prevent changes from being replicated from multiple sources. This is why in addition to USNs, Windows 2000 domain controllers also store *up-to-date vectors*. An up-to-date vector identifies the source of the *originating write* to a property. The originating write to any property identifies the source domain controller for the change. If a user changes his password, for instance, and that change is made to the copy of the directory stored on Server1, on Server1 the change would be considered an originating write; the change made there is directly related to some action performed by a user. In contrast, a *non-originating write* would be a change that was received through the replication process.

Another way to look at this is to consider the server where the change originates as the source of the originating writes.

As an example, let's look at the process of updating a change in an environment with three domain controllers: Server1, Server2, and Server3. If a user changes her password at Server1, the server updates the value in the database and assigns that change the next incremental value for its USN. What is actually stored in the directory will contain this:

```
Password, Server1, USN-7
```

The USN value will follow the rules outlined earlier.

When this change is replicated to Server2, Server2 writes the change and increments its own USN. The actual record in the directory database remains the same as it was at Server1:

```
Password, Server1, USN-7
```

Server1 has also replicated this change to Server3. Server3 stores the same information, including the up-to-date vector information. When Server2 begins the replication process with Server3, Server3 will send its current USN value *and* all of its up-to-date vectors. Server2 compares the up-to-date vectors received from Server3 to its own. Server3 will not send any changes that have already been replicated to Server2.

In Short

Domain database replication between domain controllers in a Windows 2000 Server and ADS environment is a complex process that generates traffic on the network. This traffic can be controlled (but not eliminated) through proper implementation of ADS sites. The bottom line is that we can control the replication traffic generated between sites, but we cannot control the traffic generated to replicate the directory database within a site. Site boundaries define physical groupings of TCP/IP subnets and allow us to control how updates should be performed.

In the next chapter, we will look at various ways that Microsoft could leverage the power of Active Directory to the benefit of other Microsoft products, namely the BackOffice Suite. I say "could" because one never knows exactly what surprises Microsoft is going to throw at the computer industry.

PART

III

The Future of Active
Directory Services

CHAPTER
14

ADS and BackOffice

You enter a dark and gloomy room: The smell of incense hangs in the air like fog on a London morning, and the candlelight creates shadows that dance across the corners of your mind. You approach a woman of indeterminate age, who sits behind a small table upon which rests a ball of crystal. Now is the time to ask that question that has haunted your dreams:

"What will Microsoft do next?"

Sometimes it seems as if accessing the spiritual realm is the only way to stay one step ahead of Microsoft, let alone the computer industry. Unfortunately, keeping abreast of developments and understanding new technologies (often before they hit the streets) is part and parcel of most LAN administrators' jobs.

In Part III, I intend to play the part of the "industry expert" and imagine—or guess, if you prefer—the impact that Microsoft Active Directory Services will have on the networking industry. To tell the truth, such forecasting isn't really that difficult. All I have to do is look at current directory implementations and extrapolate their functionality to the Microsoft realm.

I always wonder about anyone who calls himself an *expert*, especially in this industry! Things change so quickly that keeping up, let alone trying to stay ahead, is nearly impossible. In the next three chapters, you'll see just a few of the possibilities made available by the implementation of a directory-based network.

I tend to agree with my father, who always said, "An expert is just someone from over five miles away who carries a briefcase."

How Might ADS Affect Microsoft BackOffice?

A network administrator's job usually does not end with the network operating system (NOS). Most networks will provide numerous services to their users—everything from file storage to printing to e-mail. Many of these services are not part of the actual operating system but are additional applications that must be installed and configured.

One of the best things about using Microsoft NT as your network operating system is that Microsoft offers many additional packages that integrate easily into an NT domain environment. Okay, maybe "easily" is an overstatement, but at least the Microsoft products can be configured to work well together.

Knowing that a good NOS alone does not a network make, Microsoft has released add-on applications to provide much of the additional functionality that you might need on your network. Those applications that are network-centric (in other words, a network is an important part of the services they offer) are grouped together under a common name: *Microsoft BackOffice*. The BackOffice product line is dedicated to the goal of providing easy integration between the various network services that you use on your network. The BackOffice suite has grown over the years to reflect Microsoft's dedication to the networking market. Currently, BackOffice is made up of the following products:

Exchange Server   A high-end messaging solution capable of managing information in remarkable ways, Exchange Server has the ability to send and receive e-mail over the Internet with cc:Mail systems, with Microsoft Mail systems, with any X.400-compliant mail system, or with any messaging product for which a gateway has been written. Exchange is much more than just an e-mail application, however. It allows for the creation of *public folders*, which can hold just about any kind of information. These public folders let users connect to this information via a comfortable interface.

Proxy Server   This product has grown from a very simple add-on to a powerful Internet firewall. Proxy was originally designed to allow multiple users to share a single access point to the Internet. Proxy allows an administrator to lease one valid Internet IP address and share it among multiple clients. This offers an inexpensive solution for sitewide Internet access. Proxy Server has expanded to include all of the abilities of many higher-priced Internet firewalls.

Site Server This product allows for advanced management of Web-site servers.

Systems Management Server Originally intended as a software distribution package, SMS has grown into a full-fledged network management tool. SMS gives administrators the ability to take control of a client's computer remotely, schedule the installation or upgrade of software remotely, analyze network traffic, map a network environment, and perform hardware and software inventories across the network. SMS is a great overall tool for managing a large network.

SNA Server A gateway to environments using IBM's SNA protocol for communication, this product is usually seen as a gateway to mainframe environments.

SQL Server This product is a client/server database application capable of handling large databases. Since SQL Server is a full-fledged development environment, it can be customized to perform just about any data-management task.

Each of these applications plays a distinct role in the overall direction of Microsoft and its products. Over the last few years, Microsoft has placed a major emphasis on the role of the Internet in business. As you can see from this list, many of the core components of BackOffice are directly related to Internet functionality. Even those few applications that are not directly Internet-dependent offer functions that can enhance the Internet capabilities of a network. Given the direction of Microsoft, it's fairly easy to predict a few of the effects that a directory-based network will have on the BackOffice suite.

Exchange Server

Currently, Exchange Server uses its own X.500 hierarchical database to contain configuration information. There are snap-in modules that add Exchange functionality to NT management tools, such as User Manager for Domains, but an Exchange environment is completely separate from your NT domain environment. Since you can manage user mailboxes with the same tool you use to manage NT user accounts, this hasn't been a big draw-back for most administrators.

The simple fact, however, is that the overhead of a second database—for example, the Exchange database and the NT SAM—can place a heavy load on an NT server. It also means that a large portion of the information is stored in multiple locations. As you saw earlier, the NT domain database is replicated from the PDC to the BDCs. Exchange has its own mechanism for replicating Exchange environmental information between Exchange servers—to paraphrase Jerry Lee Lewis, "We got a whole lotta replicatin' goin' on." The traffic necessary to synchronize both the domain database and the Exchange database can place a heavy load on your network.

Now let's switch gears and look at the client environment. Current client software (Outlook, Outlook Express, and so on) needs to store configuration information at the local machine. The client must store information (such as the user's mail server, e-mail name, and certificates of authenticity), and address books are usually located in one of two places: the local machine or the user's mail server. This means that the software must first read this configuration before it can access your mail. This system works fine for a user sitting at her own desk, but what about a user who moves from place to place? Must that user remember the process of setting up the client software everywhere she goes? Even if a user moves permanently from one location to another, the client software will have to be reconfigured and the user's mailbox moved from one server to another.

Merging ADS and Exchange

Exchange might benefit more than any other piece of the BackOffice suite by a move to a directory-based solution. One of the biggest benefits would be the removal of the Exchange database. Since Exchange already uses a directory-enabled management set, why not just have the Exchange installation routine extend the ADS schema to include Exchange-specific objects and attributes? A user object could include attributes that define Exchange aspects such as the following:

- Mail server
- Security certificates
- Address lists
- Phone numbers

- Addresses

- E-mail names

This list can go on and on. Every configuration currently managed internally by the Exchange database will be moved to the ADS structure. The biggest benefit is that all of this data is automatically distributed, replicated, and available from anywhere within the network! Imagine a system where a user could sit down anywhere, log on to the network, and access his e-mail without having to perform any other configuration. Since the directory has already identified that user, there is no reason why the Exchange server can't accept that authentication and automatically make the appropriate mail available to the client.

ADS could even store the network address of a user's "home" machine. This would allow Exchange to sense whether the user is "at home" or at some other computer. If the user was not at her desk, mail would not be moved to the local machine—even if the user was configured for local storage.

Since ADS includes the ability to replicate and distribute its content, mail administrators would never again have to worry about the loss of a single server cutting off a user from mail-based services. ADS could even be configured to route mail around a downed server. Since all of the configuration information is stored in ADS, why not have ADS sense when the mail server is unavailable and store incoming mail on another Exchange server in the network? Since ADS would manage this process, a user could still access any new mail—ADS could just route the request from the client computer to the new mail server.

I don't think we'll see all of these suggestions in the next couple of releases of Exchange Server. I think Microsoft will start by moving Exchange configuration information to ADS. As with most software, the first release or two might not be that stable—but in time, Exchange will become fully integrated with the directory. Once it is, there is no telling what might happen!

Proxy Server

The current release of Proxy Server offers many services to a network connected to the Internet. At first, Proxy Server had two main functions:

- Allowing a network to *share* a single IP address
- Caching Internet content for faster access

Both of these functions could benefit from integration with a network directory.

Using ADS to Ease Proxy Management

Right now, each client must be configured with the IP address of the Proxy server to take advantage of its services. If this configuration information were stored as part of the ADS database, a client could query ADS for the IP address of the nearest active Proxy server. In other words, rather than storing a static configuration at each client, the client software would request up-to-date information each time it needed the service. This type of configuration would allow for easy fail-over to a secondary Proxy server in the event of a failure of the primary server.

If ADS were used to assign IP addresses—in other words, if Dynamic Host Configuration Protocol (DHCP) services were fully integrated with ADS—Proxy could use the directory database as its source for client communication. As it stands right now, Proxy must learn a client's address and build an internal table that correlates this address with any request made to the Internet. Using ADS as the repository for IP addressing information would remove the overhead of keeping this table up to date.

NOTE　DHCP is an industry-standard method of automatically configuring TCP/IP clients as they attach to the network. For more information, see *MCSE: TCP/IP for NT Server 4 Study Guide,* 4th ed., by Todd Lammle with Monica Lammle and James Chellis (ISBN 0-7821-2725-8, Sybex, 2000).

Proxy Server also has the ability to cache both incoming and outgoing Web content. When an internal user requests a Web page from the Internet, the proxy software can cache that page locally for faster access next time (it is assumed that any Web site of interest will be requested many times). A Proxy server could easily be configured to search the directory for a server physically near the user. The content could then be cached at that server. This would speed access to the materials even more *and* reduce traffic across the local network segments.

While placing cached Web content physically close to a user is a great advantage, we can take this concept a step further. Without ADS, each Proxy server acts as a stand-alone environment. In other words, the servers do not communicate with each other regarding the users and user requests that they are handling. This means that if two users who are utilizing the services of different Proxy servers download the same Web page, that page will be cached on each server. In an ADS environment, the proxy services could be configured and maintained from a single location (the ADS database). When one server downloaded a Web page, information about that page could be updated in a "master cache list" stored as an attribute of the proxy services. With this information available in ADS, only one copy of the material would have to be downloaded from the Internet.

Proxy Server has developed beyond these two basic functions. The latest version is also a fully functional firewall. An administrator can configure a Proxy server to filter packets based on numerous criteria. Unfortunately, each Proxy server must be manually configured as a separate entity. By placing this configuration information in ADS, an administrator could easily create a "master template" that all Proxy servers would use for their configuration. This would also facilitate changes, since you would make the changes only to the master template.

Site Server

Site Server is software designed to make the job of managing a Web site easier. It gives an administrator the ability to design a structured process for submitting, posting, and approving Web content. Having a defined process for publishing content can help to define a consistent look and feel for the corporate Web site.

Another function of Site Server is to provide users with the ability to search for specific Web content across multiple Web sites, servers, databases, and Microsoft Exchange public folders. In a large environment, finding information can be a daunting task for end-users.

Site Server also promotes the delivery of information to users by providing personalized Web pages, channels of information (as seen in Microsoft Internet Explorer 4), and e-mail. Site Server provides the tools necessary to analyze Web usage so that you can maximize your site's effectiveness.

Adding Functionality to Site Server with ADS

There are many aspects of Site Server that could benefit from the power of ADS, especially when combined with a few other pieces of the BackOffice suite. Style sheets for Web content, for instance, could be an attribute of Web page objects stored in ADS. A user who is working with a compatible product could create content and have the appropriate style applied to the page as it was posted to the Web server. The Web page object could also include an attribute that defined an "approval route" for new content, passing each page through an e-mail route automatically. Exchange Server could easily route the content to various mailboxes and include some sort of markup function for annotating the content.

As for the search functionality, ADS is the perfect solution. If each Web page were an ADS object, some of its attributes could easily contain information used by any search engine. Web sites in an ADS environment could open with a page that contains an LDAP lookup feature for searching the ADS database. This search could be based upon a number of attributes of the Web page object: a series of keywords defined by the author, a text description field, or even such simple things as department or author. Imagine a Web site where the opening page contained a search for content that was so effective you *always* found what you were looking for! You could type in a series of keywords and receive a list of relevant pages. This list could automatically contain links to the description attribute of each page. Rather than spending valuable time accessing each page, you could browse this list for more information about each page.

Since each Web page could contain keywords and description attributes, it would be fairly easy to build custom "home pages" for each user. By this, I don't mean content that the user has created (although we'll talk about that a little later), but rather the default site that the user's client software attaches to. Imagine opening Internet Explorer and having your first page consist of a list of sites that might be of interest to you. Each link could be associated with a small amount of text describing the site's content. Configuring this would be as easy as having the client software store a series of keywords used to search ADS for relevant content. Every time you opened IE4, it could perform an LDAP search for matches to your list of interests. Bingo! A dynamically built home page that is updated each time you open your client!

ADS could also be used to access a user's personal home page (content the user has created) by adding a Web-page path attribute to the user object class. Client software could then use an LDAP query to find the location of a particular user's home page. Better yet—why not add the Web-page attribute to other object classes as well? If you wanted the home page for a particular department, you could search for the Web page location of that department's object.

Since the purpose of ADS is resource location, it is a perfect match for the function of Site Server. I think this is one of the first Microsoft BackOffice products that will offer ADS integration.

Systems Management Server (SMS)

SMS was originally designed as a software distribution tool but has since developed into a complete network-management product. SMS can be configured to provide the following services on the network:

Remote software installation   The SMS administrator can create software installation *packages* that can be used to install software on a remote location. While a complete discussion of this procedure is beyond our scope, the basic process is to roll the installation of a piece of software into a single file (called a *package*), distribute that package to various SMS servers around your network, and have the client computers run the package. The administrator can schedule the installation based on numerous criteria. The software can be installed automatically at next logon, on a certain date, if the version on the target computer is older than that of the package, or even at the user's option.

Network packet analysis   SMS includes the commercial version of Network Monitor, a software-based packet analysis tool. Network Monitor allows an administrator to capture packets on the network and analyze their content. This function can help both in troubleshooting network-related problems and in network optimization.

Remote control of client computers   SMS includes the tools necessary to take control of a client computer from a remote location. This ability allows Help desk personnel to troubleshoot client computers without physical access to the machines. It also allows an administrator to show users the solutions to their needs on their own screens—you could, for instance, take control of a user's computer and show her how to apply italics to text in her word processor.

The remote control tools also include a chat utility that allows the administrator and the end-user to type comments to each other during the process. Many administrators feel that this feature alone is worth the price of admission to SMS. Many person-hours are spent physically moving to a client location and troubleshooting software or configuration problems that do not really require physical access to the computer. The only drawback to this process is that software must be running on the client computer that is to be controlled.

Software as an Object?

Each of the capabilities listed can be streamlined through integration with a network directory such as ADS. As a matter of fact, Microsoft has announced that many of the specific management capabilities now found in SMS will be built into the final version of Active Directory Services. Most of the software installation and client configuration capabilities of SMS, for instance, could be included as standard features of Windows 2000 Server.

The possibilities are plentiful for a network-management tool that takes advantage of the capabilities of ADS. Software distribution is just one small piece of the overall management puzzle, but it exemplifies the integration of SMS and ADS in a directory-based network—the software package has become an object in the directory database. Since ADS includes the appropriate services to replicate itself to multiple servers, the package distribution process need no longer be a part of the SMS application. Using ADS to manage the placement of the packages will also reduce the overhead on various servers. Imagine a process that would check for the location of home folders for all members of the "Word Processor" group and automatically place a copy of the newest word processing software on those servers. While it's at it, the same process could set up an installation schedule that would include a version check; if the new copy was a newer version, the process could automatically start an upgrade.

We've seen that Windows 2000 group policies can be configured to either assign or publish an application to users—basically replacing the software distribution capabilities of SMS.

The packet analysis process could also benefit from access to ADS. Since a directory can easily (and dynamically) store the IP and MAC addresses of computers, Network Monitor could easily display the NetBIOS names of the originator and destination for each packet it captures. It could also query ADS for the name of the user currently logged on to that computer. Inappropriate traffic could easily be identified—Network Monitor would only need to search the ADS database for matching MAC addresses. Any packets originating from a computer not registered with ADS could be flagged as potentially dangerous.

Remote control of client machines could also benefit from integration with ADS. When a user calls the Help desk, the remote control software could be configured to search ADS for the MAC address of the proper client computer. ADS could even be given the right to "log on as a service" so that the appropriate software could be started on the client computer at the point of contact (rather than having this software loading each time the client machine booted).

SMS is a perfect example of an add-on product that can utilize the information stored within the directory to perform its functions. Since network management seems to be a hot topic these days, we can assume that SMS will be quickly configured to this end.

SNA Server

SNA Server acts as a gateway to AS/400 and mainframe environments. Using software such as SNA Server allows companies to leverage their investment in such systems. Microsoft has promised that SNA Server will become the premier LAN-to-host and Web-to-host software.

As a gateway, SNA Server can take advantage of the type of information stored within ADS. Remember that one of the primary functions of any directory is to act as a resource locator. When moving from the LAN to the SNA environment, users could use ADS to find the server upon which the SNA gateway is running. When moving from the AS/400 or mainframe world, the SNA Server software can utilize ADS to find the requested resource.

Probably the most spectacular additions to the SNA Server software will be in the area of Web access. As the SNA environment becomes more closely integrated with the network, we will see applications that use ADS to authenticate to large databases stored on AS/400 or mainframe computers.

Once this becomes common, we will begin to see Web pages taking advantage of this connection. Imagine a Web page that contains a link to your order-entry database. Rather than gathering the information using CGI or Perl scripts and then batch-processing those orders to the mainframe, there could be a direct link to this process from any Web page.

SQL Server

As companies grow, so does the amount of data that they need to manipulate. SQL Server is a server-based database application capable of processing the large databases used in enterprise environments. SQL Server includes numerous fault-tolerant functions designed to ensure the integrity of the data, as well as a security system to control access to information. It can act as a powerful development environment for creating custom database applications.

The first change we will probably see in SQL Server will be the removal of its internal security system. SQL will trust the authentication process built into ADS and will use ADS user and group accounts to control access to information. This change alone should increase performance considerably by removing the security overhead from the SQL Server computer.

Since both ADS and SQL are basically database environments, it would not surprise me to see SQL begin to utilize some of the replication and distribution techniques used by ADS. A database that can distribute itself across multiple servers should be able to grow beyond the capacities of today's hardware. A database that can replicate itself to other servers is fault tolerant beyond the level of what is available today. ADS will help with both of these functions. One of the main functions of any directory is resource location. If SQL databases are treated like any other resource, there is no reason why client software cannot query ADS for the location of a particular database. ADS could also be used to balance the load of data access; if a database is "located" using ADS, there is no reason why ADS couldn't measure access and route clients to a less busy server that contains a replica of the database.

Office 2000

Although Office 2000 is not a part of the BackOffice suite, it deserves mention here as a Microsoft product that could benefit from the implementation of a network directory. There are two major issues in administering any client software:

- Licensing
- Providing fault-tolerant access

If the Office suite were represented by an object in the directory, both of these issues could be dealt with in a straightforward manner. If users found their copy of a particular piece of software through an ADS query, the directory could control the number of users accessing a given copy simultaneously. This would provide automatic software metering, ensuring that a company's use of an application would always be legal.

ADS could also contain the location of other network installations of the software and redirect users to another copy if a server goes offline or is experiencing a heavy load. Such service ensures network functionality and optimization. Best of all, it can happen automatically, without any administrative intervention!

In Short

Due to the extensibility of the ADS schema, the database can be configured to provide support for a wide range of applications. As administrators, developers, and even Microsoft begin to see ADS as another resource for services, we will start to see ADS taking a larger and larger role in day-to-day network access.

By providing a central point of control and consistent management utilities, ADS should soon begin to reduce the administrative load on overworked IS professionals. This will allow the implementation of new technologies to make end-users more productive, which, in turn, will benefit the bottom line.

Microsoft's goal seems to be to make ADS the central point of management for your entire network. We should see *everything* being integrated with the directory—from the obvious, like Windows 2000 servers and BackOffice applications, to the not-so-obvious, like Microsoft Office. Even third-party developers will soon be using ADS as an entry point into a Microsoft network. When all is said and done, your Windows 2000 network and most of the services it provides will revolve around Active Directory Services.

CHAPTER
15

ADS and
Third-Party Products

In our discussion of the possible effects of ADS on the Microsoft BackOffice suite of products, we saw what could be done if a developer had access to the internal organization, or *schema*, of the directory. We can assume that Microsoft's internal developers have such access and that Microsoft has a unique incentive to integrate its products with ADS—market share! Microsoft promises that third-party developers will also have complete access to the directory schema. Since the old adage "You can't get fired for buying IBM" has changed to "You can't get fired for buying Microsoft," it is safe to assume that third-party developers will also have an incentive to write programs that leverage ADS.

Microsoft has a couple of strong incentives to ensure that *all* developers have access to the directory database and its schema. First, given the antitrust suits that have been filed against it, Microsoft needs to maintain the appearance of offering fair access. Second, no product, no matter how technically advanced or well marketed, has succeeded in the networking realm without developer support. Microsoft has already promised that hundreds of ADS-enabled products will be available as soon as ADS hits the streets.

Software

There are literally thousands of software development companies around the globe. While I tend to avoid marketing terms, I do think that the release of ADS has ushered in a new paradigm for NT development. Writing programs that can take advantage of the power of a directory requires a completely different mindset than writing code for a domain-based environment. Regardless of the propaganda released by Microsoft, NT 4 is still a "server"-based operating system. Writing directory-based applications requires developers to change their viewpoint from the server to the network.

The move from using a small-scale *server*-based accounts database—or even the *enterprise*-capable domain accounts database for user authentication—is as drastic as the move from procedural programming to object-oriented programming. Developers need to analyze the capabilities and weaknesses of a directory and learn new techniques to maximize the benefits and minimize the drawbacks. Learning these new skills will take time.

I expect that the first ADS-compliant programs will be little more than programs that use the user authentication functions of the directory to control access to internal functions. I am sure that we will soon see a database engine that uses ADS account information to control access to files within a database—or maybe even fields within a specific file. An employee records database, for instance, could certainly contain information that is highly confidential. Today, such data is often placed in a separate file to ensure security. In an ADS environment, however, each field within the directory could include its own ACL made up of the security identifiers of ADS objects. It would then be easy to assign permissions to individual fields within a complex database. From an administrative perspective, such an arrangement reduces the number of databases that must be maintained, backed up, and managed.

Using the directory to authenticate users for data access, however, is just the tip of the iceberg. Before developers can begin to take advantage of the directory for more complex functions, they will have to redefine how they look at network-based applications.

The Application as an Object

While the scope of many applications is seen as networkwide—meaning that they provide services to the network, across the network, or are themselves dependent on the network—most are still written using the same process that was used to write programs years ago. Applications are written to be self-sufficient: They run as a separate process, control their own internal security, and manage their own data. Before we can begin to see true directory-integrated applications, developers will need to change some basic concepts about how a program should interact with a network.

The first step will be moving configuration information from a local (to the application) source, such as an .INI file or the Registry, to ADS. To accomplish this, we must first see applications as objects within the directory. There are two basic ways to accomplish this. One way would be to have each developer create his own customized application object class specific to the needs of his product. While this would ensure a "perfect fit," it would also force a high level of expertise when developing products for Windows 2000. This might not be in Microsoft's best interests (Microsoft wants as many "ADS-enabled" products on the market as possible). The better route might be to define a standard application object class as part of the standard schema for ADS. This option would make life easier for both developers and administrators, since all application objects would then have similar attributes. Some of the attributes of such an object might include the following:

- Location of program files

- User permissions

- Licenses purchased

- A link to the installation program (or better yet, to an SMS package that automatically installs the program)

- A link to application-specific help, such as online training materials

- Application version

- Minimum hardware requirements (and perhaps a program to test the user's machine to see if it meets those minimums)

- The e-mail address of the administrator of the application

The possibilities are endless! Most of these attributes are nothing more than a central location for normal configuration information. Some of these attributes could revolutionize the way that networked applications are accessed or managed.

Location of Program Files

Many companies install applications on multiple servers. They might do this to reduce the overhead on any single server or to ensure that a mission-critical application is available in the event of a server crash. Sometimes applications are stored on multiple servers to ensure that users have access to a local copy. Traveling users, for instance, might need to use an application at multiple sites. Whatever the reason, managing multiple copies of the same program can add a lot of administrative overhead. You must perform upgrades at each location, grant users permissions for each copy that they might use, and define shortcuts for each location (to avoid pulling a copy from the user's home location). And you must perform all of these tasks as though each copy were the *only* copy of the application.

If an application were accessed through a directory object, you could handle each of these tasks from a central location and eliminate many of the redundant management tasks.

Using network addresses, ADS could easily redirect a user's request to the closest server containing an application, as shown in Figure 15.1. I've seen numerous laptops that are configured with multiple shortcuts to the same application: Database–Tampa, Database–St. Paul, Database–Reno, and so on. In an ADS-enabled solution, the directory would read the current address of the user's computer, determine which ADS site the user was in, compare that with the locations of the application, and automatically send the user to the closest copy.

F I G U R E 15.1

Automatic redirection process

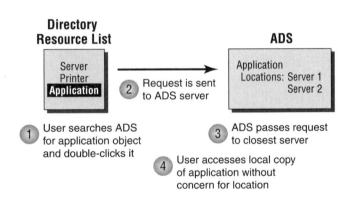

To run an ADS-aware application, the client would follow these steps:

1. The user would access a tool that presented the directory graphically. The tool could have an automatic filter in place so that only applications are displayed, or the user might just double-click an icon for the application on his Desktop.

2. The client software would forward the request to an ADS server. The server would compare the user's network address with those of the various servers that contain the application.

3. Based on defined criteria, the user's request would be forwarded to the appropriate server.

4. The user would access the application without having to be concerned with the physical aspect of the network.

You could configure ADS to use many different kinds of criteria when choosing the appropriate server for a user:

- Using the network address of the requesting computer, ADS could ensure that only local copies of the application would be offered to the user.

- ADS could be configured to alternate among the various copies available in an effort to ensure that no single server would be overburdened.

- ADS could be configured to check Performance Monitor statistics (such as %processor time or Available Memory) and use this information to help load-balance application use across several servers.

- In a company where software is purchased on a departmental level, ADS could check a user's membership in a department and offer only software owned by that user's department.

Once access to an application is controlled by a directory, the physical location of the software becomes a function of the network—not of the client's configuration.

Licensing

To protect themselves against possible civil lawsuits, many companies have policies against software piracy. Even the most skilled administrators can have trouble, however, enforcing such a policy across large networks. Installing applications in multiple locations only adds to the problem.

The application object within the directory could be configured with an attribute used to store the number of software licenses purchased. It would be a simple matter then for ADS to keep a running count of the number of users accessing a given application. When the maximum number of licenses has been reached, subsequent users requesting the application could be denied access. The effect would be automatic software metering that is managed from a central location—the directory.

Authentication

Since one of the main purposes of a network directory is user identification and authentication to resources, programs will likely begin to take advantage of these directory functions. At first, we will probably see ADS being used to determine which users can access a particular program. This approach is really no different from the traditional approach of using file permissions to determine access.

Developers could also use ADS identification as a basis for controlling access to internal application services. Perhaps certain features of a program should be available only to particular users. An example of this function might be an application used to design new products. The program might allow anyone in the engineering department the ability to work on product designs, but only certain users could copy or print this type of data. This would prevent unauthorized distribution of new product designs.

Upgrades

Most vendors release new and improved versions of their software on a regular basis. One of the more difficult tasks of a network administrator is keeping up with these new releases. The rollout of a new version can often involve a considerable amount of your time and effort. Companies often end up using multiple versions of the same software. In a perfect world, this would not be a major problem; all software would be backward compatible with earlier versions. Unfortunately, the latest release of an application is not always compatible with earlier versions—for example, files created with version 2 might not be accessible using version 3. With ADS application objects, each version could be configured as a separate object and assigned to users as appropriate.

Another interesting option would be an ADS-enabled installation process. Since the directory could be configured to hold the location of all copies of a particular application, it should be fairly easy for a developer to create an upgrade process that reads the location from ADS and upgrades all copies simultaneously. Imagine an upgrade process that was run only once—but upgrades every copy of the application on your network.

Installation

With the complexity of today's programs, installing software is more than just copying files to a directory. While most configuration information can be stored in the directory, certain configuration issues still must be handled at the client computer. Certain files, such as .DLLs, must be stored at the client machine. Installing software on local computers is a large part of the job for most network administrators.

ADS could be configured to automate most of the tasks associated with software installation. As a user attempts to access the application, ADS could check for the existence of necessary files, folders, or configuration information at the local computer. If ADS did not find these items, it could automatically install them, either through an interactive solution in which the user must provide configuration information or through an automated setup routine. ADS could also be configured to reverse these changes when the user closes the program. This would provide a truly dynamic environment where all applications were available to all users from any point on the network.

As the bandwidth available on most networks increases, many experts think we will see a shift back to server-installed applications. A central location gives administrators much more control over use, configuration, and security of applications. There will always be situations, however, that mandate a local installation of software. Laptops, for instance, where users need access to software when they are not attached to the network, will require local installation. ADS could be used to store automated installation routines for these situations. If a user needed a particular program on his computer, he could just access the installation object in ADS (while in the office and attached to the network), perhaps answer a few configuration questions, and then have the software installed on his laptop for use when out of the office.

External Access through LDAP

As we discussed earlier, Lightweight Directory Access Protocol (LDAP) defines a set of functions to be used when accessing the directory. One of the biggest benefits of LDAP is that it allows diverse clients the ability to access directory objects remotely. Combining the functionality of an LDAP-enabled directory with directory-aware applications results in a few interesting possibilities.

There has been a lot of discussion over the last few years about changing the way that software is purchased. Rather than buying an entire package—often for one feature or, even worse, for one project—you could start "renting" access to applications from vendors. Your company would not need to purchase software; rather, you would purchase the use of that software. Your company would be billed for each use (or perhaps for the amount of time you used the software), just as you are billed for your use of long-distance phone services.

Once implemented, this type of billing arrangement should benefit both the software company and its customers. The vendor would see reductions in hard costs, since customers would no longer receive a CD-ROM or floppy disk with the program on it. Renting software would also reduce support costs, since the software is stored at the vendor's site rather than on customer computers. Most installation and configuration support costs would probably become negligible.

Customers would see a reduction in initial costs, since they would not begin to pay for the software until it was actually in use. Since the software is the responsibility of the vendor, upgrades, enhancements, and bug fixes would also cease to be local problems. Just the reduction in the cost of upgrading software to stay current should be enough to justify the switch.

A directory service is the perfect technology for managing a pay-as-you-use software distribution system. The directory can hold authentication information to control access to the software, store configuration information for installation, and provide remote access to this information.

Reporting Features

In many companies, management seems to want reports more than performance. Administrators are required to justify expenses, measure bandwidth availability, and even extrapolate current conditions to include additional personnel or hardware. We use spreadsheets, graphs, analogies, and external sources to create reports that often seem to go unread.

Here's a hint for dealing with upper-level management: pictures and colors! Try to include eye-catching graphs printed with bright colors in your reports and presentations. Remember that most upper-level managers have little understanding of the technical side of networking. Creating a visual message is often the most effective way to present your information.

One area that is often ignored is the use and maintenance of software. Administrators are often asked to maintain current licensing information, to evaluate new products or upgrades, and to provide end-user training and Help desk support. Using software that pulls information from a directory, administrators could conceivably create reports that would include the following:

Peak usage and average usage   This information could be used to help justify the purchase of additional software licenses.

Data access   ADS could include an auditing feature that would allow an administrator to report the usage of confidential data.

Resource utilization   Using statistics available through Performance Monitor, ADS could be configured to report the overhead placed upon server resources during actual user access.

Software in Short

Once software developers start to view their products as another object in the ADS database, we should begin to see applications that take advantage of the services ADS can provide. Beyond simple user authentication, true ADS-aware applications will store their configuration information in the database, use the directory to control access to internal functions, and even provide installation and upgrade information.

While none of the innovations presented in this chapter is likely to be available tomorrow, moving to a directory-based network will have a great impact on how you view network applications.

Hardware

In the early days of networking, many components had to be configured by hand. Dip switches, jumpers, and custom internal setup routines were the norm. Today, however, most hardware uses a software interface of some sort for configuration. Any product that is configured using software is a candidate for configuration through a directory database. To make effective use of directories, hardware vendors must make the same kinds of changes as software developers. First and foremost, hardware manufacturers must begin to see their products as an integral part of the whole, rather than as a separate entity. Some vendors, because of the way their products are currently used, will have an easier time with this switch than others.

As with software, most early ADS-enabled hardware will probably just use the authentication services of ADS. The configuration software will count on ADS to confirm the identity of a user in order to control who has the right to use or manage a product. As time goes on, however, we should start to see some sophisticated uses of ADS for hardware management. Before this can happen, though, vendors must begin to view their products as objects in the tree.

Hardware as Objects

With software, it might be possible to create a generic "application" object that could be used to represent most types of applications. With hardware, however, there are so many different types in use—each with a completely different set of configuration and management parameters—that I believe that each vendor will have to define its own object class for the ADS tree. While Microsoft has promised that the ADS schema will be extensible, extending the schema will probably not be an easy task. Because of this, hardware manufacturers will need to train their developers in the methods necessary to ensure a clean install.

WARNING   Remember: If the extension *should* corrupt the directory, *all* network functions could be affected.

On the plus side, since each vendor will customize the object class that describes its hardware, there should never be a problem with compatibility or lack of functionality. Vendors should be able to include *every* piece of configuration information in the directory. Some common object will probably be defined as a "standard," just as some vendors create *de facto* standards now. Hewlett Packard, for instance, in many ways defines the direction of the printing industry. Many brands of printers can be configured to use a "standard" HP print driver. It is not inconceivable that HP would define a printer object to manage its printer, and that other manufacturers would create printers compatible with it.

Much of the work of moving hardware management has already been accomplished. Most vendors currently allow remote management and configuration using Simple Network Management Protocol (SNMP) Tools. Since SNMP is based on a series of hierarchical databases, known as *MIBs* (Management Information Bases), it should not be too difficult to transfer the process to a directory-based solution.

Although we may think of ADS as the perfect solution, there will always be a few types of hardware that are not easily managed or configured remotely. On the other hand, certain hardware lends itself quite nicely to a directory-based solution.

Computer Objects

Perhaps no other object is as critical to our networks and as hard to manage from a central location as the plain old desktop computer. Administrators spend thousands of dollars on software that can perform some of the following routine desktop management tasks:

- Remote control of the computer

- Hardware inventory

- Software inventory

- Remote diagnostics

- Network mapping

The biggest problem with computer management has always been that there is no standard way to connect to, manage, or configure the various makes and models available. Many administrators enforce a strict "single vendor" rule, limiting purchases to a single provider. While this approach does solve the standard access problem, it creates another problem—single vendor dependency. Personal computers have almost become an appliance device. By this I mean that there are not many differences between the various makes of computers on the market. This situation should be good for administrators, since they can shop around for the lowest price when purchasing new computers. A single-source approach negates this benefit.

Before I get a lot of nasty e-mail from computer manufacturers, let me explain. In most cases a PC is a PC: Most are based on the same basic chip set, use the same components, and are capable of pretty much the same performance. How these components are installed and configured can make a difference in overall performance, but the basic underlying concepts are the same!

Microsoft NT already provides the basic capabilities for remote management of many workstation-related issues. Most of the tools provided with the NT operating system can be used for either local or remote management. Server Manager, for instance, allows an administrator to create, modify, and delete share points on all members of the domain. Windows NT Diagnostics also allows remote access to the configuration of various parameters on an NT computer. Even the Registry editing tool REGEDIT.EXE allows for remote manipulation of the Registry files. Active Directory Services should just extend these capabilities.

From a hardware perspective, there is really nothing difficult about allowing remote access to the configuration of a computer. As long as the machine has a network interface card installed and the appropriate protocols configured, remote management should physically be a breeze. The problem lies in authentication of configuration requests. Without a centrally located and trusted authority in place, each computer manufacturer would have to design some sort of authentication routine. These routines could be as simple as a password or as complex as an encrypted certificate–driven process. At either end of the spectrum, though, administrators would need to know the particular process used by a specific vendor.

This is where ADS comes in—its main function is user authentication. Since it can be accessed by any client using industry standard protocols (LDAP), manufacturers will not have to develop the methods used. They will, in fact, only need to define the extension to the ADS schema that will store configuration information. In effect, while ADS is a commercial product, its acceptance could drive hardware vendors to a single standard for remote management. The more successful ADS is, the greater the likelihood that manufacturers will include ADS support in their products. With

Microsoft's track record of operating system dominance, it seems likely that ADS will become the preferred method of device management.

One of the first ADS-enabled PC management functions will probably involve asset tracking and inventory. As long as the computer object in the directory includes the appropriate attributes, having the PC automatically update configuration information would be a fairly simple process. Such information could include serial numbers, amount of memory, total disk space, and even the type (and number) of processors present. ADS could even include a process that would send automatic alerts to an administrator if a PC's configuration changes.

Once the simple act of inventory has been accomplished, the next step would be proactive management. Imagine a PC that automatically informs an administrator when a hard disk is going bad or, even better, when disk space is getting low.

Network Components

Anyone who has ever had to reconfigure a complex router at 3:00 A.M. will appreciate a system that allows for redundant configuration locations and automatic reconfiguration as needed. Some day, ADS will act as the repository of the configuration information for all of your network devices. Since ADS is distributed and replicated, you will never have to worry about reconfiguration again. In the event of a device problem or replacement, ADS will be able to provide a complete configuration of the device over the network. Since ADS is able to use industry standard LDAP, all devices should be able to use this feature.

We'll discuss the future of networking in more detail in Chapter 16. For now, the following is just a general discussion of the possibilities.

Due to the complex nature of their function, network devices are notoriously difficult to configure and maintain. Routers, bridges, gateways, switches—even the network cable—itself could easily be documented and managed through directory objects. Using industry standard protocols like

LDAP opens the field for a standard remote-management procedure. Here are just a few of the possibilities:

- Devices that allow access to their service based on an ADS-authenticated account

- Devices that measure bandwidth and reroute network traffic based on preferences stored in ADS

- Switches that guarantee bandwidth for certain processes or users

- Routers that route traffic only for members of a particular ADS group

This list can go on and on. The point is that once network devices are configured through a network directory, there is no limit to the types of management open to administrators.

Printers

Printers are one of the most common network peripherals—and one of the most important. It is surprising, then, how little control we have over our printing environment. We spend thousands of dollars creating fault-tolerant, stable, and secure networks, but we seem to balk at spending any time optimizing our printing process.

NT has made great gains in the area of printer management. Even without the benefit of ADS, NT print servers can automatically download the correct print driver to a client, printers can be redirected to another device with just a few mouse clicks, and the process of sharing a printer has been made so easy that just about any end-user can figure it out (sometimes without our approval). While these are all improvements over the network printing of 10 years ago, there is really nothing revolutionary in any of these functions. ADS should provide a playing field in which network printing can become a stable and reliable process.

Printing is so important in most environments that when a printer goes offline, at least a few people are no longer able to perform their work. The more important the ability to print, the more important a directory solution becomes. When a printer is unavailable, the current answer is to "resubmit the job to another printer." This quick fix places the burden on the end-user—a person who is not always computer or network savvy. ADS should be able to perform automatic print job redirection based on printer make and model or even print driver version. A typical scenario is shown in Figure 15.2.

FIGURE 15.2

Automatic print job redirection

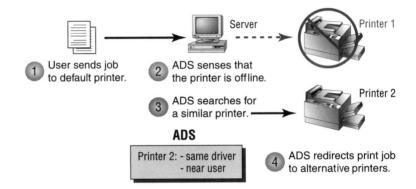

1. User sends job to default printer.
2. ADS senses that the printer is offline.
3. ADS searches for a similar printer.

ADS

Printer 2: - same driver
          - near user

4. ADS redirects print job to alternative printers.

Here's what the figure illustrates:

1. The user submits a print job to Printer 1.

2. Printer 1 is offline due to a mechanical failure.

3. ADS searches the directory for a printer near the user that can use the same print driver as the original printer.

4. ADS redirects the job to the new printer and sends a notification to that effect to all users whose jobs have been redirected.

If a location attribute exists, ADS could even send directions to the alternative printer.

The user receives her output without fuss *and* without having to be aware of the network or its physical layout.

Another possible ADS enhancement to the printing environment would be automatic distribution of print services. In the event of a print server going offline (a server crash, disk failure, or other unexpected event), ADS could automatically move the print server service to another server in the directory tree. Since the data in ADS is distributed and replicated, the loss of a single server should never disable the print environment. In a more advanced configuration, ADS could actually measure system overhead and move the print server service from a busy server to a less busy Windows 2000 server.

Fax Services

Fax servers have become an integral part of many organizations. Most do an adequate job, but I have yet to find one that is really enterprise capable. My dream fax server would include the following:

- First and foremost, it must automatically identify the recipient for incoming faxes. Once identified, the user would receive his fax as e-mail or through some other mechanism.

- The user's physical location would have no bearing on her receipt of faxed materials. If the user is logged on anywhere in the network, the fax would be forwarded to her computer.

- In a multisite environment, the outgoing faxes would be routed through a server that is local to the recipient. Put another way, the fax software would be smart enough to choose a local call over a long-distance call.

All of the information necessary to perform these tasks can be stored within the ADS database. Incoming faxes can be searched for names that match various attributes: name, full name, department, and so on. Any match should result in a fax delivered to the appropriate e-mail box.

PBX Services

One of the most exciting Microsoft technologies is the service available through the use of the Telephony API (Application Programming Interface), also known as *TAPI*. TAPI allows your operating system (both client and server) some measure of control over the telephone system. Most of us are already familiar with the user side of the TAPI environment. Anyone who has installed Dial-Up Networking on Windows 95 has experienced TAPI. Basically, TAPI defines a set of functions designed to interface with a telephone system.

Since ADS will contain the telephone numbers for all user accounts, using ADS to route calls will be fairly easy. Your PBX system will submit the number or extension requested, ADS will search for a matching value, and the call will be routed to the appropriate desk.

A new twist, however, is that your calls will automatically follow you around the company. ADS stores the MAC address of the machine where you are currently logged in. Using this information, ADS should be able to route calls to you, no matter where you are sitting. Imagine a telephone system smart enough to follow a user from desk to desk, without any user intervention. Once companies begin to adopt voice over IP technologies, this will get even easier. A user could move from site to site, and, as long as he was logged on to the network, his telephone calls would be forwarded to his current location.

ADS should also be able to route voice mail into your e-mail inbox. Since one of the attributes of a user account is the e-mail address, this should be a simple process. The client software for Exchange Server has always promoted the concept of a *Universal Inbox* as a single interface to all types of incoming information. These applications are already set to contain everything from e-mail messages to voice mail.

ADS should also be able to connect to various other database applications. Once ADS has found your current physical location, it should be able to read a SQL database and use call-ID to identify the caller's location. Your SQL server could then locate the appropriate client and put the caller's information on your computer screen.

Inventory Control

Since any device can be defined within the ADS database, we should soon begin to see some interesting uses of this technology. One example has been given at many seminars on directory services. Imagine a vending machine that informs its owner when it is out of a particular brand of soft drink. Using some sort of Internet connection, the device could pass its inventory along to ADS. ADS could, in turn, pass this information to the dispatcher, who could then dump all of the information into a program that designed a custom-built routing for delivery drivers.

The vending machine example is probably some distance down the road. The cost of installing the cellular connectivity, the processing power, and the sensors is still too high for implementation in a production environment. The same feature, however, could be cost-justified in many systems. Printers, for instance, could contain sensors that measure the amount of paper or toner available. At a certain threshold, the printer could send an e-mail message to the appropriate user—or even add a new toner cartridge to your next order from the office supply store.

Facilities Management

Facilities management and security systems use tools that are already capable of connecting to a network. High-end furnaces and air conditioners for large environments already drop statistics to a program for analysis, and many are already configured through a software interface. One of the biggest drawbacks with today's systems is that most use proprietary protocols. ADS provides a standard interface and access mechanism. Some day, you might change the temperature of your office by accessing the furnace object in an Active Directory Services database.

In Short

Third-party vendors of hardware and software stand to gain greatly from the capabilities of Active Directory Services. Before they can take advantage of the possibilities, though, most will have to redefine how they look at their products, networks, and the world. The biggest challenge will be to begin looking at products as just another object in the directory tree. Once this view is established, ADS-enabled products will flourish!

On the software front, moving to ADS-enabled configuration and management involves rethinking the way in which most software is designed. Once a program has been written to store its configuration information in ADS, however, consumers will begin to see the benefits, including central management, easy upgrades, load balancing, and license control. Software developers who jump on the ADS bandwagon will have the opportunity to define the direction of the networking industry.

The same can be said for the next generation of network hardware. By using industry standard methods of access, manufacturers will be able to move all of their configuration information to a central repository—ADS.

Once there, the information can be replicated, copied, and used for various reports to upper management.

The development and release of ADS-aware software and hardware might just change the very core of our perspective on networking. Although I hate to use it, the phrase *paradigm shift* really is appropriate. Tomorrow's networks will use a directory service to provide network services on a global scale.

In Chapter 16 we will take this idea of "ADS-enabled" to the next level. One of the most complex pieces of today's networks is the network itself. In other words, the physical devices that allow information to flow from one place to another have become an administrator's nightmare! Maintaining the physical devices, configuring security policies, and controlling user access can be a full-time job. Two companies—Microsoft and Cisco—have teamed up to create a standard way to manage network devices through a directory. This standard is known as the *Directory Enabled Networks* (DEN) model. Given the market penetration of the two principals, DEN warrants a very close look.

CHAPTER

16

Directory-Enabled
Networks (DENs)

We have discussed Active Directory Services as a tool to ease the administrative overhead of managing a large network. Microsoft ADS provides a Windows 2000 network with a single point of management and the flexibility necessary for complex environments. ADS is a single database designed to be used by the Windows 2000 operating system to authenticate users to the network and the resources on that network. From the administrative perspective, ADS reduces the amount of redundant management that is the norm for nondirectory-based operating systems. The ability to distribute the ADS database across servers reduces the overhead on each server, and the ability to replicate pieces of the database to multiple servers provides a level of fault tolerance not found in earlier versions of NT. All in all, Active Directory Services should make the life of most network administrators easier, leaving more time for adding user-specific functionality to their networks.

We've also discussed the benefits of ADS for typical users. Using ADS to authenticate to resources is really no different from using any other network operating system available: Users run whatever program is necessary to log on, provide a name and password, and are on the network. The logon procedure hasn't changed much since the dawn of networking. ADS does, however, offer certain advantages over a nondirectory solution. By providing a logical interface to the resources on a network, ADS reduces the level of "network literacy" necessary to take advantage of network functionality. Put another way, a common user with little knowledge of the network can access and use resources and services across a complex network. Users no longer need to be aware of the physical layout of the resources. A user can access a local printer in the same way she would access a resource in a remote location. ADS provides the link between the logical presentation and the physical location of resources on the network. From a user's perspective, this is probably the biggest benefit of a move to a directory-based network operating system.

While both perspectives are important—and are probably the key to understanding Microsoft Active Directory Services—they do not cover the entire gamut of services that can be provided by a networkwide directory. We have yet to discuss the benefits of ADS to the physical aspect of a network. Many administrators think of a network as a group of computers and peripherals tied together by some sort of cable. The *cable* (which includes the physical media used to transport data, and also includes routers, switches, and every other piece of equipment between one computer and another on a network) is often thought of as a separate area of expertise. In fact, many companies have a completely different set of professionals to handle connectivity issues. These devices need as much management as any other peripheral on a network (actually, they often seem to require *more* management than most other devices). Due to the complex nature of what they do, things like routers and switches often have extremely complex management methods.

A directory service is a database designed to hold information about network resources. Since the network infrastructure is just another resource, albeit a complex one, we should be able to use ADS to provide central management for infrastructure devices, as well as the more traditional peripherals discussed earlier. The management of network devices is what the *Directory-Enabled Networks (DEN)* initiative is all about.

Challenges in Today's Networking Environments

In the early days of networking, a network consisted of a few computers with some coaxial cable strung between them, as you can see in Figure 16.1. There were only a few rules to remember:

- Each segment could be no longer than 185 meters.

- Each end of the segment had to have a terminating resistor.

- Each segment had to be grounded.

- No more than 30 devices could be on a segment.

- The *5-4-3* rule must be observed. This rule allowed a maximum of five segments connected through four repeaters, with only three segments populated with computers (the other two segments were used to extend length).

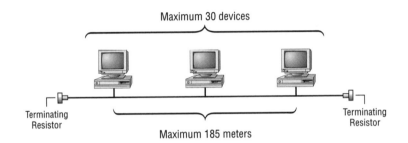

The biggest infrastructure problems were cable breaks and putting too many devices on a single segment. Of course, administrators had other problems to deal with: unstable operating systems, arcane and confusing management interfaces, and equipment prone to failure. The bottom line, though, was that we were not pushing the limits of the network infrastructure. Ten Mbps Ethernet was really overkill, given the uses to which we put our networks.

Today, it's a completely different world. It's common to see 100Mbps segments, and many of these are running out of available bandwidth. Gigabit backbones are being put in place, and still we talk about limited bandwidth. Users are demanding more and more sophisticated services from the company network. Some user reads a copy of *Byte* magazine and suddenly everyone wants real-time stock quotes as a tickertape screen saver. Another user has a friend who uses the Internet for real-time chats, and suddenly we must provide the same service. The executive committee reads about a company (obviously with a much larger IS budget) that is using the Internet as the network for video conferencing—could you have that working by next week? The pressures being placed on our networks are growing at an alarming rate. Solutions are often not available in a timely manner—due not to lack of technology but rather to lack of budget or a need for upgraded equipment. New technologies appear every day. Here are some of the hot topics:

- Streaming multimedia content across the network. This technology is used for everything from providing sales and marketing information to potential clients to end-user training.

- The use of public networks, such as the Internet, to connect to internal resources. Virtual Private Networks, which use a public network as the medium for secure exchange of data, are becoming a necessary part of most networks. Telecommunications costs have gotten out of hand and anything that can reduce them *must* be considered.

- Security concerns about public networks. Data encryption is becoming commonplace. Firewalls are a mandatory piece of equipment on any network connected to the Internet.

- The effect of network size on functionality. With the number of mergers and buyouts that happen each day, the average size of commercial networks is growing by leaps and bounds. Even without adding functionality, this increase in the number of people using the network would *still* affect performance.

Information offered in a timely, efficient, and user-friendly manner is the key to success in today's markets. The importance of the Information Services department has risen to new highs—of course, that means that the drop is longer, as well! It's a constant struggle to balance technical solutions with return on investment. Executives seem to see only two things: a service they want and the bottom line. Often the two views don't match. The cost of implementing new technologies cannot always be measured by the cost of equipment or software; the intangible costs are often much higher (as are the intangible benefits). Hidden costs can include:

- Downtime due to implementing solutions that are not mature enough for a production environment

- Increased bandwidth needs to support new services, resulting in a slowdown of networkwide services as segments become saturated

- Person-hours spent installing new technologies

- Training costs of new capabilities

- On-the-job mistakes due to lack of experience

The challenge facing network administrators is to provide the latest technologies while working within the constraints of budget, experience, and person-hours. Meeting these challenges is what DEN is all about!

What Is DEN?

DEN is really both a model and a set of specifications describing methods for managing network devices through a directory, specifically Microsoft Active Directory Services. Two companies, Microsoft and Cisco, provided the driving force behind DEN, although numerous other companies have contributed to the overall concept. The plan was turned over to the International Standards Organization and is now under ISO's control. As defined by the document *DEN: Information Model and Base Schema*, there are two goals to this initiative:

- To bind users to services available from the network according to a consistent and rational set of policies

- To provide the foundation to build intelligent networks and network-enabled applications

To accomplish these goals, DEN attempts to define how network resources should use the directory to complete the following:

- Publish information about themselves

- Discover other resources

- Obtain information about other resources

If a device can accomplish these three tasks, applications for that device can begin to interact with the network as a whole. These devices can then begin to make intelligent decisions about how to best perform their functions.

Increasing Efficiency and Consistency

As an example, let's look at routers as a directory object and how they would use the three actions just listed to increase network efficiency.

First, a router would need to publish information about itself in the directory. This basically means that the router would be represented by an object in the database, and would automatically provide the values of certain attributes. A typical router, for instance, might publish its rated throughput capacity as an attribute of its object. If a router were to become congested due to high network traffic, that router might query ADS for the location of other routers on the network. These routers would also have provided their throughput ratings to ADS. The congested router could use ADS to find routers that have routes to specific destinations (in other words, routers that can handle some of its traffic) and then query them to see how busy they are. Based on this information, the congested router can make intelligent decisions about the rerouting of traffic, as you can see in Figure 16.2.

F I G U R E   16.2

Intelligent rerouting of
network traffic

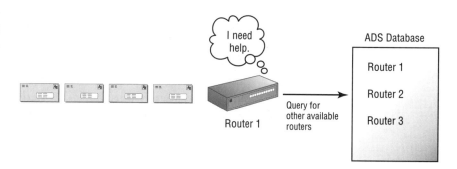

One of the main goals of the DEN initiative is to allow administrators to create consistent policies for resource access. We have already discussed the hierarchical nature of the ADS database. We've also discussed how security decisions flow down the structure so that an administrator can set up security in one location and have it affect multiple containers within the tree. DEN defines how network resources should take advantage of this system to allow the implementation of a consistent set of rules that govern resource use. An administrator might create a group object in ADS that contains all of the users within the executive committee. A policy might then be created that grants members of this group guaranteed bandwidth at all routers. Rather than configuring each device separately, this single policy would be implemented across the entire network (or any portion, as desired).

The DEN Information Model

The entire purpose of integrating a directory service with the network is to provide an environment where network information is made available to applications. This allows the applications to better leverage the various resources and services available and provide enhanced functionality to users. In other words, knowledge is power. The more information available about the network, the more intelligent the choices made by applications can be.

The *DEN information model* is an abstraction of knowledge so that the organization of that information can be understood before implementation. Using the information model as a guide, application developers can better utilize the data stored in the directory database. This, in turn, allows them to design applications that are aware of the network and able to make informed choices. The DEN information model defines how network resources should be defined within the directory and how these objects can interact with resources such as users, applications, and other network devices.

ADS defines objects that represent users and groups and a multitude of other objects. The DEN information model defines a hierarchy of network-related objects. Essentially, DEN is the definition of an extension to the existing schema. This extension not only defines a new set of objects; it defines how these objects should interact with each other and with other objects within the directory.

What's in the DEN Information Model?

The information model consists of three parts:

- Six base classes of objects that define the basic elements and services added to the directory schema. These six classes are the following:

  - NetworkElement

  - NetworkProtocol

  - NetworkMedia

  - NetworkService

  - Profile

  - Policy

We'll look at each class in detail later in this chapter.

- An extensible schema based on the format of the ADS schema. It uses the same inheritance principles as ADS.

- Mechanisms for establishing relationships between objects.

Interoperability

The information model is the key to providing networks that are truly *network enabled*. It is this set of standards that ensures that multivendor solutions will be available. Using the DEN extensions, an administrator could choose management products from multiple vendors, and those products would be able to share information through the directory. This interoperability is a major goal of the DEN initiative. It should be possible for any vendor to create an object within the tree, have the device populate that object (automatically provide values for its attributes), and publish that information to the directory. Another vendor's application could then interrogate the directory, pull that information out, and use it for its own purposes. Since all of the information is stored in a common format, with common access and security procedures, there should be no problem with compatibility.

History shows us that a committee might have lofty interoperability goals, but actual implementation is another story. While the theory makes for a great story, I'm not sure that the reality will be quite as rosy. It will be interesting to look back on the development of ADS-enabled applications 10 years from now and see just how interoperable they really were.

DEN Operational Models

Network objects are much more complex than the other types of ADS objects we have discussed. This is because the resources they represent are, by nature of their function, more complex than users, groups, or any of the other standard ADS object classes. The hierarchical structure of ADS cannot, by itself, describe the relationships between network object classes. To understand these relationships, it is necessary to model the network resources and services. A *model* is an abstraction of something that is used to help understand that thing. There are three states to complex objects within the directory, each of which is described within a different operational model:

Object model   Used to describe the static aspects of the schema. Things like object classes, attributes, and relationships between objects are described in an object model.

Dynamic model   Used to describe the behavior of objects as they interact with each other and how each component is controlled as a function of time or change in state. In other words, a dynamic model defines how objects interrelate and the changes within the environment that control these relationships.

Functional model   Used to describe the relationships between values and the process used to determine the final value of an attribute. For example, an attribute of one object might be set to an active state based on the value of an attribute of another object.

DEN Attributes

Each object defined within the schema will contain attributes. The DEN initiative defines four different types of attributes:

Intrinsic   Information that rarely or never changes. This information can be used to uniquely identify the device, such as a MAC or IP address.

Configurable   Information that defines the operation of a device. This data remains static until the configuration of the device changes. For a router object, for instance, configurable attributes might be the number and types of interfaces. This information would not change until another interface was added to the device.

Operational   Information that describes how a device interacts with its environment. This information determines how the device functions without any manual intervention. A dynamically built routing table, for example, defines the routing parameters of a router and is built automatically.

Contextual Defines how a device relates to other objects on the network. These attributes use the other types of information available, especially intrinsic and operational, to define relationships.

Defining Relationships between Objects

The definition of relationships between objects within the directory tree is one of the most important functions of DEN. This ability is what gives devices the knowledge to make intelligent choices about the way they provide their services. A switch might be related to an application object so that the application is provided a guaranteed amount of bandwidth. A live video feed, for instance, is the type of data that requires a large amount of bandwidth on a consistent basis. DEN defines three different types of relationships between objects:

Link A physical or conceptual relationship between two objects. A link is an instance of an association.

Association A group of links that work together in a common way. An association is a separate object class that depends upon two or more other objects within the tree. Associations have their own attributes, which are usually dependent upon the value of an attribute in another object. In an association that defines the communication between two devices, for instance, the TCP/IP attribute might be set to an "on" state if both devices are configured to use the TCP/IP protocol.

Aggregation A special type of association where some objects are part of another object. DEN defines four types of aggregate relationships:

Transitivity If A is part of B and B is part of C, then A is part of C.

Anti-symmetricity If A is part of B, then B is not part of A.

Separability If an object contains multiple aggregate relationships, each must be treated as a separate entity.

Property propagation Properties of the whole propagate to its components.

As you can see, defining objects within the DEN extensions to ADS is much more complex than building a simple object like a user class. Each of these models (object, dynamic, and functional) should first be considered singly for each object class, and then viewed as a whole when appropriate.

Defining Objects

For any LDAP-accessible directory, each object must be defined within a set of parameters. Specifically, each object must define a set of object classes. Each class will contain the following lists:

- A list of attributes that a class *must* have to be stored in the directory

- A list of optional attributes that the class *may* have

- A list of classes that are parents of the class

- A list of classes from which the class is derived

NOTE Remember that an object can be a collection of attributes defined in other classes.

The DEN schema is based on these four rules, but it is also more than this. The DEN initiative defines both the schema *and* the associated information model. The primary goal of DEN is to separate the specification and representation of network devices and services from the information necessary to implement them. In other words, there are two parts to the DEN schema:

- The object classes, representing resources and services

- The definition of relationships, defining how devices and services are actually implemented

Since many of the implementation methods used will be vendor specific, the main goal of DEN is to provide an extensible schema that can be extended for vendor-specific purposes. The DEN schema extension is therefore made up of some very basic object classes. Vendors will group these classes to begin the representation of their products within the directory structure.

While DEN defines a schema of its own, it builds on the work of Microsoft. Microsoft, in turn, relied on the work of a few other standards committees when building the ADS schema. Before we can begin to discuss the DEN object classes, we must first describe the schemas on which they rely.

X.500

The X.500 model provides the following object classes that are critical to DEN:

Top   This object serves as the root of the directory.

Person   This object represents a person, an organizational role within the structure, a person associated with the organization (perhaps an outside vendor), or a person associated with a residence. The X.500 recommendations also define a StrongAuthenticationUser to outline the attributes of a person using some strong authentication service. DEN uses these classes of objects for two distinct purposes:

- To allow a user access to a device or service
- To authenticate administrative permissions on a device or service

Group   This is basically an administrative object used to ease administration of multiple users with similar needs.

Organization   There are three classes of organizational objects:

- Organization
- Organizational Unit
- Organizational Role

The X.500 recommendations assume that these organizational objects will represent businesses, subdivisions, and positions within an organization, respectively. DEN extends this concept so that devices and services can base their services on these same divisions.

Application   There are two classes of application objects within the X.500 recommendations:

- ApplicationProcess
- ApplicationEntity

DEN adds attributes so that these objects can be associated with network resources.

Other Object Classes

The X.500 recommendations define numerous other classes of objects, such as alias and DSA (Directory Service Agent). These objects are critical to the function of the directory, but DEN does not utilize or define such objects. As an extension to an existing directory service, DEN assumes that these objects exist and function properly.

Common Information Model (CIM)

The *Common Information Model (CIM)* is an object-oriented model for the information necessary to manage many common features of complex computer systems. CIM is an open standard defined by the Desktop Management Task Force (DMTF). CIM has gained acceptance throughout the industry as a method of providing a consistent view of the managed environment, regardless of the protocols or data formats used by the various devices being managed. Many of today's most popular enterprise management tools use the CIM object definitions as the basis for their communication with devices and services on the network.

CIM and DEN

CIM is primarily concerned with managing individual components of an enterprise network, as opposed to DEN, which is more concerned with the relationships between these objects. CIM and DEN share a common goal: the management of devices and services from a central location using a consistent model. DEN is really just an extension of the schema defined by CIM.

While a complete discussion of the CIM schema is beyond the scope of this book, a few CIM concepts are critical for DEN:

Product, FRU, and so on This collection of objects represents a product and replaceable parts of a product. DEN will not directly use these object classes, but applications such as inventory and asset tracking will use them. They are included in the DEN schema for completeness.

ManagedSystemElement This object acts as the base class for any system or component that can be managed. This is a critical part of the DEN standard. All of the DEN object classes are derived from this CIM object.

Configuration   This object defines a group of settings that represent the desired functionality of a ManagedSystemElement. DEN extends this object class to include network components.

Service   This object represents the configuration point of any service (as opposed to the actual hardware).

ServiceAccessPoint   This object defines the methods used to access a given service.

Software   This object is used to describe the basic functionality of any product or application.

System   This object has many subclasses. Each represents a discrete component of some product or service. Some examples include the ComputerSystem, FileSystem, and OperatingSystem objects.

Location   This object specifies the address of a particular device or application.

Check and Action   Check is a condition that is expected to be true for a particular computer system. Action is an operation that moves software from one state to another. DEN extends these two objects to include network resources—this is the basis for all relationships.

Application   This object allows an application to be managed as a discrete body of functions with business goals.

As you can see, between the X.500 recommendations and the CIM standard, most of the base objects and attributes have already been defined. DEN is basically an effort to bring network-specific functionality to an existing directory service. Since it was originally driven by Cisco and Microsoft, the directory of choice was Active Directory Services.

Many articles seem to imply that DEN is strictly an ADS implementation. Nothing could be further from the truth. Now that the specifications have been released to a standards committee, many other companies (including Novell) are getting involved. If DEN is successful, we should start to see directories from different vendors interacting to manage network devices. Actually, as companies begin to comply more and more with the X.500 recommendations and the CIM standard, this interoperability should extend into all aspects of the network.

DEN Object Classes

Den defines six different base object classes that are subdivided into numerous subclasses. Each main division describes a different aspect of the network. Three of the main classes are just enhancements of either X.500 or CIM object classes. These three are the following:

- NetworkService
- NetworkProtocol
- NetworkElement

NetworkService is the base upon which all DEN objects are made. It follows the guidelines of the CIM Service object but adds new associations between itself and other classes.

Three of the DEN object classes present new concepts not found in either the X.500 recommendations or the CIM standard. These three classes are:

- Policy
- Profile
- NetworkMedia

While a complete discussion of each of the subclasses and their attributes is beyond our scope, a short description of each of the main classes, with a few of the more important subclasses, is important. This should give you a better feel for the functionality of DEN.

NetworkService

This class describes objects that provide a service of a *non-informational nature*. Non-informational means services that do not return any data to the client computer. In other words, non-informational describes the background services that exist on most networks but do not interact directly with the end-user.

NetworkService Subclasses

Some of the key subclasses of the NetworkService class are:

MultiMediaService   Objects that represent various multimedia services on the network. A streaming video application, for example, could be defined as a MultiMediaService object.

AAAAService   There are four subclasses to the AAAAService object class. Each represents an area of network management:

AuthenticationService   Used during the authentication of one object to another

AuthorizationService   Represents the various methods that can be used to authenticate users or applications to a service or device

AccountingService   Represents different methods of providing accountability on the network

AuditingService   Represents different methods of providing auditing on the network

SecurityService   Defines the objects that will represent the various types of security services used on a network. Due to the popularity of TCP/IP and Internet connections, one of the more important subclasses of the SecurityService object is the IPSECService object class. This class defines the use of IPSEC security, a fairly new standard for securing IP traffic in a hostile environment on a network.

QOSService   Defines the methods to be used when building *Quality of Service* (QOS) applications. QOS applications attempt to provide a guaranteed level of bandwidth or performance to a particular application, service, or user.

The NetworkService objects are the backbone of the DEN schema. Most of these services will be used to provide support for other services within the directory. As stated earlier, NetworkService objects are non-informational in nature, meaning that they do not provide information to the client. The function of NetworkService objects is to do exactly what the name implies— provide network management services to other objects within the directory structure.

NetworkProtocol

Out of the six major DEN object classes, NetworkProtocol is the least complete. The intention is to provide a series of subclasses that will allow for the configuration of protocols and their use through a network. Due to the number of protocols available today and the different ways of describing them, the DEN schema has not been fully fleshed out in this area. Protocols can be described as a suite, such as the TCP/IP suite, or by the types of services that are offered, such as connection-oriented or connectionless communication. While the descriptions vary, the services offered by most communication protocols are quite similar. So far, the DEN standard includes three subclasses to the NetworkProtocol object class. These are Layer1Protocol, Layer2Protocol, and Layer3Protocol, referring to the bottom three layers of the OSI networking model. Provisions have yet to be made for the inclusion of protocols that do not map well to the OSI model.

For more information on the OSI model, see *MCSE: Networking Essentials Study Guide,* 3rd ed., by James Chellis, Charles Perkins, and Matthew Strebe (ISBN 0-7821-2695-2, Sybex, 1999).

The goal of this object class appears to be making the communication services of the network transparent to users and applications. In other words, neither the user nor the application will have to be aware of the protocol used for communication. All configuration information will be handled within the directory.

NetworkElement

The object class NetworkElement is based on the CIM computer object. This object was chosen as the base for the NetworkElement object class because many network devices share basic elements of computers—the use of an operating system, processors, memory, slots, and the ability to compute.

DEN adds specific attributes to the computer object class that pertain to network functionality. These include the ability to have files that control the functionality of the device, the mechanisms used to access and manage the device (also known as the *semantics* of the device), special interface requirements like routing tables, and attributes that can describe the networking software used by the device.

Many of the functions of network devices are installed as either software upgrades or add-on cards, both of which are defined through other object classes: card and application. NetworkElement objects build relationships with these classes to make available a full description of the devices' capabilities.

NetworkElement Subclasses

Some of the subclasses of the NetworkElement object class are the following:

NetworkElementSoftwareFeatures   This is basically a description of the capabilities of the networking software that is running on the device.

NetworkElementSoftwareElements   These objects represent add-on features that have been installed on the base device, through additional hardware or software.

RoutedProtocols   This is really an aggregate of information stored in other classes of objects. The end result is a description of the protocols used by the device for each network interface.

RoutingProtocols   This is basically the same as RoutedProtocols, except that it pertains to a specific type of protocol: those that perform routing calculations.

The NetworkElement objects within a directory tree will represent the physical devices (and the software they run) that provide connectivity services on the network. As such, they are critical to the concept of remote management of these devices.

Policy

Policies are objects that contain a set of conditions that determine the *function* of network services (as opposed to the *use* of those services, which is controlled though profiles). This can be a bit confusing, since profiles and policies are closely related. All policies contain two components:

- A set of conditions under which the policy applies. A redundant WAN link, for instance, might be activated only upon the failure of the primary link.

- A set of actions that either maintain the current state or change the state of an object. In the case of our redundant link, the actions would be the steps necessary to activate the second WAN link.

Simple and Complex Policies

There are two classifications of policy objects: simple and complex. *Simple* policies are those that can be represented with a simple statement, such as a Boolean comparison. *Complex* policies are made up of groups of simple policies.

Another way to think of this is to think of the simple policy as the individual steps taken to achieve a goal, and the complex policy as the grouping of these steps into a complete procedure.

In our redundant-link example, the following simple steps, illustrated in Figure 16.3, might need to be taken:

1. The directory receives an indication that the primary link has gone down. At this point the policy is initiated.

2. The policy directs a test to confirm the unavailability of the primary link (perhaps a Ping across the router).

3. The policy begins the process of updating routing information held in all network objects.

4. The policy initiates any software necessary to bring the secondary link online (such as by accessing a COM port and dialing a remote number).

FIGURE 16.3

Redundant-link policy

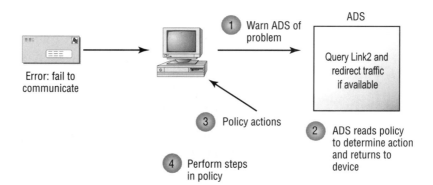

Each of these four steps would represent a simple policy. The entire procedure would constitute a complex policy.

Implementing Effective Policies

The goal of including policies in the DEN schema was to allow administrators to enforce business goals and objectives. In our example, the business goal was to provide a fault-tolerant link between two sites without the expense of two dedicated lines. Many network services can be configured to augment business goals, but as an administrator you must have a complete understanding of both the network needs *and* the business needs of your organization in order to implement effective policies.

Policy Subclasses

A few of the subclasses of the policy object class are:

ContainedPolicies   The set of policies that make up this policy. In other words, this subclass is a list of the simple policies in an overall procedure.

ContainedPolicyConditions   The conditions that this policy contains. In a simple policy, this would be its conditions. In a complex policy, this would be the conditions that initiate the simple policies it contains.

ContainedPolicyActions   The actions for the ContainedPolicyConditions attribute described in the preceding item.

One of the main goals of DEN is to provide an environment where network devices and services can make intelligent decisions about how they will perform their functions. Policies are the embodiment of that goal. Policies provide the decision tree that those objects will use when making their decisions.

Profile

Profiles define the *characteristics* and *needs* of an object in general terms. These general aspects of an object can include behavioral, semantic, and control information that can be passed between applications from different vendors. These applications can use different implementations, but the directory service acts as a standard format. This allows products from diverse environments to share information in a standard manner.

Profile Subclasses

DEN defines six subclasses of profiles; each applies to a different type of object:

UserProfile   A definition of how different profiles should be applied to individual users. For instance, a UserProfile might define how a user connects to the network (characteristic) and what services are available to that user once connected (needs).

GroupProfile   Basically, a UserProfile that applies to a group of users.

OrganizationProfile   A profile that applies to a branch of the directory structure.

OUProfile   A profile that affects users in a particular Organizational Unit.

DeviceProfile   A profile that can be applied to a network device.

ServiceProfile   A profile that can be applied to a network service.

 These last two subclasses might simply control who can use a device or service on the network. They can, however, be much more complex, using time, address, and even departmental information to determine appropriate access controls.

Policies determine *what* will happen on a network; profiles determine *who* can do something. These two object classes work hand in hand to provide an intelligent networking environment.

NetworkMedia

The NetworkMedia object class helps applications determine the protocols in use on any given network interface. It works in conjunction with the CIM object class PhysicalLink (which defines wire type and physical characteristics) to fully define the options available for communication through any network interface.

In Short

The Directory-Enabled Networks initiative extends the capabilities of an Active Directory Services environment into the network. DEN defines the objects and attributes necessary to access and manage network-related devices. DEN was designed to provide two services:

- To bind users to services available from the network according to a consistent and rational set of policies

- To provide the foundation to build intelligent networks and network-enabled applications

To accomplish these goals, three actions must occur:

- Develop a directory service that is DEN compliant. In our case, this is ADS.

- Define a model that describes the physical, behavioral, and functional relationships between objects in that directory. This is the DEN standard schema extension.

- Add protocols for accessing and managing directory information. Both DAP and LDAP fill this need.

Today's networks are complex entities that must be able to manage all aspects of the network from a single location. Administrators have sophisticated needs that must be met if we are to move to the next level of network services. Some of these needs include:

- The ability to manage Internet access in a secure and consistent manner.

- The ability to manage the multitude of services that networks provide, including DHCP, DNS, QOS, and authentication, with a minimum of administrative overhead.

- End-to-end security of applications over the network. This is especially true in an environment using VPNs over the Internet.

- Merging the management of physical resources with that of users and groups. This allows these devices access to the directory in order to enforce usage policies.

- Authentication services for network applications and services.

- Single-point management for a class of device.

- Configuring devices and service based on a set of conditions.

- Inventory and asset tracking services.

This list could go on and on. The bottom line is that network resources—both services and devices—need to better integrate into common management techniques. This is the goal of DEN.

APPENDICES

APPENDIX A

The Active Directory Schema

A complete description of the ADS schema is really beyond the scope of this book. There are, however, some of us who always have to see the minutiae of the operating system. In this appendix, you'll find a complete list of the attributes available with the default schema, so that you can see what the object classes are made of. Then we'll look at a few object classes in detail so you can see how those attributes are used.

Documentation on some of these objects is spotty at best. Most of the classes do not have names that indicate their purpose—except maybe to a software developer. Don't expect detailed explanations of most of the object classes. That type of information probably won't be available until Windows 2000 has been on the market for quite some time and people start developing value-added products. As it stands, my take is that Microsoft would just as soon we didn't know much about the schema. (This is the exact same stance that Novell took when it released NetWare 4. It was a few years before that attitude changed.)

As you saw in Chapter 12, you can access the ADS schema through the Microsoft Management Console (MMC) by adding the Active Directory Schema Manager snap-in.

Expanding the Classes container will show you a list of the 50-plus classes of objects available in the default schema and the attributes of each class. Expanding the Attributes folder will show you a list of the hundreds of attributes used to populate the classes. We'll start with the attributes.

Available Attributes

$\mathbf{A}$DS attributes are the "fields" for each record in the database. They are combined to create object classes: records that represent network resources. Table A.1 lists all of the attributes included in the schema.

T A B L E A.1 ADS Attributes		
	accountExpires	aCSMaxNoOfLogFiles
	accountNameHistory	aCSMaxPeakBandwidth
	aCSAggregateTokenRatePerUser	aCSMaxPeakBandwidthPerFlow
	aCSAllocableRSVPBandwidth	aCSMaxSizeOfRSVPAccountFile
	aCSCacheTimeout	aCSMaxSizeOfRSVPLogFile
	aCSDirection	aCSMaxTokenBucketPerFlow
	aCSDSBMDeadTime	aCSMaxTokenRatePerFlow
	aCSDSBMPriority	aCSMinimumDelayVariation
	aCSDSBMRefresh	aCSMinimumLatency
	aCSEnableACSService	aCSMinimumPolicedSize
	aCSEnableRSVPAccounting	aCSNonReservedMaxSDUSize
	aCSEnableRSVPMessageLogging	aCSNonReservedMinPolicedSize
	aCSEventLogLevel	aCSNonReservedPeakRate
	aCSIdentityName	aCSNonReservedTokenSize
	aCSMaxAggregatePeakRate- PerUser	aCSNonReservedTxLimit
	aCSMaxDurationPerFlow	aCSNonReservedTxSize
	aCSMaximumSDUSize	aCSPermissionBits
	aCSMaxNoOfAccountFiles	aCSPolicyName

TABLE A.1 *(cont.)* ADS Attributes	aCSPriority	altSecurityIdentities
	aCSRSVPAccountFilesLocation	aNR
	aCSRSVPLogFilesLocation	applicationName
	aCSServerList	appliesTo
	aCSServiceType	appSchemaVersion
	aCSTimeOfDay	assetNumber
	aCSTotalNoOfFlows	assistant
	additionalTrustedServiceNames	assocNTAccount
	addressBookRoots	attributeDisplayNames
	addressEntryDisplayTable	attributeID
	addressEntryDisplayTableMSDOS	attributeSecurityGUID
	addressSyntax	attributeSyntax
	addressType	attributeTypes
	adminContextMenu	auditingPolicy
	adminCount	authenticationOptions
	adminDescription	authorityRevocationList
	adminDisplayName	auxiliaryClass
	adminPropertyPages	badPasswordTime
	allowedAttributes	badPwdCount
	allowedAttributesEffective	birthLocation
	allowedChildClasses	bridgeheadServerListBL
	allowedChildClassesEffective	bridgeheadTransportList

T A B L E A.1 *(cont.)* ADS Attributes	builtinCreationTime	cOMClassID
	builtinModifiedCount	cOMCLSID
	businessCategory	cOMInterfaceID
	bytesPerMinute	comment
	c	cOMOtherProgId
	cACertificate	company
	cACertificateDN	cOMProgID
	cAConnect	cOMTreatAsClassId
	canonicalName	cOMTypelibId
	canUpgradeScript	cOMUniqueLIBID
	catalogs	contentIndexingAllowed
	categories	contextMenu
	categoryId	controlAccessRights
	cAUsages	cost
	cAWEBURL	countryCode
	certificateAuthorityObject	createDialog
	certificateRevocationList	createTimeStamp
	certificateTemplates	createWizardExt
	classDisplayName	creationTime
	cn	creationWizard
	co	creator
	codePage	cRLObject

T A B L E A.1 *(cont.)*
ADS Attributes

cRLPartitionedRevocationList	dhcpIdentification
crossCertificatePair	dhcpMask
currentLocation	dhcpMaxKey
currentParentCA	dhcpObjDescription
currentValue	dhcpObjName
currMachineId	dhcpOptions
dBCSPwd	dhcpProperties
dc	dhcpRanges
defaultClassStore	dhcpReservations
defaultGroup	dhcpServers
defaultHidingValue	dhcpSites
defaultLocalPolicyObject	dhcpState
defaultObjectCategory	dhcpSubnets
defaultPriority	dhcpType
defaultSecurityDescriptor	dhcpUniqueKey
deltaRevocationList	dhcpUpdateTime
department	directReports
description	displayName
desktopProfile	displayNamePrintable
destinationIndicator	distinguishedName
dhcpClasses	dITContentRules
dhcpFlags	division

T A B L E A.1 *(cont.)* ADS Attributes	dMDLocation	dSASignature
	dmdName	dSCorePropagationData
	dNReferenceUpdate	dSHeuristics
	dnsAllowDynamic	dSUIAdminMaximum
	dnsAllowXFR	dSUIAdminNotification
	dNSHostName	dSUIShellMaximum
	dnsNotifySecondaries	dynamicLDAPServer
	dNSProperty	eFSPolicy
	dnsRecord	employeeID
	dnsRoot	employeeNumber
	dnsSecureSecondaries	employeeType
	dNSTombstoned	Enabled
	domainCAs	enabledConnection
	domainCrossRef	enrollmentProviders
	domainID	extendedAttributeInfo
	domainIdentifier	extendedCharsAllowed
	domainPolicyObject	extendedClassInfo
	domainPolicyReference	extensionName
	domainReplica	facsimileTelephoneNumber
	domainWidePolicy	fileExtPriority
	driverName	flags
	driverVersion	flatName

T A B L E A.1 (cont.)		
ADS Attributes	forceLogoff	fRSReplicaSetType
	foreignIdentifier	fRSRootPath
	friendlyNames	fRSRootSecurity
	fromEntry	fRSServiceCommand
	fromServer	fRSServiceCommandStatus
	frsComputerReference	fRSStagingPath
	frsComputerReferenceBL	fRSTimeLastCommand
	fRSControlDataCreation	fRSTimeLastConfigChange
	fRSControlInboundBacklog	fRSUpdateTimeout
	fRSControlOutboundBacklog	fRSVersion
	fRSDirectoryFilter	fRSVersionGUID
	fRSDSPoll	fRSWorkingPath
	fRSExtensions	fSMORoleOwner
	fRSFaultCondition	garbageCollPeriod
	fRSFileFilter	generatedConnection
	fRSFlags	generationQualifier
	fRSLevelLimit	givenName
	fRSMemberReference	globalAddressList
	fRSMemberReferenceBL	governsID
	fRSPartnerAuthLevel	gPCFileSysPath
	fRSPrimaryMember	gPCFunctionalityVersion
	fRSReplicaSetGUID	gPCMachineExtensionNames

T A B L E A.1 *(cont.)* ADS Attributes	gPCUserExtensionNames	initialAuthOutgoing
	gPLink	initials
	gPOptions	installUiLevel
	groupAttributes	instanceType
	groupMembershipSAM	internationalISDNNumber
	groupPriority	interSiteTopologyFailover
	groupsToIgnore	interSiteTopologyGenerator
	groupType	interSiteTopologyRenew
	hasMasterNCs	invocationId
	hasPartialReplicaNCs	ipPhone
	helpData16	ipsecData
	helpData32	ipsecDataType
	helpFileName	ipsecFilterReference
	homeDirectory	ipsecID
	homeDrive	ipsecISAKMPReference
	homePhone	ipsecName
	homePostalAddress	iPSECNegotiationPolicyAction
	iconPath	ipsecNegotiationPolicyReference
	implementedCategories	iPSECNegotiationPolicyType
	indexedScopes	ipsecNFAReference
	info	ipsecOwnersReference
	initialAuthIncoming	ipsecPolicyReference

TABLE A.1 *(cont.)*		
ADS Attributes		

isCriticalSystemObject	linkTrackSecret
isDefunct	lmPwdHistory
isDeleted	localeID
isEphemeral	localizationDisplayId
isMemberOfPartialAttributeSet	localizedDescription
isPrivilegeHolder	localPolicyFlags
isSingleValued	localPolicyReference
keywords	location
knowledgeInformation	lockoutDuration
l	lockOutObservationWindow
lastBackupRestorationTime	lockoutThreshold
lastContentIndexed	lockoutTime
lastKnownParent	logonCount
lastLogoff	logonHours
lastLogon	logonWorkstation
lastSetTime	lSACreationTime
lastUpdateSequence	lSAModifiedCount
lDAPAdminLimits	machineArchitecture
lDAPDisplayName	machinePasswordChangeInterval
lDAPIPDenyList	machineRole
legacyExchangeDN	machineWidePolicy
linkID	mail

T A B L E A.1 *(cont.)* ADS Attributes		
	mailAddress	meetingKeyword
	managedBy	meetingLanguage
	managedObjects	meetingLocation
	manager	meetingMaxParticipants
	mAPIID	meetingName
	marshalledInterface	meetingOriginator
	masteredBy	meetingOwner
	maxPwdAge	meetingProtocol
	maxRenewAge	meetingRating
	maxStorage	meetingRecurrence
	maxTicketAge	meetingScope
	mayContain	meetingStartTime
	meetingAdvertiseScope	meetingType
	meetingApplication	meetingURL
	meetingBandwidth	member
	meetingBlob	memberOf
	meetingContactInfo	mhsORAddress
	meetingDescription	middleName
	meetingEndTime	minPwdAge
	meetingID	minPwdLength
	meetingIP	minTicketAge
	meetingIsEncrypted	mobile

TABLE A.1 *(cont.)* ADS Attributes		
	modifiedCount	mSMQCSPName
	modifiedCountAtLastProm	mSMQDependentClientService
	modifyTimeStamp	mSMQDependentClientServices
	moniker	mSMQDigests
	monikerDisplayName	mSMQDigestsMig
	moveTreeState	mSMQDsService
	mscopeId	mSMQDsServices
	mS-DS-ConsistencyChildCount	mSMQEncryptKey
	mS-DS-ConsistencyGuid	mSMQForeign
	mS-DS-CreatorSID	mSMQInRoutingServers
	ms-DS-MachineAccountQuota	mSMQInterval1
	mS-DS-ReplicatesNCReason	mSMQInterval2
	msiFileList	mSMQJournal
	msiScript	mSMQJournalQuota
	msiScriptName	mSMQLabel
	msiScriptPath	mSMQLabelEx
	msiScriptSize	mSMQLongLived
	mSMQAuthenticate	mSMQMigrated
	mSMQBasePriority	mSMQNameStyle
	mSMQComputerType	mSMQNt4Flags
	mSMQComputerTypeEx	mSMQNt4Stub
	mSMQCost	mSMQOSType

T A B L E A.1 *(cont.)* ADS Attributes	mSMQOutRoutingServers	mSMQSiteID
	mSMQOwnerID	mSMQSiteName
	mSMQPrevSiteGates	mSMQSiteNameEx
	mSMQPrivacyLevel	mSMQSites
	mSMQQMID	mSMQTransactional
	mSMQQueueJournalQuota	mSMQUserSid
	mSMQQueueNameExt	mSMQVersion
	mSMQQueueQuota	msNPAllowDialin
	mSMQQueueType	msNPCalledStationID
	mSMQQuota	msNPCallingStationID
	mSMQRoutingService	msNPSavedCallingStationID
	mSMQRoutingServices	msRADIUSCallbackNumber
	mSMQServices	msRADIUSFramedIPAddress
	mSMQServiceType	msRADIUSFramedRoute
	mSMQSignCertificates	msRADIUSServiceType
	mSMQSignCertificatesMig	msRASSavedCallbackNumber
	mSMQSignKey	msRASSavedFramedIPAddress
	mSMQSite1	msRASSavedFramedRoute
	mSMQSite2	msRRASAttribute
	mSMQSiteForeign	msRRASVendorAttributeEntry
	mSMQSiteGates	mS-SQL-Alias
	mSMQSiteGatesMig	mS-SQL-AllowAnonymous Subscription

T A B L E A.1 *(cont.)* ADS Attributes	mS-SQL-AllowImmediate-UpdatingSubscription	mS-SQL-Language
	mS-SQL-AllowKnownPull-Subscription	mS-SQL-LastBackupDate
	mS-SQL-AllowQueuedUpdating-Subscription	mS-SQL-LastDiagnosticDate
	mS-SQL-AllowSnapshotFilesFTP-Downloading	mS-SQL-LastUpdatedDate
	mS-SQL-AppleTalk	mS-SQL-Location
	mS-SQL-Applications	mS-SQL-Memory
	mS-SQL-Build	mS-SQL-MultiProtocol
	mS-SQL-CharacterSet	mS-SQL-Name
	mS-SQL-Clustered	mS-SQL-NamedPipe
	mS-SQL-ConnectionURL	mS-SQL-PublicationURL
	mS-SQL-Contact	mS-SQL-Publisher
	mS-SQL-CreationDate	mS-SQL-RegisteredOwner
	mS-SQL-Database	mS-SQL-ServiceAccount
	mS-SQL-Description	mS-SQL-Size
	mS-SQL-GPSHeight	mS-SQL-SortOrder
	mS-SQL-GPSLatitude	mS-SQL-SPX
	mS-SQL-GPSLongitude	mS-SQL-Status
	mS-SQL-InformationDirectory	mS-SQL-TCPIP
	mS-SQL-InformationURL	mS-SQL-ThirdParty
	mS-SQL-Keywords	mS-SQL-Type

T A B L E A.1 *(cont.)*	mS-SQL-UnicodeSortOrder	netbootSCPBL
ADS Attributes	mS-SQL-Version	netbootServer
	mS-SQL-Vines	netbootSIFFile
	mustContain	netbootTools
	name	networkAddress
	nameServiceFlags	nextLevelStore
	nCName	nextRid
	nETBIOSName	nonSecurityMember
	netbootAllowNewClients	nonSecurityMemberBL
	netbootAnswerOnlyValidClients	notes
	netbootAnswerRequests	notificationList
	netbootCurrentClientCount	nTGroupMembers
	netbootGUID	nTMixedDomain
	netbootInitialization	ntPwdHistory
	netbootIntelliMirrorOSes	nTSecurityDescriptor
	netbootLimitClients	o
	netbootLocallyInstalledOSes	objectCategory
	netbootMachineFilePath	objectClass
	netbootMaxClients	objectClassCategory
	netbootMirrorDataFile	objectClasses
	netbootNewMachineNamingPolicy	objectCount
	netbootNewMachineOU	objectGUID

T A B L E A.1 *(cont.)* ADS Attributes	objectSid	otherMobile
	objectVersion	otherPager
	oEMInformation	otherTelephone
	oMObjectClass	otherWellKnownObjects
	oMSyntax	ou
	oMTGuid	owner
	oMTIndxGuid	packageFlags
	operatingSystem	packageName
	operatingSystemHotfix	packageType
	operatingSystemServicePack	pager
	operatingSystemVersion	parentCA
	operatorCount	parentCACertificateChain
	optionDescription	parentGUID
	options	partialAttributeDeletionList
	optionsLocation	partialAttributeSet
	originalDisplayTable	pekKeyChangeInterval
	originalDisplayTableMSDOS	pekList
	otherFacsimileTelephoneNumber	pendingCACertificates
	otherHomePhone	pendingParentCA
	otherIpPhone	perMsgDialogDisplayTable
	otherLoginWorkstations	perRecipDialogDisplayTable
	otherMailbox	personalTitle

T A B L E A.1 *(cont.)* ADS Attributes		
	physicalDeliveryOfficeName	prefixMap
	physicalLocationObject	presentationAddress
	pKICriticalExtensions	previousCACertificates
	pKIDefaultCSPs	previousParentCA
	pKIDefaultKeySpec	primaryGroupID
	pKIEnrollmentAccess	primaryGroupToken
	pKIExpirationPeriod	primaryInternationalISDNNumber
	pKIExtendedKeyUsage	primaryTelexNumber
	pKIKeyUsage	printAttributes
	pKIMaxIssuingDepth	printBinNames
	pKIOverlapPeriod	printCollate
	pKT	printColor
	pKTGuid	printDuplexSupported
	policyReplicationFlags	printEndTime
	portName	printerName
	possibleInferiors	printFormName
	possSuperiors	printKeepPrintedJobs
	postalAddress	printLanguage
	postalCode	printMACAddress
	postOfficeBox	printMaxCopies
	preferredDeliveryMethod	printMaxResolutionSupported
	preferredOU	printMaxXExtent

TABLE A.1 (cont.) ADS Attributes	printMaxYExtent	priorValue
	printMediaReady	privateKey
	printMediaSupported	privilegeAttributes
	printMemory	privilegeDisplayName
	printMinXExtent	privilegeHolder
	printMInYExtent	privilegeValue
	printNetworkAddress	productCode
	printNotify	profilePath
	printNumberUp	proxiedObjectName
	printOrientationsSupported	proxyAddresses
	printOwner	proxyGenerationEnabled
	printPagesPerMinute	proxyLifetime
	printRate	publicKeyPolicy
	printRateUnit	purportedSearch
	printSeparatorFile	pwdHistoryLength
	printShareName	pwdLastSet
	printSpooling	pwdProperties
	printStaplingSupported	qualityOfService
	printStartTime	queryFilter
	printStatus	queryPoint
	priority	queryPolicyBL
	priorSetTime	queryPolicyObject

TABLE A.1 *(cont.)* ADS Attributes		
	rangeLower	rIDNextRID
	rangeUpper	rIDPreviousAllocationPool
	rDNAttID	rIDSetReferences
	registeredAddress	rIDUsedPool
	remoteServerName	rightsGuid
	remoteSource	roleOccupant
	remoteSourceType	rootTrust
	remoteStorageGUID	rpcNsAnnotation
	replicaSource	rpcNsBindings
	replInterval	rpcNsCodeset
	replPropertyMetaData	rpcNsEntryFlags
	replTopologyStayOfExecution	rpcNsGroup
	replUpToDateVector	rpcNsInterfaceID
	repsFrom	rpcNsObjectID
	repsTo	rpcNsPriority
	requiredCategories	rpcNsProfileEntry
	retiredReplDSASignatures	rpcNsTransferSyntax
	revision	sAMAccountName
	rid	sAMAccountType
	rIDAllocationPool	schedule
	rIDAvailablePool	schemaFlagsEx
	rIDManagerReference	schemaIDGUID

T A B L E A.1 (cont.)	schemaInfo	serviceDNSNameType
ADS Attributes	schemaUpdate	serviceInstanceVersion
	schemaVersion	servicePrincipalName
	scopeFlags	setupCommand
	scriptPath	shellContextMenu
	sDRightsEffective	shellPropertyPages
	searchFlags	shortServerName
	searchGuide	showInAddressBook
	securityIdentifier	showInAdvancedViewOnly
	seeAlso	sIDHistory
	seqNotification	signatureAlgorithms
	serialNumber	siteGUID
	serverName	siteLinkList
	serverReference	siteList
	serverReferenceBL	siteObject
	serverRole	siteObjectBL
	serverState	siteServer
	serviceBindingInformation	sn
	serviceClassID	sPNMappings
	serviceClassInfo	st
	serviceClassName	street
	serviceDNSName	streetAddress

T A B L E A.1 *(cont.)* ADS Attributes	subClassOf	terminalServer
	subRefs	textEncodedORAddress
	subSchemaSubEntry	thumbnailLogo
	superiorDNSRoot	thumbnailPhoto
	superScopeDescription	timeRefresh
	superScopes	timeVolChange
	supplementalCredentials	title
	supportedApplicationContext	tokenGroups
	syncAttributes	tokenGroupsGlobalAndUniversal
	syncMembership	tokenGroupsNoGCAcceptable
	syncWithObject	tombstoneLifetime
	syncWithSID	transportAddressAttribute
	systemAuxiliaryClass	transportDLLName
	systemFlags	transportType
	systemMayContain	treatAsLeaf
	systemMustContain	treeName
	systemOnly	trustAttributes
	systemPossSuperiors	trustAuthIncoming
	telephoneNumber	trustAuthOutgoing
	teletexTerminalIdentifier	trustDirection
	telexNumber	trustParent
	templateRoots	trustPartner

T A B L E A.1 *(cont.)* ADS Attributes		
	trustPosixOffset	uSNDSALastObjRemoved
	trustType	USNIntersite
	uASCompat	uSNLastObjRem
	uNCName	uSNSource
	unicodePwd	validAccesses
	upgradeProductCode	vendor
	uPNSuffixes	versionNumber
	url	versionNumberHi
	userAccountControl	versionNumberLo
	userCert	volTableGUID
	userCertificate	volTableIdxGUID
	userParameters	volumeCount
	userPassword	wbemPath
	userPrincipalName	wellKnownObjects
	userSharedFolder	whenChanged
	userSharedFolderOther	whenCreated
	userSMIMECertificate	winsockAddresses
	userWorkstations	wWWHomePage
	uSNChanged	x121Address
	uSNCreated	

Object Classes

An object class acts as a container for the attributes (or fields) of a specific type of record in the Active Directory database. There are well over 50 object classes defined in the default ADS database, each with numerous attributes. Just as a visual object lesson (pardon the pun), we'll look at the attributes that make up a few of them.

The aCSPolicy Class

The aCSPolicy object class contains the attributes listed in Table A.2.

TABLE A.2 Attributes of the aCSPolicy Class		
	aCSTotalNoOfFlows	aCSIdentityName
	aCSTimeOfDay	aCSDirection
	aCSServiceType	aCSAggregateTokenRatePerUser
	aCSPriority	url
	aCSPermissionBits	wWWHomePage
	aCSMinimumDelayVariation	whenCreated
	aCSMinimumLatency	whenChanged
	aCSMaximumSDUSize	wellKnownObjects
	aCSMinimumPolicedSize	wbemPath
	aCSMaxTokenRatePerFlow	uSNSource
	aCSMaxTokenBucketPerFlow	uSNLastObjRem
	aCSMaxPeakBandwidthPerFlow	USNIntersite
	aCSMaxDurationPerFlow	uSNDSALastObjRemoved
	aCSMaxAggregatePeakRate-PerUser	uSNCreated

T A B L E A.2 *(cont.)* Attributes of the aCSPolicy Class	uSNChanged	objectGUID
	systemFlags	distinguishedName
	subSchemaSubEntry	nonSecurityMemberBL
	subRefs	netbootSCPBL
	siteObjectBL	mS-DS-ConsistencyGuid
	serverReferenceBL	mS-DS-ConsIstencyChIldCount
	sDRightsEffective	modifyTimeStamp
	revision	masteredBy
	repsTo	managedObjects
	repsFrom	lastKnownParent
	directReports	isPrivilegeHolder
	replUpToDateVector	memberOf
	replPropertyMetaData	isDeleted
	name	isCriticalSystemObject
	queryPolicyBL	showInAdvancedViewOnly
	proxyAddresses	fSMORoleOwner
	proxiedObjectName	fRSMemberReferenceBL
	possibleInferiors	frsComputerReferenceBL
	partialAttributeSet	fromEntry
	partialAttributeDeletionList	flags
	otherWellKnownObjects	extensionName
	objectVersion	dSASignature

T A B L E A.2 *(cont.)* Attributes of the aCSPolicy Class	dSCorePropagationData	allowedChildClasses
	displayNamePrintable	allowedAttributesEffective
	displayName	allowedAttributes
	description	adminDisplayName
	createTimeStamp	adminDescription
	cn	objectClass
	canonicalName	objectCategory
	bridgeheadServerListBL	nTSecurityDescriptor
	allowedChildClassesEffective	instanceType

The aCSSubnet Class

The aCSSubnet object class contains the attributes listed in Table A.3.

T A B L E A.3 Attributes of the aCSSubnet Class	aCSServerList	aCSMaxSizeOfRSVPLogFile
	aCSRSVPLogFilesLocation	aCSMaxSizeOfRSVPAccountFile
	aCSRSVPAccountFilesLocation	aCSMaxPeakBandwidthPerFlow
	aCSNonReservedTxSize	aCSMaxPeakBandwidth
	aCSNonReservedTxLimit	aCSMaxNoOfLogFiles
	aCSNonReservedTokenSize	aCSMaxNoOfAccountFiles
	aCSNonReservedPeakRate	aCSMaxDurationPerFlow
	aCSNonReservedMinPolicedSize	aCSEventLogLevel
	aCSNonReservedMaxSDUSize	aCSEnableRSVPMessageLogging
	aCSMaxTokenRatePerFlow	aCSEnableRSVPAccounting

T A B L E A.3 *(cont.)* Attributes of the aCSSubnet Class		
aCSEnableACSService	serverReferenceBL
aCSDSBMRefresh	sDRightsEffective
aCSDSBMPriority	revision
aCSDSBMDeadTime	repsTo
aCSCacheTimeout	repsFrom
aCSAllocableRSVPBandwidth	directReports
url	replUpToDateVector
wWWHomePage	replPropertyMetaData
whenCreated	name
whenChanged	queryPolicyBL
wellKnownObjects	proxyAddresses
wbemPath	proxiedObjectName
uSNSource	possibleInferiors
uSNLastObjRem	partialAttributeSet
USNIntersite	partialAttributeDeletionList
uSNDSALastObjRemoved	otherWellKnownObjects
uSNCreated	objectVersion
uSNChanged	objectGUID
systemFlags	distinguishedName
subSchemaSubEntry	nonSecurityMemberBL
subRefs	netbootSCPBL
siteObjectBL	mS-DS-ConsistencyGuid

T A B L E A.3 *(cont.)* Attributes of the aCSSubnet Class	mS-DS-ConsistencyChildCount	displayNamePrintable
	modifyTimeStamp	displayName
	masteredBy	description
	managedObjects	createTimeStamp
	lastKnownParent	cn
	isPrivilegeHolder	canonicalName
	memberOf	bridgeheadServerListBL
	isDeleted	allowedChildClassesEffective
	isCriticalSystemObject	allowedChildClasses
	showInAdvancedViewOnly	allowedAttributesEffective
	fSMORoleOwner	allowedAttributes
	fRSMemberReferenceBL	adminDisplayName
	frsComputerReferenceBL	adminDescription
	fromEntry	objectClass
	flags	objectCategory
	extensionName	nTSecurityDescriptor
	dSASignature	instanceType
	dSCorePropagationData	

The addressBookContainer Class

The addressBookContainer object class contains the attributes listed in Table A.4.

T A B L E A.4 Attributes of the addressBook-Container Class	purportedSearch	sDRightsEffective
	displayName	revision
	url	repsTo
	wWWHomePage	repsFrom
	whenCreated	directReports
	whenChanged	replUpToDateVector
	wellKnownObjects	replPropertyMetaData
	wbemPath	name
	uSNSource	queryPolicyBL
	uSNLastObjRem	proxyAddresses
	USNIntersite	proxiedObjectName
	uSNDSALastObjRemoved	possibleInferiors
	uSNCreated	partialAttributeSet
	uSNChanged	partialAttributeDeletionList
	systemFlags	otherWellKnownObjects
	subSchemaSubEntry	objectVersion
	subRefs	objectGUID
	siteObjectBL	distinguishedName
	serverReferenceBL	nonSecurityMemberBL

T A B L E A.4 *(cont.)* Attributes of the addressBook-Container Class	netbootSCPBL	dSCorePropagationData
	mS-DS-ConsistencyGuid	displayNamePrintable
	mS-DS-ConsistencyChildCount	displayName
	modifyTimeStamp	description
	masteredBy	createTimeStamp
	managedObjects	cn
	lastKnownParent	canonicalName
	isPrivilegeHolder	bridgeheadServerListBL
	memberOf	allowedChildClassesEffective
	isDeleted	allowedChildClasses
	isCriticalSystemObject	allowedAttributesEffective
	showInAdvancedViewOnly	allowedAttributes
	fSMORoleOwner	adminDisplayName
	fRSMemberReferenceBL	adminDescription
	frsComputerReferenceBL	objectClass
	fromEntry	objectCategory
	flags	nTSecurityDescriptor
	extensionName	instanceType
	dSASignature	

The addressTemplate Class

The addressTemplate object class contains the attributes listed in Table A.5.

T A B L E A.5 Attributes of the addressTemplate Class		
proxyGenerationEnabled	USNIntersite
perRecipDialogDisplayTable	uSNDSALastObjRemoved
perMsgDialogDisplayTable	uSNCreated
addressType	uSNChanged
addressSyntax	systemFlags
displayName	subSchemaSubEntry
originalDisplayTableMSDOS	subRefs
originalDisplayTable	siteObjectBL
helpFileName	serverReferenceBL
helpData32	sDRightsEffective
helpData16	revision
addressEntryDisplayTableMSDOS	repsTo
addressEntryDisplayTable	repsFrom
cn	directReports
url	replUpToDateVector
wWWHomePage	replPropertyMetaData
whenCreated	name
whenChanged	queryPolicyBL
wellKnownObjects	proxyAddresses
wbemPath	proxiedObjectName
uSNSource	possibleInferiors
uSNLastObjRem	partialAttributeSet

T A B L E A.5 *(cont.)* Attributes of the addressTemplate Class	partialAttributeDeletionList	flags
	otherWellKnownObjects	extensionName
	objectVersion	dSASignature
	objectGUID	dSCorePropagationData
	distinguishedName	displayNamePrintable
	nonSecurityMemberBL	displayName
	netbootSCPBL	description
	mS-DS-ConsistencyGuid	createTimeStamp
	mS-DS-ConsistencyChildCount	cn
	modifyTimeStamp	canonicalName
	masteredBy	bridgeheadServerListBL
	managedObjects	allowedChildClassesEffective
	lastKnownParent	allowedChildClasses
	isPrivilegeHolder	allowedAttributesEffective
	memberOf	allowedAttributes
	isDeleted	adminDisplayName
	isCriticalSystemObject	adminDescription
	showInAdvancedViewOnly	objectClass
	fSMORoleOwner	objectCategory
	fRSMemberReferenceBL	nTSecurityDescriptor
	frsComputerReferenceBL	instanceType
	fromEntry	

The applicationProcess Class

The applicationProcess object class contains the attributes listed in Table A.6.

T A B L E A.6 Attributes of the applicationProcess Class		
	seeAlso	serverReferenceBL
	ou	sDRightsEffective
	l	revision
	cn	repsTo
	url	repsFrom
	wWWHomePage	directReports
	whenCreated	replUpToDateVector
	whenChanged	replPropertyMetaData
	wellKnownObjects	name
	wbemPath	queryPolicyBL
	uSNSource	proxyAddresses
	uSNLastObjRem	proxiedObjectName
	USNIntersite	possibleInferiors
	uSNDSALastObjRemoved	partialAttributeSet
	uSNCreated	partialAttributeDeletionList
	uSNChanged	otherWellKnownObjects
	systemFlags	objectVersion
	subSchemaSubEntry	objectGUID
	subRefs	distinguishedName
	siteObjectBL	nonSecurityMemberBL

T A B L E A.6 *(cont.)* Attributes of the applicationProcess Class		
netbootSCPBL	dSCorePropagationData
mS-DS-ConsistencyGuid	displayNamePrintable
mS-DS-ConsistencyChildCount	displayName
modifyTimeStamp	description
masteredBy	createTimeStamp
managedObjects	cn
lastKnownParent	canonicalName
isPrivilegeHolder	bridgeheadServerListBL
memberOf	allowedChildClassesEffective
isDeleted	allowedChildClasses
isCriticalSystemObject	allowedAttributesEffective
showInAdvancedViewOnly	allowedAttributes
fSMORoleOwner	adminDisplayName
fRSMemberReferenceBL	adminDescription
frsComputerReferenceBL	objectClass
fromEntry	objectCategory
flags	nTSecurityDescriptor
extensionName	instanceType
dSASignature	

The applicationSettings Class

The applicationSettings object class contains the attributes listed in Table A.7.

T A B L E A.7	notificationList	repsFrom
Attributes of the applicationSettings Class	applicationName	directReports
	url	replUpToDateVector
	wWWHomePage	replPropertyMetaData
	whenCreated	name
	whenChanged	queryPolicyBL
	wellKnownObjects	proxyAddresses
	wbemPath	proxiedObjectName
	uSNSource	possibleInferiors
	uSNLastObjRem	partialAttributeSet
	USNIntersite	partialAttributeDeletionList
	uSNDSALastObjRemoved	otherWellKnownObjects
	uSNCreated	objectVersion
	uSNChanged	objectGUID
	systemFlags	distinguishedName
	subSchemaSubEntry	nonSecurityMemberBL
	subRefs	netbootSCPBL
	siteObjectBL	mS-DS-ConsistencyGuid
	serverReferenceBL	mS-DS-ConsistencyChildCount
	sDRightsEffective	modifyTimeStamp
	revision	masteredBy
	repsTo	managedObjects

T A B L E A.7 *(cont.)* Attributes of the applicationSettings Class	lastKnownParent	description
	isPrivilegeHolder	createTimeStamp
	memberOf	cn
	isDeleted	canonicalName
	isCriticalSystemObject	bridgeheadServerListBL
	showInAdvancedViewOnly	allowedChildClassesEffective
	fSMORoleOwner	allowedChildClasses
	fRSMemberReferenceBL	allowedAttributesEffective
	frsComputerReferenceBL	allowedAttributes
	fromEntry	adminDisplayName
	flags	adminDescription
	extensionName	objectClass
	dSASignature	objectCategory
	dSCorePropagationData	nTSecurityDescriptor
	displayNamePrintable	instanceType
	displayName	

The attributeSchema Class

The attributeSchema object class contains the attributes listed in Table A.8.

T A B L E A.8 Attributes of the attributeSchema Class	systemOnly	wWWHomePage
	searchFlags	whenCreated
	schemaFlagsEx	whenChanged
	rangeUpper	wellKnownObjects
	rangeLower	wbemPath
	oMObjectClass	uSNSource
	mAPIID	uSNLastObjRem
	linkID	USNIntersite
	isMemberOfPartialAttributeSet	uSNDSALastObjRemoved
	isEphemeral	uSNCreated
	isDefunct	uSNChanged
	extendedCharsAllowed	systemFlags
	classDisplayName	subSchemaSubEntry
	attributeSecurityGUID	subRefs
	schemaIDGUID	siteObjectBL
	oMSyntax	serverReferenceBL
	lDAPDisplayName	sDRightsEffective
	isSingleValued	revision
	cn	repsTo
	attributeSyntax	repsFrom
	attributeID	directReports
	url	replUpToDateVector

T A B L E A.8 *(cont.)* Attributes of the attributeSchema Class	replPropertyMetaData	isDeleted
	name	isCriticalSystemObject
	queryPolicyBL	showInAdvancedViewOnly
	proxyAddresses	fSMORoleOwner
	proxiedObjectName	fRSMemberReferenceBL
	possibleInferiors	frsComputerReferenceBL
	partialAttributeSet	fromEntry
	partialAttributeDeletionList	flags
	otherWellKnownObjects	extensionName
	objectVersion	dSASignature
	objectGUID	dSCorePropagationData
	distinguishedName	displayNamePrintable
	nonSecurityMemberBL	displayName
	netbootSCPBL	description
	mS-DS-ConsistencyGuid	createTimeStamp
	mS-DS-ConsistencyChildCount	cn
	modifyTimeStamp	canonicalName
	masteredBy	bridgeheadServerListBL
	managedObjects	allowedChildClassesEffective
	lastKnownParent	allowedChildClasses
	isPrivilegeHolder	allowedAttributesEffective
	memberOf	allowedAttributes

TABLE A.8 *(cont.)*	adminDisplayName	objectCategory
Attributes of the attributeSchema Class	adminDescription	nTSecurityDescriptor
	objectClass	instanceType

The builtinDomain Class

The builtinDomain object class contains the attributes listed in Table A.9.

TABLE A.9	uASCompat	lockoutDuration
Attributes of the builtinDomain Class	serverState	lockOutObservationWindow
	serverRole	forceLogoff
	revision	domainReplica
	pwdProperties	creationTime
	pwdHistoryLength	url
	oEMInformation	wWWHomePage
	objectSid	whenCreated
	nTSecurityDescriptor	whenChanged
	nextRid	wellKnownObjects
	modifiedCountAtLastProm	wbemPath
	modifiedCount	uSNSource
	minPwdLength	uSNLastObjRem
	minPwdAge	USNIntersite
	maxPwdAge	uSNDSALastObjRemoved
	lockoutThreshold	uSNCreated

T A B L E A.9 *(cont.)*		
Attributes of the builtinDomain Class	uSNChanged	objectGUID
	systemFlags	distinguishedName
	subSchemaSubEntry	nonSecurityMemberBL
	subRefs	netbootSCPBL
	siteObjectBL	mS-DS-ConsistencyGuid
	serverReferenceBL	mS-DS-ConsistencyChildCount
	sDRightsEffective	modifyTimeStamp
	revision	masteredBy
	repsTo	managedObjects
	repsFrom	lastKnownParent
	directReports	isPrivilegeHolder
	replUpToDateVector	memberOf
	replPropertyMetaData	isDeleted
	name	isCriticalSystemObject
	queryPolicyBL	showInAdvancedViewOnly
	proxyAddresses	fSMORoleOwner
	proxiedObjectName	fRSMemberReferenceBL
	possibleInferiors	frsComputerReferenceBL
	partialAttributeSet	fromEntry
	partialAttributeDeletionList	flags
	otherWellKnownObjects	extensionName
	objectVersion	dSASignature

T A B L E A.9 *(cont.)*	dSCorePropagationData	allowedChildClasses
Attributes of the builtinDomain Class	displayNamePrintable	allowedAttributesEffective
	displayName	allowedAttributes
	description	adminDisplayName
	createTimeStamp	adminDescription
	cn	objectClass
	canonicalName	objectCategory
	bridgeheadServerListBL	nTSecurityDescriptor
	allowedChildClassesEffective	instanceType

The categoryRegistration Class

The categoryRegistration object class contains the attributes listed in Table A.10.

T A B L E A.10	managedBy	wbemPath
Attributes of the category-Registration Class	localizedDescription	uSNSource
	localeID	uSNLastObjRem
	categoryId	USNIntersite
	url	uSNDSALastObjRemoved
	wWWHomePage	uSNCreated
	whenCreated	uSNChanged
	whenChanged	systemFlags
	wellKnownObjects	subSchemaSubEntry

TABLE A.10 *(cont.)* Attributes of the category-Registration Class	subRefs	netbootSCPBL
	siteObjectBL	mS-DS-ConsistencyGuid
	serverReferenceBL	mS-DS-ConsistencyChildCount
	sDRightsEffective	modifyTimeStamp
	revision	masteredBy
	repsTo	managedObjects
	repsFrom	lastKnownParent
	directReports	isPrivilegeHolder
	replUpToDateVector	memberOf
	replPropertyMetaData	isDeleted
	name	isCriticalSystemObject
	queryPolicyBL	showInAdvancedViewOnly
	proxyAddresses	fSMORoleOwner
	proxiedObjectName	fRSMemberReferenceBL
	possibleInferiors	frsComputerReferenceBL
	partialAttributeSet	fromEntry
	partialAttributeDeletionList	flags
	otherWellKnownObjects	extensionName
	objectVersion	dSASignature
	objectGUID	dSCorePropagationData
	distinguishedName	displayNamePrintable
	nonSecurityMemberBL	displayName

TABLE A.10 *(cont.)*		
Attributes of the category-Registration Class	description	allowedAttributes
	createTimeStamp	adminDisplayName
	cn	adminDescription
	canonicalName	objectClass
	bridgeheadServerListBL	objectCategory
	allowedChildClassesEffective	nTSecurityDescriptor
	allowedChildClasses	instanceType
	allowedAttributesEffective	

The certificationAuthority Class

The certificationAuthority object class contains the attributes listed in Table A.11.

TABLE A.11		
Attributes of the certification-Authority Class	teletexTerminalIdentifier	enrollmentProviders
	supportedApplicationContext	domainPolicyObject
	signatureAlgorithms	domainID
	searchGuide	dNSHostName
	previousParentCA	deltaRevocationList
	previousCACertificates	currentParentCA
	pendingParentCA	crossCertificatePair
	pendingCACertificates	cRLObject
	parentCACertificateChain	certificateTemplates
	parentCA	cAWEBURL

TABLE A.11 *(cont.)* Attributes of the certification-Authority Class	cAUsages	siteObjectBL
	cAConnect	serverReferenceBL
	cACertificateDN	sDRightsEffective
	cn	revision
	certificateRevocationList	repsTo
	cACertificate	repsFrom
	authorityRevocationList	directReports
	url	replUpToDateVector
	wWWHomePage	replPropertyMetaData
	whenCreated	name
	whenChanged	queryPolicyBL
	wellKnownObjects	proxyAddresses
	wbemPath	proxiedObjectName
	uSNSource	possibleInferiors
	uSNLastObjRem	partialAttributeSet
	USNIntersite	partialAttributeDeletionList
	uSNDSALastObjRemoved	otherWellKnownObjects
	uSNCreated	objectVersion
	uSNChanged	objectGUID
	systemFlags	distinguishedName
	subSchemaSubEntry	nonSecurityMemberBL
	subRefs	netbootSCPBL

TABLE A.11 *(cont.)* Attributes of the certification-Authority Class	mS-DS-ConsistencyGuid	dSCorePropagationData
	mS-DS-ConsistencyChildCount	displayNamePrintable
	modifyTimeStamp	displayName
	masteredBy	description
	managedObjects	createTimeStamp
	lastKnownParent	cn
	isPrivilegeHolder	canonicalName
	memberOf	bridgeheadServerListBL
	isDeleted	allowedChildClassesEffective
	isCriticalSystemObject	allowedChildClasses
	showInAdvancedViewOnly	allowedAttributesEffective
	fSMORoleOwner	allowedAttributes
	fRSMemberReferenceBL	adminDisplayName
	frsComputerReferenceBL	adminDescription
	fromEntry	objectClass
	flags	objectCategory
	extensionName	nTSecurityDescriptor
	dSASignature	instanceType

The classRegistration Class

The classRegistration object class contains the attributes listed in Table A.12.

T A B L E A.12 Attributes of the classRegistration Class	requiredCategories	subRefs
	managedBy	siteObjectBL
	implementedCategories	serverReferenceBL
	cOMTreatAsClassId	sDRightsEffective
	cOMProgID	revision
	cOMOtherProgId	repsTo
	cOMInterfaceID	repsFrom
	cOMCLSID	directReports
	url	replUpToDateVector
	wWWHomePage	replPropertyMetaData
	whenCreated	name
	whenChanged	queryPolicyBL
	wellKnownObjects	proxyAddresses
	wbemPath	proxiedObjectName
	uSNSource	possibleInferiors
	uSNLastObjRem	partialAttributeSet
	USNIntersite	partialAttributeDeletionList
	uSNDSALastObjRemoved	otherWellKnownObjects
	uSNCreated	objectVersion
	uSNChanged	objectGUID
	systemFlags	distinguishedName
	subSchemaSubEntry	nonSecurityMemberBL

TABLE A.12 *(cont.)*	netbootSCPBL	dSCorePropagationData
Attributes of the classRegistration Class	mS-DS-ConsistencyGuid	displayNamePrintable
	mS-DS-ConsistencyChildCount	displayName
	modifyTimeStamp	description
	masteredBy	createTimeStamp
	managedObjects	cn
	lastKnownParent	canonicalName
	isPrivilegeHolder	bridgeheadServerListBL
	memberOf	allowedChildClassesEffective
	isDeleted	allowedChildClasses
	isCriticalSystemObject	allowedAttributesEffective
	showInAdvancedViewOnly	allowedAttributes
	fSMORoleOwner	adminDisplayName
	fRSMemberReferenceBL	adminDescription
	frsComputerReferenceBL	objectClass
	fromEntry	objectCategory
	flags	nTSecurityDescriptor
	extensionName	instanceType
	dSASignature	

The classSchema Class

The classSchema object class contains the attributes listed in Table A.13.

T A B L E A.13 Attributes of the classSchema Class	systemPossSuperiors	url
	systemOnly	wWWHomePage
	systemMustContain	whenCreated
	systemMayContain	whenChanged
	systemAuxiliaryClass	wellKnownObjects
	schemaFlagsEx	wbemPath
	rDNAttID	uSNSource
	possSuperiors	uSNLastObjRem
	mustContain	USNIntersite
	mayContain	uSNDSALastObjRemoved
	lDAPDisplayName	uSNCreated
	isDefunct	uSNChanged
	defaultSecurityDescriptor	systemFlags
	defaultHidingValue	subSchemaSubEntry
	classDisplayName	subRefs
	auxiliaryClass	siteObjectBL
	subClassOf	serverReferenceBL
	schemaIDGUID	sDRightsEffective
	objectClassCategory	revision
	governsID	repsTo
	defaultObjectCategory	repsFrom
	cn	directReports

TABLE A.13 *(cont.)* Attributes of the classSchema Class	replUpToDateVector	memberOf
	replPropertyMetaData	isDeleted
	name	isCriticalSystemObject
	queryPolicyBL	showInAdvancedViewOnly
	proxyAddresses	fSMORoleOwner
	proxiedObjectName	fRSMemberReferenceBL
	possibleInferiors	frsComputerReferenceBL
	partialAttributeSet	fromEntry
	partialAttributeDeletionList	flags
	otherWellKnownObjects	extensionName
	objectVersion	dSASignature
	objectGUID	dSCorePropagationData
	distinguishedName	displayNamePrintable
	nonSecurityMemberBL	displayName
	netbootSCPBL	description
	mS-DS-ConsistencyGuid	createTimeStamp
	mS-DS-ConsistencyChildCount	cn
	modifyTimeStamp	canonicalName
	masteredBy	bridgeheadServerListBL
	managedObjects	allowedChildClassesEffective
	lastKnownParent	allowedChildClasses
	isPrivilegeHolder	allowedAttributesEffective

TABLE A.13 *(cont.)* Attributes of the classSchema Class	allowedAttributes	objectCategory
	adminDisplayName	nTSecurityDescriptor
	adminDescription	instanceType
	objectClass	

The classStore Class

The classStore object class contains the attributes listed in Table A.14.

TABLE A.14 Attributes of the classStore Class	versionNumber	uSNCreated
	nextLevelStore	uSNChanged
	lastUpdateSequence	systemFlags
	appSchemaVersion	subSchemaSubEntry
	url	subRefs
	wWWHomePage	siteObjectBL
	whenCreated	serverReferenceBL
	whenChanged	sDRightsEffective
	wellKnownObjects	revision
	wbemPath	repsTo
	uSNSource	repsFrom
	uSNLastObjRem	directReports
	USNIntersite	replUpToDateVector
	uSNDSALastObjRemoved	replPropertyMetaData

TABLE A.14 *(cont.)* Attributes of the classStore Class	name	isDeleted
	queryPolicyBL	isCriticalSystemObject
	proxyAddresses	showInAdvancedViewOnly
	proxiedObjectName	fSMORoleOwner
	possibleInferiors	fRSMemberReferenceBL
	partialAttributeSet	frsComputerReferenceBL
	partialAttributeDeletionList	fromEntry
	otherWellKnownObjects	flags
	objectVersion	extensionName
	objectGUID	dSASignature
	distinguishedName	dSCorePropagationData
	nonSecurityMemberBL	displayNamePrintable
	netbootSCPBL	displayName
	mS-DS-ConsistencyGuid	description
	mS-DS-ConsistencyChildCount	createTimeStamp
	modifyTimeStamp	cn
	masteredBy	canonicalName
	managedObjects	bridgeheadServerListBL
	lastKnownParent	allowedChildClassesEffective
	isPrivilegeHolder	allowedChildClasses
	memberOf	allowedAttributesEffective

T A B L E A.14 *(cont.)*	allowedAttributes	objectCategory
Attributes of the classStore Class	adminDisplayName	nTSecurityDescriptor
	adminDescription	instanceType
	objectClass	

The computer Class

The computer object class contains the attributes listed in Table A.15.

T A B L E A.15	volumeCount	managedBy
Attributes of the computer Class	siteGUID	machineRole
	rIDSetReferences	location
	policyReplicationFlags	localPolicyFlags
	physicalLocationObject	dNSHostName
	operatingSystemVersion	defaultLocalPolicyObject
	operatingSystemServicePack	cn
	operatingSystemHotfix	catalogs
	operatingSystem	userCertificate
	networkAddress	userWorkstations
	netbootSIFFile	userSharedFolderOther
	netbootMirrorDataFile	userSharedFolder
	netbootMachineFilePath	userPrincipalName
	netbootInitialization	userParameters
	netbootGUID	userAccountControl

TABLE A.15 (cont.) Attributes of the computer Class		
	unicodePwd	mSMQSignCertificatesMig
	terminalServer	mSMQSignCertificates
	servicePrincipalName	mSMQDigestsMig
	scriptPath	mSMQDigests
	pwdLastSet	mS-DS-CreatorSID
	profilePath	maxStorage
	primaryGroupID	logonWorkstation
	preferredOU	logonHours
	otherLoginWorkstations	logonCount
	operatorCount	lockoutTime
	ntPwdHistory	localeID
	networkAddress	lmPwdHistory
	msRASSavedFramedRoute	lastLogon
	msRASSavedFramedIPAddress	lastLogoff
	msRASSavedCallbackNumber	homeDrive
	msRADIUSServiceType	homeDirectory
	msRADIUSFramedRoute	groupsToIgnore
	msRADIUSFramedIPAddress	groupPriority
	msRADIUSCallbackNumber	groupMembershipSAM
	msNPSavedCallingStationID	dynamicLDAPServer
	msNPCallingStationID	desktopProfile
	msNPAllowDialin	defaultClassStore

TABLE A.15 *(cont.)* Attributes of the computer Class	dBCSPwd	userSMIMECertificate
	controlAccessRights	userCert
	codePage	textEncodedORAddress
	badPwdCount	telephoneNumber
	badPasswordTime	showInAddressBook
	adminCount	legacyExchangeDN
	aCSPolicyName	garbageCollPeriod
	accountExpires	info
	supplementalCredentials	cn
	sIDHistory	x121Address
	securityIdentifier	comment
	sAMAccountType	title
	rid	co
	tokenGroupsNoGCAcceptable	primaryTelexNumber
	tokenGroupsGlobalAndUniversal	telexNumber
	tokenGroups	teletexTerminalIdentifier
	nTSecurityDescriptor	street
	altSecurityIdentities	st
	accountNameHistory	registeredAddress
	sAMAccountName	preferredDeliveryMethod
	objectSid	postalCode
	userCertificate	postalAddress

TABLE A.15 *(cont.)* Attributes of the computer Class	postOfficeBox	l
	thumbnailPhoto	internationalISDNNumber
	physicalDeliveryOfficeName	initials
	pager	givenName
	otherPager	generationQualifier
	otherTelephone	facsimileTelephoneNumber
	mobile	employeeID
	otherMobile	mail
	primaryInternationalISDNNumber	division
	ipPhone	destinationIndicator
	otherIpPhone	department
	otherHomePhone	c
	homePhone	countryCode
	otherFacsimileTelephoneNumber	company
	personalTitle	assistant
	middleName	homePostalAddress
	otherMailbox	streetAddress
	ou	userPassword
	o	telephoneNumber
	mhsORAddress	sn
	manager	seeAlso
	thumbnailLogo	cn

T A B L E A.15 *(cont.)* Attributes of the computer Class	url	replUpToDateVector
	wWWHomePage	replPropertyMetaData
	whenCreated	name
	whenChanged	queryPolicyBL
	wellKnownObjects	proxyAddresses
	wbemPath	proxiedObjectName
	uSNSource	possibleInferiors
	uSNLastObjRem	partialAttributeSet
	USNIntersite	partialAttributeDeletionList
	uSNDSALastObjRemoved	otherWellKnownObjects
	uSNCreated	objectVersion
	uSNChanged	objectGUID
	systemFlags	distinguishedName
	subSchemaSubEntry	nonSecurityMemberBL
	subRefs	netbootSCPBL
	siteObjectBL	mS-DS-ConsistencyGuid
	serverReferenceBL	mS-DS-ConsistencyChildCount
	sDRightsEffective	modifyTimeStamp
	revision	masteredBy
	repsTo	managedObjects
	repsFrom	lastKnownParent
	directReports	isPrivilegeHolder

T A B L E A.15 *(cont.)* Attributes of the computer Class	memberOf	createTimeStamp
	isDeleted	cn
	isCriticalSystemObject	canonicalName
	showInAdvancedViewOnly	bridgeheadServerListBL
	fSMORoleOwner	allowedChildClassesEffective
	fRSMemberReferenceBL	allowedChildClasses
	frsComputerReferenceBL	allowedAttributesEffective
	fromEntry	allowedAttributes
	flags	adminDisplayName
	extensionName	adminDescription
	dSASignature	objectClass
	dSCorePropagationData	objectCategory
	displayNamePrintable	nTSecurityDescriptor
	displayName	instanceType
	description	

The configuration Class

The configuration object class contains the attributes listed in Table A.16.

TABLE A.16	cn	directReports
Attributes of the configuration Class	url	replUpToDateVector
	wWWHomePage	replPropertyMetaData
	whenCreated	name
	whenChanged	queryPolicyBL
	wellKnownObjects	proxyAddresses
	wbemPath	proxiedObjectName
	uSNSource	possibleInferiors
	uSNLastObjRem	partialAttributeSet
	USNIntersite	partialAttributeDeletionList
	uSNDSALastObjRemoved	otherWellKnownObjects
	uSNCreated	objectVersion
	uSNChanged	objectGUID
	systemFlags	distinguishedName
	subSchemaSubEntry	nonSecurityMemberBL
	subRefs	netbootSCPBL
	siteObjectBL	mS-DS-ConsistencyGuid
	serverReferenceBL	mS-DS-ConsistencyChildCount
	sDRightsEffective	modifyTimeStamp
	revision	masteredBy
	repsTo	managedObjects
	repsFrom	lastKnownParent

TABLE A.16 *(cont.)*	isPrivilegeHolder	description
Attributes of the configuration Class	memberOf	createTimeStamp
	isDeleted	cn
	isCriticalSystemObject	canonicalName
	showInAdvancedViewOnly	bridgeheadServerListBL
	fSMORoleOwner	allowedChildClassesEffective
	fRSMemberReferenceBL	allowedChildClasses
	frsComputerReferenceBL	allowedAttributesEffective
	fromEntry	allowedAttributes
	flags	adminDisplayName
	extensionName	adminDescription
	dSASignature	objectClass
	dSCorePropagationData	objectCategory
	displayNamePrintable	nTSecurityDescriptor
	displayName	instanceType

The connectionPoint Class

The connectionPoint object class contains the attributes listed in Table A.17.

T A B L E A.17 Attributes of the connectionPoint Class	managedBy	repsTo
	keywords	repsFrom
	cn	directReports
	url	replUpToDateVector
	wWWHomePage	replPropertyMetaData
	whenCreated	name
	whenChanged	queryPolicyBL
	wellKnownObjects	proxyAddresses
	wbemPath	proxiedObjectName
	uSNSource	possibleInferiors
	uSNLastObjRem	partialAttributeSet
	USNIntersite	partialAttributeDeletionList
	uSNDSALastObjRemoved	otherWellKnownObjects
	uSNCreated	objectVersion
	uSNChanged	objectGUID
	systemFlags	distinguishedName
	subSchemaSubEntry	nonSecurityMemberBL
	subRefs	netbootSCPBL
	siteObjectBL	mS-DS-ConsistencyGuid
	serverReferenceBL	mS-DS-ConsistencyChildCount
	sDRightsEffective	modifyTimeStamp
	revision	masteredBy

T A B L E A.17 *(cont.)* Attributes of the connectionPoint Class	managedObjects	displayName
	lastKnownParent	description
	isPrivilegeHolder	createTimeStamp
	memberOf	cn
	isDeleted	canonicalName
	isCriticalSystemObject	bridgeheadServerListBL
	showInAdvancedViewOnly	allowedChildClassesEffective
	fSMORoleOwner	allowedChildClasses
	fRSMemberReferenceBL	allowedAttributesEffective
	frsComputerReferenceBL	allowedAttributes
	fromEntry	adminDisplayName
	flags	adminDescription
	extensionName	objectClass
	dSASignature	objectCategory
	dSCorePropagationData	nTSecurityDescriptor
	displayNamePrintable	instanceType

The container Class

The container object class contains the attributes listed in Table A.18.

T A B L E A.18 Attributes of the container Class	schemaVersion	repsTo
	defaultClassStore	repsFrom
	cn	directReports
	url	replUpToDateVector
	wWWHomePage	replPropertyMetaData
	whenCreated	name
	whenChanged	queryPolicyBL
	wellKnownObjects	proxyAddresses
	wbemPath	proxiedObjectName
	uSNSource	possibleInferiors
	uSNLastObjRem	partialAttributeSet
	USNIntersite	partialAttributeDeletionList
	uSNDSALastObjRemoved	otherWellKnownObjects
	uSNCreated	objectVersion
	uSNChanged	objectGUID
	systemFlags	distinguishedName
	subSchemaSubEntry	nonSecurityMemberBL
	subRefs	netbootSCPBL
	siteObjectBL	mS-DS-ConsistencyGuid
	serverReferenceBL	mS-DS-ConsistencyChildCount
	sDRightsEffective	modifyTimeStamp
	revision	masteredBy

TABLE A.18 (cont.) Attributes of the container Class		
	managedObjects	displayName
	lastKnownParent	description
	isPrivilegeHolder	createTimeStamp
	memberOf	cn
	isDeleted	canonicalName
	isCriticalSystemObject	bridgeheadServerListBL
	showInAdvancedViewOnly	allowedChildClassesEffective
	fSMORoleOwner	allowedChildClasses
	fRSMemberReferenceBL	allowedAttributesEffective
	frsComputerReferenceBL	allowedAttributes
	fromEntry	adminDisplayName
	flags	adminDescription
	extensionName	objectClass
	dSASignature	objectCategory
	dSCorePropagationData	nTSecurityDescriptor
	displayNamePrintable	instanceType

Index

Note to the Reader: Throughout this index **boldfaced** page numbers indicate primary discussions of a topic. *Italicized* page numbers indicate illustrations.

H

U

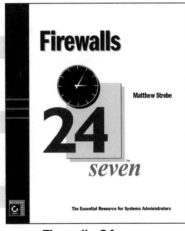

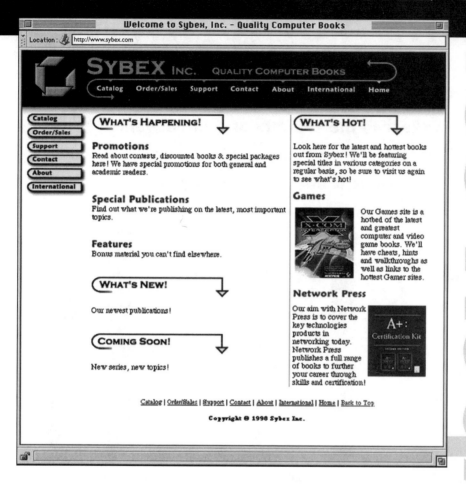

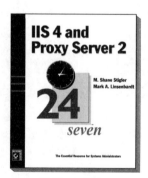